SCOTTISH SHEPHERD

SCOTTISH SHEPHERD

••• *The Life and Times of* •••

John Murray Murdoch, Utah Pioneer

KENNETH W. MERRELL

THE UNIVERSITY OF UTAH PRESS
Salt Lake City

The Defiance House Man colophon is a registered trademark of the University of
Utah Press. It is based upon a four-foot-tall, Ancient Puebloan pictograph (late PIII)
near Glen Canyon, Utah.

12 11 10 09 08   1 2 3 4 5

LIBRARY OF CONGRESS CATALOGING-IN-PUBLICATION DATA

Merrell, Kenneth W.
  Scottish shepherd : the life and times of John Murray Murdoch, Utah pioneer / by Kenneth
W. Merrell.
      p. cm.
  Includes bibliographical references and index.
  ISBN-13: 978-0-87480-931-2 (paper : alk. paper)
  ISBN-10: 0-87480-931-2 (paper : alk. paper) 1. Murdoch, John Murray, 1820-1910.
2. Mormon pioneers—Utah—Biography. 3. Sheep ranchers—Utah—Biography. 4. Scottish
Americans—Utah—Biography. 5. Frontier and pioneer life—Utah. 6. Frontier and pioneer
life—Utah—Wasatch County. 7. Utah—Biography. 8. Wasatch County (Utah)—
Biography. I. Title.
  F826.M87M47 2006
  979.2'01092—dc22
  [B]   2006019189

Lines from the song "Turning Away," by Scottish songwriter Dougie MacLean, used by
permission of Limetree Arts and Music. From the album "Indigenous" (Dunkeld Records,
1991), www.dougiemaclean.com.

Lines from the song "Talking with My Father," music and lyrics by Scottish songwriter
Dougie MacLean, used by permission of Limetree Arts and Music. From the album "Who
Am I" (Dunkeld Records, 2001), www.dougiemaclean.com.

◆ ◆ ◆

This volume is dedicated to John Murray Murdoch and to three women who are my links to the past: my mother, Eliza Janett Rasband Merrell; my grandmother, Annie McMullin Rasband; and my great-grandmother, Janett Osborne Murdoch McMullin, who was John Murdoch's daughter and the fifth born of his twenty-two children.

CONTENTS

PREFACE

America is a nation of immigrants. With the exception of Native Americans, who currently compose less than 2 percent of the population of the United States, most Americans need only trace their family lineage back a handful of generations or less before they reach their ancestors who made the break from their own homeland, left family and friends, and embarked on a path to a new life and an unknown fate in a strange land. This American quest has been a pattern for more than four hundred years and continues to this day. Each wave of immigrants has its own unique circumstances and generational challenges and faces somewhat differing patterns of stress with respect to acculturation, assimilation, and accommodation into the new culture.

The conditions under which immigrants have arrived in America differ greatly. Some were coerced here in shackles and became part of America's shameful legacy of slavery. Others made their way here by choice, trying to satisfy their restlessness and frustration, escaping problems, seeking economic opportunity, or being guided by a vision of freedom from political oppression and tyranny. Another sector of American immigrants came to this land driven by a spiritual quest for religious freedom, salvation, and the desire to gather with like-minded visionary seekers. For this latter type of immigrant, America has always represented a golden ideal, or some variation on the theme of a promised land, a Zion, or a New Jerusalem.

One of the unique migrations in the history of this nation was the large infusion of immigrants—primarily from northern and western Europe—who came to America to gather with the "Saints," members of the Church of Jesus Christ of Latter-day Saints, during the nineteenth century. From shortly after the founding of the church in the 1830s until a tapering off of conversion rates a few decades later, thousands of Europeans—especially those from the British Isles—embraced the message of Mormonism and had instilled in their hearts a desire to seek a spiritual refuge with the Saints on the frontiers of the American west.

The initial years of the gathering occurred in Ohio, Missouri, and especially in Nauvoo, Illinois, the "City of Joseph," named informally after the charismatic founding Mormon prophet, Joseph Smith. Much of the gathering occurred after the Mormons were driven west to the deserts and mountains of Utah. On foot or in wagon train, pulling handcarts or push-ing exhausted cattle, they came. Most of these pioneers were inexperienced in the ways of frontier life, having been plucked from the wastelands of the industrialized population centers of Great Britain. Most were of modest means, and many were exceptionally poor. Against mind-boggling odds and in the face of sometimes overwhelming hardships they came. Some died along the way. Others left the trail disillusioned, and some made it to Utah only to become bitter or to lose their interest in the faith and desire that had brought them there. Many suffered immeasurably along the way. But most of these immigrants ultimately made it to Zion, remained faith-ful to their new religion, established new lives, and spawned new genera-tions of Americans who would look to the lives and hardships of their pio-neer forebears with respect, pride, and a sense of purpose.

John Murray Murdoch was one such American immigrant, and this volume tells the story of his life and the unique times in which he lived. This story is also the tale of two Scottish women, Anne Steele Murdoch, John's wife who accompanied him from Scotland to America in 1852, and Isabella Crawford Murdoch, who made her own sojourn to Utah as a young woman some time after John and Ann and ultimately joined with them in a marriage to John, making the trio part of the institution of nineteenth-century Mormon polygamy.

Born and raised in the Auchinleck region of Ayrshire, Scotland, John Murdoch left his homeland with his pregnant wife, Ann, and two young children in 1852 to be part of the gathering of Saints in Utah. Along the way, they experienced the privations and suffering of many pilgrims, including hunger, life-threatening disease, the deaths of their two chil-dren, more hunger, betrayal, aching fatigue, unimaginable sorrow, and temporary despair.

After arriving in Utah, John slowly began to emerge from these trou-bles, maintained his optimism, and ultimately became a player in some of the most unusual and compelling events in the history of America's inter-mountain west region. He had close interactions and associations with notable figures, including Brigham Young and Abraham Smoot; held key ecclesiastical positions at the local level; participated in the military prepa-rations and maneuvers against the United States Army in the 1857 Utah War; fled with his family from their home in Salt Lake City during the incursion of Johnston's army; helped to settle the Wasatch County area and became one of the first elected officials of the county; built homes; established the first sheep cooperative in Wasatch County and helped to establish the sheep ranching industry in Utah; entered into the peculiar

Mormon institution of plural marriage or polygamy; led a contingent of militia in Utah's Black Hawk and Walker Indian wars; became a prosperous rancher and businessman; lost several children to premature death; became a beloved and honored leader and public figure within Heber and Wasatch County; lived through the extensive conflicts between the United States government and his church and experienced some of the unprecedented persecution of the federal government against the Mormons; saw his church renounce the practice of polygamy under the threat of extinction and then served brief jail time for refusing to abandon his polygamous wife and family; and experienced the turn of the century and the beginnings of the modern era in Utah.

John Murdoch was a somewhat prominent figure within Wasatch County and was known and respected by many others within the greater Utah region, but his life never involved the kind of high level public stature and regional prominence that is usually the case with individuals who become the subject of a biographer's work. Given that he was not a high profile politician, ecclesiastical leader, business magnate, military leader, explorer, or a controversial figure, one might wonder why his life would be the focus of this volume, and who should be interested in his life and times beyond his descendants and those persons interested in the history of Wasatch County, Utah. It is precisely this "everyman" aspect of John Murdoch's life that makes his story so compelling. Through examining his life and times in close detail, we can obtain a lens into the experience of ordinary people who lived through the extraordinary times that his lifetime comprised. John Murdoch's experience as a Scottish immigrant to America, and his role as a participant in one of the most extraordinary episodes in the history of America—the pioneer era in Utah—make his life and times compelling indeed. This tale is intended to be of interest for aficionados of Utah, Mormon, and western U.S. history. It is also intended to be of import to those persons who are interested in American social history, the immigration experience, and the idea that each generation is connected not only to the generations that came before, but to those that will come after their own time.

Although I am a descendant of John Murdoch, I did not set out to write this volume to lionize an ancestor or to put a particular spin on any controversial events that were part of his lifetime. I am also a social scientist and have spent two decades of my professional life studying how environments, contexts, and events that are unique to one's time and circumstance shape behavior, define character, and weave a path to future events. I am also fascinated by how our past experiences and those experiences and attitudes that are intergenerational in nature shape our current thoughts, behaviors, and feelings. This book is part biography and part social history. In researching and writing it, I have attempted to portray people and events fairly, to deal with controversial issues without shying away from or whitewashing them, and to always consider how the reality of the past and the ultimate potential impact on the future must be taken into account when understanding any human phenomenon.

ACKNOWLEDGMENTS

I am deeply grateful for the support and assistance of several people and institutions that played key roles in bringing this book forward. Several faculty and staff from the University of Utah, publisher of this volume, were exceptionally helpful and supportive in this process. I am indebted to Peter DeLafosse and other staff at the University of Utah Press for seeing the value of this work and for supporting and shaping it. Frederick Buchanan, Emeritus Professor of Education and author of *A Good Time Coming: Mormon Letters from Scotland*, was extremely generous with his time, his extensive knowledge of Scottish immigration to Utah, and his sage advice regarding potential sources for the topics I pursued in this project, some of which were very obscure and not easy to locate. Mr. Buchanan also served as an external reviewer for the publisher on the first complete version of the manuscript, as did Peter Goss, Professor of Architectural History and Associate Vice President for Scholarly and Creative Activities, a notable documentary photographer. Their insightful comments and suggestions on the initial version of the manuscript led to some major improvements.

Some of the current generations of descendants of John Murdoch, particularly those who were serving on the executive committee of the James and Mary Murdoch Family Organization during the development of this project, were exceptionally supportive and enthusiastic toward my idea for this book, and I simply could not have completed it without their assistance. Anne Rasband McDonald shared with me her treasure trove of prized family photographs from the nineteenth century, and she trusted me enough to let me take them from Utah to my home in Oregon for digital scanning and enhancing. Don Blanchard, Murdoch family genealogist, provided me with essential clarification and verification on birth and death dates, sent me digital images of photographs of John Murdoch and his family, and provided me with some family documents that I would not otherwise have located. Helen Hall and Gary Lloyd of the Murdoch family organization were also very supportive and generous with their time and suggestions.

More than anyone else, Dallas Murdoch, President of the James and Mary Murdoch Family Organization when I began to explore the possibility of this project, was incredibly helpful, supportive, and determined to see that my vision of this work was carried out. As the original instigator of *The James and Mary Murray Murdoch Family History*, published by the family organization in 1982, Mr. Murdoch set in motion the events that led to the creation of this unusually rich volume, which comprises biographies, articles, journal entries, photographs, and genealogical information for John Murdoch's family of origin. Known simply as *The Red Book* (for the color of its cover), this volume reflects the very best in what a family history can be, and it contains material that was invaluable in my research. Stated simply, without the richness of detail in *The Red Book*, I would not have been able to complete the story of John Murdoch's life and times. As soon as I proposed my idea for this project, Dallas began almost immediately to help me find sources that would have otherwise been irretrievable, and his frequent phone and e-mail communications with me during the two-year duration of the research and writing of this book—even when he was recovering from a near fatal heart attack and subsequent heart transplant surgery—helped me to remain motivated, focused, and determined to see this work through.

Susan Merrell, my wife and partner of a quarter century, was very generous with her extensive knowledge of family history resources, her training in accessing genealogical indexes and databases, and in serving as the first eyes for the initial draft for each chapter of this volume. I am also indebted to her for her patience and support of my work on this project, which was all done in my "spare" time and required many late nights and weekends in my writing retreat to bring it to life, as well as a necessary obsession at times to see the project through.

In my research I relied heavily on the extensive collections of several libraries, as well as some more non-traditional information sources, and I sometimes found wonderful supporting documents, inspiration, and other evidence in the most unlikely of places. The Marriott Library at the University of Utah proved to be an excellent source for works on nineteenth-century Scottish immigration to Utah, and the Frederick S. Buchanan papers in the special collections section were a virtual gold mine in this regard. The Salt Lake County public library and the research library of the Utah State Historical Society were both excellent sources for materials on pioneer-era Utah, and the latter institution provided me with some rare photographs of nineteenth-century Heber City and the sheep industry in the region. The Family History Library of the Church of Jesus Christ of Latter-day Saints—including its extensive Internet resources—was a crucial source of information on nineteenth-century Mormonism in Scotland, maps of Scotland and of the nineteenth-century American west, immigration to Utah, and Latter-day Saint history during the second half of the nineteenth century.

During one of my trips to Utah to conduct research, I serendipitously learned of a concert to be held that night featuring notable Scottish singer-songwriter Dougie MacLean, and I was lucky enough to be able to secure a ticket and attend. This experience, and my subsequent mining of his musical catalogue, inspired me to dig into the Celtic and other music traditions of Scotland in search of connections with the Murdoch family, and led me to study in more detail the work of famed eighteenth-century Scottish poet Robert Burns, who was a contemporary of John Murdoch's parents, both in age and in the region of Scotland from which they hailed. As I studied John Murdoch's own written recollections on his life, I discovered that even in his old age and many years removed from Scotland he still quoted Burns, and that the themes from some of Burns's best known works could almost perfectly describe critical scenes from Murdoch's own life. It was very purposeful that I included quotes from Burns and from McLean's lyrics in several places in this volume.

The Knight Library at the University of Oregon proved to be an excellent source for works on the social history of Scotland, and on the westward expansion of America in the nineteenth century. The Eugene, Oregon, public library also provided a surprisingly good collection of works on Scottish history, and on the pioneering period of the American west, including an extensive collection of Wallace Stegner's books. My search for primary source material on the establishment of the sheep ranching industry in Utah and the adjoining western United States—which had previously been essentially fruitless—finally paid off in the stacks of the Kerr Library at Oregon State University, where I located several comprehensive volumes that informed my research and writing. The University of Iowa library, as well as the Iowa City public library, were both a rich source of materials on the Mormon handcart encampment and launching site near Iowa City, the place that John Murdoch's mother, Mary Murray Murdoch ("Wee Granny") camped and embarked from on her fatal trek toward Utah that took her several hundred miles on foot at age seventy-two to her last moments near Chimney Rock, Nebraska. The staff of the Maine Maritime Museum in Bath were helpful and responsive to my inquiries regarding the *Kennebec*, the ship that brought John and Ann Murdoch from Liverpool to New Orleans in 1852, and their efforts resulted in important information that I would have never otherwise located.

A surprising amount of material for this volume was not available in traditional library sources, but was found only through the use of Internet search engines, which helped me to identify several fascinating websites that in some cases contained primary source materials that were both obscure and critical to my work. Such resources would not have been available in the public domain only a decade ago, and I am indebted to those individuals and organizations that have developed and maintained the websites that I have referenced in this volume.

One of the most unexpected inspirations for this book was the late rock-music journalist Timothy White's 2001 book *Long Ago and Far Away*, a biography of American singer-songwriter James Taylor. As I began to read White's book, I was surprised and fascinated to see the extensive attention paid to Taylor's prominent Scottish ancestors and their immigration patterns to America, as well as the notion that ancestral themes or archetypes continue to play out in subsequent generations. In my introduction to Chapter 2, I have included a statement from White that I discovered in an online chat session he held regarding his book, just prior to its release:

> There are three main components to one's life: heritage, identity, and destiny. Heritage is what you are given via bloodlines. Identity is your own struggle to lead an original life with your unique gifts. Destiny is the unknowable future you must confront, meanwhile discovering your purpose in life.

I found this statement to be intriguing and in a way almost revelatory, and the idea stuck with me. As I began to consider the possibility of writing a biography and social history based on the life and times of John Murray Murdoch, I kept this statement at the forefront of my thinking, and it shaped the way that I analyzed John Murdoch's life, pursued and interpreted research evidence, and tied his own life to themes from prior and subsequent generations. Indeed, heritage, identity, and destiny form essential components of our lives, and with respect to John Murdoch's life, all three components form a thread that weaves its way throughout the chapters of this book.

SCOTTISH SHEPHERD

PROLOGUE:

AN AMERICAN ODYSSEY

Sorrow is soon enough when it comes.

—Scottish proverb

It is part of the American character to consider nothing as desperate—
to surmount every difficulty by resolution and contrivance.

—THOMAS JEFFERSON

The Mississippi River dissects the United States, flowing from the north woods of Minnesota into the Gulf of Mexico near New Orleans. This fabled river has been the lifeblood of the American heartland for generations, an artery for travel, trade, and industry. The river flows south, cutting through the eastern portions of the great prairies, a few hundred miles west of where the vast hardwood forests of the east give way to native grasses and rich loess soils. West of the river lie vast stretches of prairie, which eventually turn into the more desolate high-plains regions leading to the Rocky Mountains, that great sentinel of granite that looks east toward the Big Muddy.

The characteristic murky color and lack of a visibly strong current along most of the river mask its vast power and provide few clues as to its importance in the history of the great American nation. In the early nineteenth century, the Mississippi separated the frontier of the west from the last large outposts of civilization. In the spring of 1804, Lewis and Clark's Corps of Discovery traveled through the strategically important St. Louis area along the river, in preparation for their journey up the Missouri River and into the west. Later that century, untold numbers of pioneers, immigrants, religious pilgrims, fortune-seekers, ne'er-do-wells, outlaws, and opportunists followed Lewis and Clark's paths, using the confluence of the Mississippi and Missouri rivers near St. Louis as their launching point, to a fate that would bring prosperity and satisfaction to some, and misery and destruction to many others. The fate that would await these sojourners as they traveled west proved to be a testing ground or crucible to many, sometimes strengthening their character and resolve, and sometimes reducing them to a life of disappointment, despair, and resentment.

In the mid-nineteenth century, the Mormon prophet Joseph Smith founded the city of Nauvoo, Illinois, on the eastern banks of the Mississippi, about one hundred miles north of St. Louis. From the beginnings of the church in western New York, then to Ohio, and then on to western Missouri, Joseph's beleaguered followers, members of the Church of Jesus Christ of Latter-day Saints, experienced religious persecution unparalleled in the history of this nation. Through it all, Mormonism became the quintessential American religion, following patterns and ideals that represented the American dream and the character that had forged the nation.

Joseph claimed that the biblical Garden of Eden had been in Missouri, and he prophesied that a New Jerusalem, the land of Zion, would be built on the American continent. After being driven from Missouri, the Mormons sought refuge in Nauvoo, building the city up from a disease-infested swamp into one of the largest and most culturally advanced cities along the great river. From the late 1830s until Joseph's bloody murder at the hands of a mob in Carthage, Illinois, in June 1844, Nauvoo prospered. After Joseph's death, it became increasingly obvious that the Saints would be forced to leave the heartland and follow the pattern of movement west that had been cast a few decades earlier by the great explorers. The Saints hoped to find a new refuge in the Rocky Mountains, as the prophet had previously predicted they would.

Once the Saints began to be established in the Great Basin region near the Great Salt Lake, thousands of converts to the faith from Europe continued to make their own pilgrimages west to Zion. From the late 1840s until the transcontinental railroad connected Utah with the east and west coasts in 1869, Mormon converts flocked to the new Promised Land. Sailing from the British Isles to American ports such as Boston, New York, Philadelphia, and New Orleans, this wave of immigrants reached the Mississippi and then made their way west on foot or in ox-drawn carts. They sought not only a spiritual connection with the body of the Saints in Utah, but the American dream of freedom and prosperity. Many of these immigrant Saints never made it, either dying along the way or quitting and heading back east in disillusionment as the going became increasingly difficult. Those who survived the experience and made it to Zion became part of the great epic tale of the Mormon pioneers.

In early April 1852, John Murray Murdoch, a Mormon convert from Ayrshire, Scotland, then an immigrant bound for Utah, walked dejectedly along a muddy road, not far from the banks of the Misssissippi in St. Louis, penniless and numb. His damp and tattered clothing amounted to almost the entirety of his remaining earthly possessions. He had parted with most of his possessions and given the remainder of his money to the elders of the church in Liverpool as part of his instructions to make his immigration to Zion, where he was to work as a shepherd for church president Brigham Young. He was thus in a situation where he was dependent on luck, providence, determination, and the aid of others to reach his goal. His worn boots were covered with mud from recent rains, and there was a chill in the air from the early spring weather. Where hot tears of anguish had trailed down his cheeks an hour earlier, the flesh was now dry and dirty. His eyes burned intensely, and an aching depression and massive confusion clouded his mind and caused his head to feel as if it were a great stone weight. At times his pitiful state lurched on the edge of a feeling of unreality, and he was torn between his trust and faith in God and the overwhelming feeling that he had been abandoned.

John Murdoch was experiencing his personal crucible, the lowest point of his life. He was returning to his wife, Ann, and the Mormon encampment group with whom he was traveling, after having gone to bury the body of his three-year-old daughter. She had recently died, following days of sickness while traveling up the Mississippi by steamer, lacking appropriate food and drinking impure water. Without financial resources or kin nearby, John had attempted to give her an appropriate burial in what amounted to a pauper's grave, deceitfully offered by opportunists who had appeared to sympathize with his plight. John then witnessed the fruits of their deception, a scene of horror so traumatic that it would haunt him at times for the rest of his life and ultimately be forced into the back recesses of his memory by the necessity for survival and sanity. He was now desperate and on the edge of giving up all hope. His daughter's death was the second loss of a child he had experienced in less than two weeks, and he and his pregnant wife were now childless. His twenty-two-month-old son had died of similar causes miles downriver and was buried in a wood yard, his unmarked grave soon to be forgotten by those who lived and worked nearby. Now these two immigrants were put to the ultimate test. Their new faith offered a promise of redemption and hope, yet it could not yet take away the bitter sting of how they now felt, and there was no guarantee that they would even survive the trek to Utah.

Some six weeks later, following a trek across Missouri to an area near Kansas City, Ann gave birth to a baby girl. In the midst of a spectacularly terrifying thunderstorm on the open midwestern prairie, John prepared their tent for the birth and put Ann up a few inches off the ground, to keep her out of the near river of water that was flowing under the walls. After the birth, in the dark of the tent, John saw his third child's face and held her in his arms. Under the poorest of circumstances, the spark of this new life began to lift the gloom and despair that had oppressed him for weeks, and he began to feel that he could go on, and that there might be hope for the future.

This is the story of John Murray Murdoch, a nineteenth-century Scottish immigrant to America, a convert to Mormonism who crossed the ocean and trekked halfway across the continent to live his life in Zion to be gathered with the Saints, and to seek a better life than he had in the old world. It is the story of overcoming a depth of adversity that few can imagine and of doing it all with grace, humor, conviction, and compassion. It is the story of an amazing legacy and of a place and time that are now gone. Although it is John Murdoch's story, it is a prototypical American saga. To a nation of immigrants, underdogs, and dreamers, John Murdoch is an Everyman, an ordinary person who is representative of the larger group. His story is larger than his own life.

1

◆ ◆ ◆

CALEDONIA

There's a well upon the hill from our ancient past
Where an age is standing still holding strong and fast
And there's those that try to tame it and to carve it into stone
Ah but words cannot extinguish it However hard they're thrown

On Loch Etive they have worked with their Highland dreams
By Kilcrennan they have nourished in the mountain streams
And in searching for acceptance they had given it away
Only the children of their children know the price they have to pay

— DOUGIE MacLEAN, from "Turning Away"

As a type they are hardy, tenacious, and unconquerable; an industrious and hard-spirited race, with high ideals, an insatiable thirst for knowledge, a strong love of independence ... [they] have made their mark in whatever country they have adopted. ... The Scotch were poor but their intellectual level was high; and while the country was the poorest in Christendom, the people vied in every branch of learning with the most favored peoples.

— MAUDE GLASGOW, *The Scotch-Irish in Northern Ireland
and the American Colonies*

The story of John Murray Murdoch begins with the story of Scotland, his native country and the land of his forebears, the Murdochs and the Murrays. The descendants of John Murdoch and his beloved Scottish wives, Ann Steele and Isabella Crawford, as well as the American descendants of other immigrants who came to this land during the Scottish diaspora, are now several generations removed from the land of heather, glens, and lochs. Most of their descendants are aware that their ancestral heritage runs through Scotland. How many are aware of the story of their distant ancestors and past is less clear. Although much of our knowledge of the distant past of John Murdoch's Scottish ancestry has been buried, the impact of this heritage is undisputable. The themes and patterns that have been played out in the lives of John Murdoch's descendants, and the descendants of other Scottish immigrants, are intertwined with those of their forebears, close and distant. Thus, the story of Scotland, from its known origins to the time of John Murdoch's tearful departure from his homeland, is one that must be told.

A Scottish journalist has summed up the modern stereotypes and misconceptions about Scotland in the following tongue-in-cheek paragraph:

> The Scots are tall, rugged people who live in the mountain fastnesses of their native land, on a diet of oatmeal porridge and whisky. They wear kilts of tartan weave, play a deafening musical instrument called the bagpipe, are immensely hospitable but cautious with money. They are sparing with words, but when they speak they speak the truth. They have a hard and Spartan religious faith and regard virtually any activity on Sunday as a grave sin. When they leave their native land, they immediately rise to the top in other peoples' industries and professions.[1]

Like all stereotypes, some of this recitation is based in part on truth, but much of it is also nonsense. Reality is always more complicated—and interesting—than stereotypes, a maxim that certainly holds true for the Scottish past.

THE LAND

A culture is shaped to a great extent by the physical features of its geography. In this respect, there is no question that the climate, terrain, and geographical location of Scotland all merged to create the conditions that formed the national character. Scotland is a tiny country, consisting of just over thirty thousand square miles of land. By comparison Scotland is slightly smaller than South Carolina. The state of Utah, John Murdoch's adopted home, is more than two and a half times the size of Scotland, occupying more than eighty-four thousand square miles. Despite or perhaps because of Scotland's small size, meager population (it has never had many more than five million inhabitants), and limited natural resources, the geography and position of the region ultimately helped forge a people who became influential in the modern world to an extent that is absolutely stunning. This eventual influence was hard fought. As the famed Scottish writer Walter Scott said, "I am a Scotsman; therefore I had to fight my way into the world."

Scotland covers the northern third of the island of Great Britain, and it is separated from its neighbor to the south, England, by a jagged, northeast-flowing boundary stemming from the Solway Firth (bay) of the Irish Sea on the west side of the island, to an area near where the mouth of the Tweed River flows into the North Sea on the east side. By wide-open American conventions, Scotland is surprisingly close to several other European nations on the other side of the North Sea. At the closest points, Norway is only about 250 miles northeast and Denmark only about 350 miles due east of Scotland—closer than Laramie, Wyoming, is to Salt Lake City. To the southeast, Germany is less than four hundred miles away, with Belgium and France not much farther. To the southwest, Ireland is as close as twenty-five miles at some points—no farther than a modern American suburb is from a downtown business district. The close proximity of other European landforms and peoples to Scotland is a key to understanding the origins of the Scottish people, who stem from a mixture of the inhabitants of northwestern Europe. It is also a key to understanding the constant sieges upon Scotland by conquering peoples from the south and east.

The southernmost edge of Scotland is situated at the latitude of about 55 degrees north, whereas the northernmost point—the Orkney Islands—is about 59 degrees north. For a North American equivalent perspective, this range of latitude is comparable to the region from Prince Rupert, British Columbia, to Homer, Alaska. Although the climate of Scotland is somewhat tempered because the land is surrounded by various arms of the Atlantic Ocean, it is a decidedly cool northern climate, similar in many respects to the coastal and western mountainous areas of the Pacific Northwest and British Columbia, with a copious amount of rainfall in many areas, and cold winds from Scandinavia to the east. Although it is true that much of Scotland is known for being damp and cold, its climate has always been viewed as favorable by northern European standards, especially when contrasting it with the much colder climes of the Scandinavian nations to the relatively close northeast.[2]

One additional aspect of the land has greatly shaped Scotland's culture: it has some of the thinnest, poorest soil in all of Europe, making agriculture a risky endeavor, and forcing the ancient inhabitants of the land to be exceedingly clever and industrious if they were to avoid starving to death. The largest portion of Scotland—about three fourths of the total land mass—is encompassed by the lightly populated highlands, a rocky, bare, mountainous area where the odds have always been greatly against the success of any farming endeavors, and where the difficult geography led to the development of a hardy, self-reliant system of clans. By contrast, the Scottish lowlands, where the majority of the population has always existed (including John Murdoch's immediate ancestors), is somewhat more amenable to agriculture and commerce, although it would be a stretch of the imagination to say that this area was a fertile Eden. This geographical division of Scotland resulted in the development of two separate cultures—the Highlanders and the Lowlanders—each with its own historic language, customs, and ancestry. In many respects, this separateness is still reflected somewhat in Scotland's national identity.

CONQUERORS AND CONFLICT

The proximity and relatively easy access of other European regions to Scotland had a great influence on the development of immigration patterns, culture, and the national character. The first inhabitants of the area are thought to be Neolithic people—short individuals with long heads—who eked out a living primarily through hunting and gathering, and who created dwellings that were little more than holes in the ground with branches for roofs. During the Bronze Age, new arrivals from continental Europe ultimately mixed with the aboriginal inhabitants. We know little about these new arrivals except that they buried their dead in circular graves, devised earthenware beakers for storing food and water, and must have been intelligent to be able to survive as new arrivals in a difficult land.

The first branch of Celtic immigrants, the Britons, arrived during the Iron Age, wandering to Scotland from eastern Europe. The Britons were the first inhabitants of the area to leave a record of their language, which survives to this day in the fringes of European linguistics. These people were good husbandmen, skillful with horses and carts. They tended to live in small communities, keeping mostly to themselves until they were forced to band together and with the other inhabitants of the region to try to thwart an invasion by the Romans in about AD 80.

It has been said that the Roman invasion was the first true test of Scottish character under stress, revealing and shaping a personality of dogged stubbornness, and the propensity to fight to the death for a cause. The Romans referred to the inhabitants they encountered in the north as "Caledonians," although some of them were later called "Picts," because of their custom of tattooing designs or pictures on their foreheads and other parts of their bodies. The Roman incursion into Scotland was not particularly successful, despite being led by one of the Empire's best generals, Julius Agricola. Although the Romans caused substantial death and destruction, they never conquered the whole region, and they were constantly under siege by attacking bands of northerners. By AD 117, a few years after a mass attack on them, and after the mysterious disappearance of their entire Ninth Legion, the Roman emperor Hadrian decided that the area was not worth the trouble it was causing, and the greatest military power on earth retreated south, building a fifteen foot wall about seventy-three miles long, near the current Scottish border with England.

Hadrian's Wall, eight years in the making, was designed to mark the edge of the Roman dominion and to discourage travel into the south by the Picts. By the late 300s, the Empire was under siege on many fronts, and the determined Picts continued to spread southward. After fierce attacks on the Romans by bands of *Scotti* (meaning "raiders") warriors who sailed from Northern Ireland, and after the arrival of more Germanic immigrants from the east, the Romans retreated farther south, and never again had a strong presence in the area. By then the decline of Rome was in full swing, and the Romans' retreat from Scotland was just one of many troubles that led to the Empire's ultimate fall in 476.

For several centuries following the Roman retreat little is known regarding developments in the Scottish region. When the Romans left, not only did the heavy hand of their occupation cease, but their influence on architecture, art, building construction, and other advanced cultural and scientific endeavors waned. This period is often called Scotland's Dark Ages, partly because it is so difficult to reconstruct the happenings of the era from historical artifacts. What we do know about this era is primarily what has been handed down through oral traditions.

Perhaps the single most important development of the era between about 450 and 840 was the coming of Christianity to Brittany. Much of the spread of Christianity in that region was attributable to the Romans, many of whom were Christians. Monks and priests—many of them having been trained in Rome—later moved to northern Brittany, establishing the presence of the church there. The influence that the ancient pagan religions had over many of the inhabitants of the area was gradually weakened, as Christianity became increasingly popular and powerful. Because of cultural differences and the great difficulty of centralized church and government administration at that time, there were substantial differences in the way that the Christian religion was practiced across European regions. The Irish model represented a distinct view, and the Roman model another ideal. Ultimately, the Roman model prevailed in the region, following a meeting in Yorkshire in 664, which had the result of creating a relatively uniform faith across Britain. Although the clan system of governance had taken root and a strong class system was beginning to emerge by the mid-ninth century, Scotland was beginning to become a nation, connected under an increasingly shared Christian faith, being forced to band together to ward off attacks by Viking invaders, and becoming somewhat united under Kenneth MacAlpin, who became the first King of the Scots in 839.

Defying the English: Scottish Heroes

The story of Scotland during the eleventh through fourteenth centuries involves continual conflict with England, a theme that would continue for several centuries. The arrogant English kings generally considered the Scots to be inferior, and they continually made incursions to the north, attempting to keep the Scots under their domination. However, the Scots were not easily intimidated and their resistance became legendary. William Wallace was a commoner who led a fierce revolt against the English with his small but loyal band of warriors. Wallace led his outmatched contingent to some stunning victories but was finally defeated and forced to live in hiding for several years. He was ultimately betrayed and turned over to the king by a pro-English lord in 1305. Taken to London for punishment, Wallace suffered the penalty for treason against the English and was made to be an example: he was brutally tortured, hanged, drawn and quartered, and his head was spiked on London Bridge while the four quarters of his corpse were displayed at key points in Scotland to further intimidate the Scots into accepting English domination and discouraging further rebellion. The effect of all this was quite the opposite of what the English King Edward intended: Wallace, despite his sometimes heavy-handed tactics with his own people, became the greatest hero in all of Scottish history and inspired further uprisings.

Robert Bruce ("the Bruce") was a Scottish noble and contemporary of Wallace. He regretted his prior allegiance to England, and he believed that he had a legitimate claim to the Scottish throne. Undoubtedly aided by the anger and emerging nationalistic feelings that were a by-product of Wallace's execution, Bruce rode this wave of fervor into open conflict with England and asserted his leadership within Scotland. He united a large portion of Scots in further uprisings as he led armies into battle against England over several years. He led the Scots to their most crucial military victory in history at the battle of Bannockburn in 1314. This victory united the people and put Bruce clearly in charge. Although the conflicts with England continued, Scotland had developed the unity it needed to forge a strong national character. Bruce, like Wallace before him, received much of his support from the people of the Ayrshire and Dumfries regions of Scotland, the areas that would one day be considered the ancestral home region for most of the Murdochs.

Treachery, Violence, and Oppression: A Hardscrabble Life

In recounting the glory of William Wallace, Robert Bruce, and Scotland's against-all-odds military victories over the English during the thirteenth and fourteenth centuries, one must be careful to avoid glorifying this era into some kind of bygone golden age of Scottish national pride and great attainment. On the contrary, it must be said that for most Scots who lived during those times, it was an utterly miserable existence. These two centuries were still part of the dark ages in most respects. Although Wallace and Bruce attained stunning victories against their English foes at times, they often accomplished these feats through the pale of treachery, betrayal, and a general lack of support of many of their own countrymen. The landed nobility of Scotland during these times often resorted to cruel and underhanded measures to maintain their status. For the peasants who toiled in serfdom, life was a harsh reality where starvation was always on the horizon, disease was rampant, and superstitious ignorance and violence were the norm. In addition the government oppressed its citizens most grievously, and terrible schisms and corruptions abounded within the church. These conditions were only part of the bleak fabric of daily life in Scotland. Within a few years following King Robert Bruce's victory at Bannockburn, nearly a third of the entire population living between India and Iceland died of the Black Death of 1348–50, and Scotland was certainly not spared from this pestilence. Chaos, futility, ignorance, violence, and terror reigned supreme at times, giving great credence to the notion that the fourteenth century was an incredibly bad time for humanity.[3]

The Seeds of Modernity

For the next three centuries conditions improved in many respects. Scotland generally was ruled by her own kings and queens, and the seeds of modernity were eventually sown. By about 1500, a series of legal reforms by the Scottish parliament began to rein in the power of the nobility, a rising standard of living was emerging, and there were substantial developments in industry, commerce, and the arts. By the late 1500s, an important set of reforms was enacted to curb the abuses, excesses, and increasing corruption of the Roman Catholic Church in Scotland. This Scottish Protestant reformation ultimately led to a weakening of ties with Rome and the creation of an independent Scottish church or *kirk*. It also served as a reminder of the fiercely independent Scottish character.

When Mary, Queen of Scots, returned to Scotland in 1561 after being raised a Catholic in France, she found out just how belligerent and tough the independent Scottish Protestants could be. Although a planned burning in effigy of a Roman Catholic priest was wisely abandoned during Mary's state entry at Edinburgh, her private mass was denounced by none other than John Knox, a former Catholic priest who had become the fiery voice of the Scottish reformation. Mary's own priests were physically attacked, and Knox further antagonized the queen by writing a polemic diatribe that denounced having a woman rule the nation, *A First Blast of the Trumpet against the Monstrous Regimen of Women,* which stated, among other things, that it was against natural and divine law for a woman to hold dominion over men, and warned that the judgments of God would sweep Scotland for her breach of the God-given order of things. In modern terms, Knox could accurately be called a bigot and misogynist, but he also had twice the charisma of any present-day American televangelist. He was said to be "one who neither feared nor flattered any flesh,"[4] a description that proved true on many occasions throughout his life. Knox had the ability to whip his followers into an uncontrolled frenzy, preaching hellfire and damnation to them until they quaked in their boots. His goal was to mobilize, if not bully, Scotland's nobility and urban classes into overthrowing the influence of Catholicism and adopting the Protestant dogma of John Calvin, and in the process to turn the Scots into God's chosen people. Knox's resolve was hardened during his early years, when he spent several years imprisoned for his passionate radical religious and political views, including time spent chained to the rowing benches of the king's galleys. In short, he was a force of nature. When Mary called Knox to a private meeting to account for his actions, he was neither penitent nor accommodating, and he even had the audacity to suggest that the Scottish people need not follow the Crown if the Crown did not do right by God.

The tenacity and character of the Scots during this era—both good and bad—is captured succinctly in the following statement from a modern writer of popular history of the British Isles:

> The Scots were a proud and tenacious people. Foreign visitors praised them as courageous warriors, but also found them to be uncouth and lawless, hostile to strangers and inordinately quarrelsome. Their way of life was seen as primitive. The weather was often cold and wet, and the roads, where they existed, were atrocious. The people were ignorant and superstitious, and there was a widespread belief in witchcraft. It appeared that all classes valued money more than honour. However, Scotland was in many respects a civilised land: it boasted three universities, and had thriving trade and cultural links with other countries.[5]

UNION WITH ENGLAND

By the end of the seventeenth century, Scotland had gradually drifted toward a union with her long-hated neighbor to the south. The idea of an alliance with England was something few Scots wanted, and it caused many to correctly fear that such a union would be in essence a takeover by England, something that ultimately proved to be true. The onset of Scotland's loss of independence was later mourned by Robert Burns, in his poem "Farewell To A' Our Scottish Fame":

> *Farewell to a' our Scottish fame,*
> *Faerweel to our ancient glory!*
> *Farewell ev'n to our Scottish name,*
> *Sae famed in martial story.*

With the Act of Union in 1707, the merger with England became a reality, and many Scots regretted the price that came with this new alliance. A final attempt to install a Scottish monarch occurred with a revolt by the Highlanders, the so-called Jacobite uprising in 1745, in which Charles Edward Stuart ("Bonnie Prince Charlie"), a potential heir to the Scottish throne, returned to Scotland from France with a few followers, joined with Highlander clan armies, and led them into battle against the English. At first, the English forces were easily swept away, and Charles was magnanimous and humble in victory as his forces continued to march south. But plagued by smaller numbers than their English foes, and by a lack of unity toward this cause by the Scottish people, Charles's forces were defeated at the battle of Culloden in 1746, and he was forced to escape to France. Many years later, the American descendants of John Murdoch and other Scottish immigrants would sing "My Bonnie Lies Over the Ocean" as children, with many not realizing that this tune was a sweet and mournful homage to the Highlanders' deposed leader and last hope for a Scottish monarch, "Bonnie Prince Charlie," who was separated "o'er the ocean" from Scotland by the Irish and Celtic Seas and the English Channel. As a result of the uprising, many clan chiefs were brutally executed by the English, and bagpipes and kilts were outlawed for decades.[6] The prohibition of kilts and bagpipes probably served to elevate their status as symbols of the Scottish national identity beyond what they deserved, another indicator of the proud, obstinate Scottish national character. Ultimately, kilts would become co-opted as vacation dress and ceremonial garb of English nobles and royalty, a sure sign that the merger with England was final, and that Scotland's future would be forever connected to that of England.

By the dawn of the eighteenth century the dark ages were over in Europe, and western civilization had made remarkable strides in almost every aspect of life. Scotland was no exception. The eighteenth century is still considered to be a remarkable period of development and influence for the Scottish nation. By the mid-nineteenth century many Scots were lamenting the end of this golden era, recognizing that the heady days of Scottish leadership in business, literature, and public life were waning. Again, one must be careful to not lose sight of the fact that even during the era of Scotland's greatest worldwide influence there were tremendous times of difficulty for common people, such as John Murdoch's forebears. Sandwiched between the good times were reminders that life was a constant struggle for most Scots:

> The eighteenth century opened in Scotland with dark and dismal prospects. The poorer classes were in misery, hunger, and the shadow of death. This was the result of a series of bad seasons, and a poor condition of cultivation. On the roads were to be seen dead bodies, and dying mothers lying with starved infants that had sucked dry breasts. Even in the streets of towns starving men fell down and died. These were known as the hungry years. When meal was sold in markets women were heard crying, "How shall we go home and see our children die of hunger?"[7]

THE SCOTTISH ENLIGHTENMENT

From the days of John Murdoch's earliest identified ancestors (dating back to 1620 in one case, but primarily dating only to the early eighteenth century) until his departure for America in 1852, Scotland's history is well documented, and it is an amazing tale. What is perhaps most interesting and inspiring is the story of how a tiny, poor nation was able to create a people that ultimately had so much impact and influence. Arthur Herman's 2001 book *How the Scots Invented the Modern World* may be guilty of hyperbole in the title, but it documents convincingly that the Scots created many of the basic ideals of modernity. Herman argues that the Scots transformed their own culture and society in the eighteenth century, and then carried their legacy wherever they went. Although some modern detractors might scoff at this notion and look down on the Scottish and Scots-Irish contributions to modern society as consisting primarily of stock car racing, the moonshine whisky still, and country music, the truth is that there is virtually no aspect of modern American society that has not been influenced to some extent by this heritage.

Scotland became the first modern literate society in Europe. Not only did the Scottish Protestant Reformation create a strong audience for reading the Bible, there was a virtual proliferation of books of many types, an effort that was aided greatly by the removal of religious censorship barriers. Following the failed Jacobite revolution in the mid-1700s, the cities of Glasgow and Edinburgh became the two most important centers of the "Scottish Enlightenment." Edinburgh was the center of an artistic and literary enclave, whereas Glasgow became a magnet for innovation with a focus on practicality and getting things done. Together, they created hubs of critical mass that allowed new ideas, innovations, and forms of expression to incubate. The writings of Scottish intellectuals such as David Hume and Adam Smith made enormous contributions to modern philosophical and scientific thinking. Smith is undoubtedly best known for his contributions to the field of economics, most specifically his 1776 book *The Wealth of Nations*, but he was also a philosopher who lectured at Glasgow University on the topics of ethics, rhetoric, and jurisprudence. Hume was a philosopher of science and a skeptic who wrote extensively on human tendencies to behave, think, and feel in customary and predictable ways. He aspired to apply Newtonian-like laws to predict human behavior, and he also developed a rudimentary classification scheme for the contents of the human mind.

In the literary world, writers such as Walter Scott and Robert Burns made enormous contributions that ultimately reached well beyond the borders of Scotland. Scott was a novelist and poet who became enormously popular for his historical novels, such as *Ivanhoe*, *The Talisman*, and *Rob Roy*. Scott's novels dealt with cultural conflict, and often the specific conflict between old Scottish values and newer English values. Burns, a common man and farmer, became the "Scottish Bard," and most beloved of all Scottish writers, for his song lyrics and poetry. So influential was Burns that he became the namesake and honored memory for "Burns Suppers," or "Burns Night Suppers," which are roughly the Scottish equivalent of an American Thanksgiving feast. At a Burns supper, celebrants eat a traditional Scottish meal (especially including haggis—boiled sheep stomach filled with a pudding of minced liver, oatmeal, suet, onions, and spices), drink Scotch whisky, and recite Burns poetry. The evening usually commences with a recitation of the "Selkirk Prayer," which is of unknown origin but is usually attributed to Burns:

> *Some hae meat and cannot eat.*
> *Some cannot eat that want it:*

But we hae meat and we can eat,
Sae let the Lord be thankit.

Burns's work and legend undoubtedly had some influence on young John Murdoch, who lived as a boy in Ayr (Ayrshire), Burns's home county, within one generation of the Bard. Evidence of this influence is that John Murdoch penned several poems himself and desired so badly to have the ability to create poetic verse as a young man that he prayed fervently to receive the "gift of poetry."

In addition to major developments in literature, philosophy, and the arts, the Scottish Enlightenment of the eighteenth century served as a watershed period for commerce, science, architecture, and invention. Glasgow became an emporium of commerce and manufacturing. Key merchants developed close ties to the American colonies—especially Maryland, Virginia, and North Carolina—for importation and worldwide distribution of tobacco. The Scottish merchants made their profits not so much through marketing their own unique products as through developing efficient transatlantic routes of shipping and distribution, as well as through employing ruthless cost-cutting measures. Publishing and printing became another Glasgow-based powerhouse industry, spawning many imitators across Great Britain. Engineer James Watt, best known for his remarkable improvements to the modern steam engine, helped build Glasgow's first dry dock, which further established the area as a major center of commerce and industry. Architect Robert Adam helped lead an eighteenth-century transformation in the fields of design and building, moving beyond the traditional reliance on classical Greek and Italian ideas of design architecture into a modern, sleek, functional, and artistic vision of building that became imitated throughout the modern world.

The eighteenth and early nineteenth centuries proved to be a fertile period for Scottish influence, but it is worth considering that much of this influence was not so much in the high profile inventions and contributions of Scotland's movers and shakers, but in the ways in which the work of common people developed. Although the urban areas of Edinburgh, Glasgow, and Aberdeen became focal points for high accomplishments in the arts, commerce, and invention, the Scottish people also created major innovations during this period in less glamorous endeavors such as coal mining, cattle and sheep ranching, textile weaving, and stone cutting. Two of these occupations of common people—sheep ranching and coal mining—would become pursuits of young John Murdoch. The narrow but densely populated region between the Firth of Clyde to the west and the

Firth of Ford to the east (spanning the region from Glasgow to Edinburgh) also contained some of the richest coalfields in Britain. Perhaps not coincidentally, this coal mining region proved to be the area of Scotland that was the most fertile ground for Mormon missionaries in the 1840s and 1850s.[8] Although John Murdoch apparently had no great love of coal mining and had seen it take his father's life, he earned his stripes in this most difficult and grimy of occupations as he labored to earn money for his family. Because sheep ranching had long been a part of Scotland's tradition, the state of the craft there was said to be several cuts above what existed in America and other places in the New World, and there was a demand for the skills of Scottish shepherds.[9] It would ultimately be his skills as a shepherd that gave John Murdoch his opportunity to emigrate to America.

HER GREATEST EXPORT: THE SCOTTISH DIASPORA

Scotland's contributions in the arts, sciences, and business were extraordinary but it has been said that its greatest export was its people. Because the physical size and lack of natural resources have kept Scotland's population at a relatively small level, and because the Scottish character became so connected to innovation and creativity, it was inevitable that many Scots would leave their homeland in search of adventure and opportunity, particularly as the world opened up in the sixteenth through nineteenth centuries.[10] When John Murdoch, Ann Steele, and Isabella Crawford made their own journeys to America in the mid-nineteenth century, they were following a pattern that had become an aspiration of many of their countrymen for at least two hundred years, and they became part of the fabled "Scottish Diaspora." The term *diaspora* may be a misnomer, because in sheer numbers Scottish immigrants during this period amounted to about three quarters of a million, in comparison to the staggering five million Irish who left their homeland. However, the influence these Scottish immigrants ultimately had in their new lands was disproportionate to their numbers and was aided by the fact that most Scottish immigrants were reasonably well educated and nearly all spoke English. Although Scottish people immigrated to many regions of the world during this period, the most common targets were the English-speaking British colonies in Canada, America, New Zealand, and Australia. North America in particular became a magnet for Scottish resettlement. The Canadian province of Nova Scotia ("New Scotland") was originally a scheme for a new Scottish colony, hatched by King James I. As it turned out, the difficult climate and heavy excise taxes conspired to make this effort ill-fated.

In contrast, America proved to be the foremost magnet and center of success for Scottish immigration. Scots, especially the Ulster Scots or Scots-Irish (a branch of Calvinists who moved from Scotland to northern Ireland) became indispensable to the management and cultural life of the American colonies, especially in the southern and mid-Atlantic states during the seventeenth and early eighteenth centuries. Many of these immigrants moved to the Appalachian mountain regions of Virgina, West Virginia, Kentucky, the Carolinas, and Tennessee, where their Scottish mannerisms are still reflected in traditional mountain dialects (such as "critter" for "creature," "thar" for "there," "nekkid" for "naked," and "widder" for "widow"), where their musical traditions evolved into the high and lonesome sound of the mountains, and where their propensity for independence and stubbornness became legendary.[11] One of the favored explanations for the word *redneck* is that it is a Scottish border term meaning Presbyterian. It has been said that the Lowland Presbyterians who signed a solemn covenant and left Scotland for Ireland during a period of English oppression signed this covenant in their own blood, and sometimes wore pieces of red cloth around their neck as a token of this covenant. The term *redneck* thus may have been later reinforced in America when some southern Presbyterian ministers wore red ministerial collars in memory of the solemn covenant of their forebears.[12] The word *cracker* is said to come from the Scots word "crak" or "craik," meaning one who is a loud talker or a trait that apparently also became associated with some of the Scottish immigrants to the American south. Although the meaning of these words has changed over time, their continuance in the dialects of the deep south and the southern Appalachian mountain regions shows the widespread influence of the Scots. It is also worth noting that the famous feuding families of Kentucky and West Virginia—the Hatfields and McCoys—both had Scottish roots, and were in a sense re-enacting the famous Highlander clan feuds of some of their Scottish predecessors, the Campbells and MacDonalds.

Although the Ulster Scots made the earliest large migrations to America, the Highland and Lowland Scots also began emigration on a large scale by the late eighteenth century, spreading to every part of the new United States, and carrying with them their culture and traditions. Some of the most influential and powerful Americans of this era were Scottish immigrants who had come to the land of opportunity to seek their fortune: inventor Alexander Graham Bell, industrialist Andrew Carnegie, scientist-physician Benjamin Rush, and the federalist Alexander Hamilton were all Scottish immigrants or otherwise had recent Scottish roots. In

American politics, eleven U.S. presidents, thirty-five Supreme Court justices, fifty-six signatories of the Declaration of Independence, nearly half of all secretaries of the treasury, nearly one third of the U.S. secretaries of state, and nine of the thirteen governors of the newly created United States were of recent Scottish ancestry.

The reasons for immigration of the many Scots who came to the United States varied considerably, but in a sense they were all driven by the promise of opportunity. To John Murdoch and his fellow Zion-bound Saints, those opportunities were spiritual as well as economic. Although nineteenth-century Scotland had many advantages if one were in the right situation, there was still a stiff class system in place, and the lot of common men and women was often one of grinding poverty. Over time, the upper and middle classes of Scotland began to lose the hard-driving edge that had long been part of their heritage and the fuel of their success, and were instead settling into a lifestyle of English gentility. In turn, the social, economic, and religious climate in Scotland became increasingly stale and unattractive. By the mid to late nineteenth century, the intellectual capital and economic engine of Scotland was on the wane, and its days as the incubator of modernity and generator of Europe's most innovative ideas were over. To young John Murdoch, a poor man with high aspirations but few possibilities, and other working class Scots in his shoes, the promise of a new life in America must have seemed sweet indeed.

NOTES

1. Clifford Hanley, *The Scots* (New York: Times Books, 1980), 1.

2. Peter Frye and Fiona Somerset Fry, *The History of Scotland* (London: Routledge, 1982), 3.

3. Barbara W. Tuchman, *A Distant Mirror: The Calamitous 14th Century* (New York: Alfred Knopf, 1978), xiii.

4. Alison Wier, *Mary, Queen of Scots and the Murder of Lord Darnley* (New York: Ballantine Books, 2003), 29.

5. Ibid., 21.

6. Nigel Blundell, *Scotland* (New York: Barnes & Noble Books, 1998), 146.

7. James Edward Shaw, *Ayrshire, 1745–1950: A Social and Industrial History* (Edinburgh, Scotland: Oliver and Boyd, 1953), 137.

8. Frederick S. Buchanan, ed., *A Good Time Coming: Mormon Letters to Scotland* (Salt Lake City: University of Utah Press, 1988), 1–2.

9. "Scotland and the Victorian West Reality," Electric Scotland, http://www.electricscotland.com/history/world/victorian_west.htm (accessed October 28, 2004).

10. T. M. Devine, *Scotland's Empire and the Shaping of the Americas, 1600–1815* (Washington, DC: Smithsonian Books, 2003), 94–97.

11. Arthur Herman, *How the Scots Invented the Modern World: The True Story of How Western Europe's Poorest Nation Created Our World and Everything in It* (New York: Crown Publishers, 2001).

12. "Scottish Hillbillies and Rednecks?" Scottish History Online, Todd J. Wilkinson, http://www.scotshistoryonline.co.uk/rednecks/rednecks.html (accessed October 28, 2004).

2

•••

THE MURDOCHS

There are three main components to one's life: heritage, identity, and destiny. Heritage is what you are given via bloodlines. Identity is your own struggle to lead an original life with your unique gifts. Destiny is the unknowable future you must confront, meanwhile discovering your purpose in life.

— TIMOTHY WHITE

I'm talking with my father across these gentle Perthshire hills
It's timeless mysteries that we gather to make the memories that we fill
He says don't fix what is not broken no need to find what's not been lost
It's a heavy gate we have to open an endless field we have to cross

— DOUGIE MACLEAN, from "Talking with My Father"

John Murdoch's Scottish ancestors have been traced as far back as the early seventeenth century. The earliest currently known ancestor, Moses Loudon, was born in 1620. The known ancestors of John Murdoch lived primarily in the adjoining shires (or counties) of Ayr and Dumfries, which are also referred to as Ayrshire and Dumfrieshire. This general area is in the southwest sector of Scotland, separated from England to the southeast by the Cheviot Hills, and surrounded by the Irish Sea where Ayr juts out to the southwest. Although this sector of Scotland is considered to be the lowlands, much of Ayr and Dumfries is within a geographical region that is referred to as the Southern Uplands, because it is covered with hills and small mountains. John Murdoch's ancestors and their fellow Scots in this region would have survived by small-scale farming, raising sheep and cattle, fishing, extracting coal, and perhaps engaging in some limited trade. In later years, as the industrial revolution swept Britain, the coal mining industry increased dramatically, and the ironworks, textile, and shipbuilding industries became established in Scotland and would have provided additional economic opportunities, resulting in increased urbanization in the cities to the north, including Kilmarnock, Glasgow, and Edinburgh, and spread to some extent into Ayr and Dumfries.

John's parents, James Murdoch and Mary Murray, were married January 10, 1811, nine years before John's birth. James was born about 1786 in the village of Commondyke in Ayr. His wife, Mary (later known as "Wee Granny"), was born October 13, 1782, in the village of Glencairn in Dumfries. James Murdoch's immediate family heritage included the Murdochs and the Osbornes of Ayr, whereas Mary Murray's immediate lineage included the Murrays of Ayr and Dumfries and the McCalls of Dumfries. Other surnames that have been traced in John Murray Murdoch's family lines include Wyllie, Watson, Muckle, Loudon, and Miller.

The Family Name

The Murdoch family name has been traced to two Gaelic names, *Muireach* and *Murchadh*. The two names apparently coalesced into the current family name at some point in time, and they have been linked historically to either Gaels or Norseman of Irish descent.[1] A less common Scottish spelling of this name is Murdock (with a *k* substituted for the *h*). The primary reason that many Murdochs changed the spelling of their name to Murdock after emigrating to America was to make it conform to the Americanized way of pronouncing the hard *k* consonant at the end of the word. The name Murdock was also used in Scotland, although much less frequently than the Murdoch spelling for this name. A recent survey of names found in published phone directories has indicated that in Scotland the proportion of Murdoch to Murdock spellings (about 120 Murdochs for every one Murdock) is much different than in the United States (where there are four Murdocks for every one Murdoch).[2] It is interesting to consider that John Murdoch, like many other Scottish emigrants to the United States, changed the spelling of his last name to Murdock after his arrival. He sometimes used the two spellings of his surname interchangeably within the same document. When the Murdoch family dedicated a new gravestone for John Murdoch and his two wives on August 24, 2002, officers of the family organization elected to use the *k*-ending spelling, because John increasingly adopted it after he left Scotland. At a family program connected to the gravestone dedication, Dallas Murdoch, who was then serving as president of the James and Mary Murdoch family organization, explained that following John's passing, many family members chose to revert to the original Scottish spelling with the *h*-ending, as a tribute to their heritage, a change that has resulted in two spellings of the same name within the extended family.[3]

Another interesting detail is that although the Murdoch name is not uncommon in Scottish history, it is clearly not among the most common or popular surnames in that nation, either currently or in the past. In a 1995 list of the one hundred most frequent surnames appearing in Scottish marriage, birth, and death registries compiled by the government of Scotland, Murdoch did not even make the list.[4] By contrast, *Murray* was the twelfth most common name, whereas *Osborne* and *McCall* also failed to make the top-hundred list. The most common name in the registry—by a rather wide margin—is *Smith*, with *Brown* in distant second place. Neither of these two most common Scottish names would automatically inspire thoughts of Scotland among present-day Americans, who are more likely to attach a Scottish connection to names such as MacDonald, Campbell, and Mackenzie.

Although the Murdoch name may not be among the most common in Scotland, John Murdoch's ancestors of the Murdoch line, both near and distant, have an interesting story, and they played important roles in the development of the Scottish nation. As is true with John Murdoch's own known ancestry, most Scots of that surname can trace their ancestral homeland to the southern uplands region of Scotland, particularly the Dumfries and Galloway areas, which are closely connected to Ayr. Some of the Murdochs from this region are known to have departed for Ulster in northern Ireland about 1600, as part of the emergence of Protestantism. Some of these Murdochs and their descendants became the Scots-Irish or Ulster Scots who eventually emigrated to the American colonies during the seventeenth century, particularly to the mountainous regions of the southern colonies.

The Murdoch name and its close derivations have been traced to about the ninth or tenth centuries. Some of the early Murdochs were apparently associated with the prominent MacDonald and Macpherson highland clans, a fact that has led some modern Murdoch descendants to perhaps mistakenly adopt the tartans of those groups. Most informed accounts consider these familial connections to be marginal and make the case that the large majority of Murdochs were not related by either geography or kinship group to these better known clans.[5] A much better case can be made that the large majority of Murdochs descended from the peoples of the southern uplands region, and that the Galloway, Dumfries, and Ayr areas of this region are the closest thing there is to a Murdoch ancestral homeland.

A Gift from the Bruce: The Ravens and Cumloden

One of the most enduring tales handed down to present generations regarding the Murdoch name is the story of the ravens and Cumloden.[6] Stories such as these were handed down through the oral tradition and it is thus hard to tell how much is truth and how much is myth. Nevertheless it is an interesting and inspiring story that bears repeating. According to legend, King Robert Bruce and a few score of his troops and followers, after some initial victories against the English, found themselves outmatched and on the run in 1307 in the Galloway region, fleeing from the armies of their English foe John of Lorn. To outwit his pursuers, the Bruce ordered his forces to split into three groups, go separate ways, and rendezvous the next day at a house on Loch (lake) Dee. After his own group was scattered in the ferocious pursuit, the Bruce found himself alone but did make his way to Loch Dee, where he found lodging at the home of a widow in Craigencallie.

In the morning the widow observed some of the ornaments of royalty that the Bruce was wearing and guessed his true identity. King Robert confirmed his identity and asked the woman if she had any sons who could assist him in his time of distress. She told the king that she had three sons who would be at his service. The Bruce asked her for something to eat, being famished from his flight. She offered him a bit of oatmeal and goat's milk—the only food she had in the house. While the food was being prepared, the woman's sons—all of whom were stout men—appeared and willingly accepted the king's invitation. After finishing his meal King Robert asked them if they had any weapons and skill in using them. The brothers stated that they used only bow and arrow. Accepting the king's invitation to demonstrate their skill in archery, the oldest brother, Mackie, took aim at two ravens that were perched atop a large rock near the house. His arrow was dead-on, going directly through the heads of both birds. The second oldest son, Murdoch, then took aim at a raven in flight, and shot him through the body. The youngest lad, MacClurg, likewise took aim but did not meet with success.

The English were camped at Moss Raplock, a great marsh on the other side of Loch Dee. Seeing that their king's forces were greatly outnumbered, the three young men offered Robert a plan: they would round up all of the goats and horses in the vicinity and use them to cloak the king and his small band, who would conceal themselves in the middle of the herd. The English, upon hearing the noise from this herd, mistakenly assumed that a much larger force of Robert's armies were in the area, and they decided to stay put at their encampment another day. At dawn the following day King Robert and his men attacked the English with great fury. Although outnumbered greatly, these men defeated their enemies in a fierce battle that became known as the battle of Glentrool of 1307. For years afterward Scots who dug peat from the marsh for fuel found broken swords and battle-axe heads.

The three young men remained close to Robert the Bruce in all of his wars with the English. After the English were (temporarily) forced out of the region, and after the nobles who had sided with the English were dispossessed of their lands, King Robert allocated these lands for the men who had stuck with him and served him in his battles. Upon asking the three young men what lands they desired in return for their service, they claimed that they had not expected a reward, but modestly asked for only a three-by-five-mile strip of land in the Hassock and Cumloden area, just northeast of Newton Stewart. The Bruce agreed to their request, and Murdoch became known henceforth as Murdoch of Cumloden. To this day there are many Murdochs in the Newton Stewart area. The killing of the two ravens with one arrow by the oldest of the three young men is today commemorated prominently on a Murdoch coat of arms.

AUCHINLECK, AYR: THE ANCESTRAL HOMELAND

The presence of individuals with the Murdoch surname in southwest Scotland during the eighteenth century can be illustrated by snippets and footnotes mined from some of the voluminous correspondence of James Boswell (1740–95), a famed Scottish writer, lawyer, and socialite. Boswell is best known for his work as a writer, especially for his masterpiece *The Life of Samuel Johnson*, a work that has long been hailed as one of the best and most influential biographies ever written in the English language. Those who are acquainted with Boswell the writer seldom realize that he simultaneously had another prominent role during the last two decades of his life, as a wealthy landowner who became the ninth laird of Auchinleck (a large estate and parish in Ayr) in 1782. Boswell's prodigious correspondence to his overseers James Bruce and Andrew Gibb regarding the condition of his Auchinleck estate and the details of their dealings with his tenants has been carefully preserved and compiled into a collection that allows a glimpse not only of the lives of some Murdochs in that time and place, but of life in rural eighteenth-century Scotland under conditions that were not far removed from the ancient feudal system.[7]

In his "lord and master" role as laird of Auchinleck, Boswell was known to be a landowner who became well acquainted with his tenants, who was fair and often lenient in the conditions of rent payment, and who strove to honor the feudal principle of mutual obligation between a master and his vassals to the well-being of both. He apparently took a personal interest in the business not only of his estate (where he did not live) but of the people who populated it.

In these letters and accompanying documents the Murdoch name figures prominently. The editors of this collection noted that when Boswell became the laird of Auchinleck, he understood that some families (the Murdochs are specifically mentioned by name) had lived on the estate for several generations, a fact that instilled his feelings of feudal obligation toward them. In these documents there are twenty-six different Murdochs mentioned specifically by name and circumstance. Those so mentioned include seven women: Bess Murdoch, two Euphemia Murdochs, Jean Murdoch, Joan Murdoch, Margaret Murdoch, and Mary Murdoch. Nineteen Murdoch men are specifically mentioned: David Murdoch, George Murdoch, five James Murdochs, five John Murdochs, Patrick Murdoch, Peter Murdoch, two Robert Murdochs, and three William Murdochs. Most of these people were apparently common laborers, farmers, and tradesmen such as masons, weavers, wrights, and tinkers.

A few of the Murdochs of Auchlinleck attained somewhat greater prominence. David Murdoch (who died in 1782) was a teacher at Auchinleck school who also sold horses for Boswell. One of the several John Murdochs (he who died in 1812) was the sheriff, clerk, and provost (chief magistrate) of Ayr, a position of great influence. William Murdoch (1754–1839), a onetime resident of Auchlineck, distinguished himself through his pioneering inventions and is best known for developing and refining coal gas for use in lighting—a tremendous advance at that time.[8]

Although none of the Murdochs mentioned in Boswell's correspondence and in related documents can be traced with *certainty* at the present time to John Murdoch, the similarity in their names is striking, as is the close proximity in time and location along with the fact that Auchinleck was considered to be a multigenerational homeland for many Murdochs. These facts suggest that at a minimum, some of the Murdochs listed as tenants of Auchinleck estate were probably close kin to John Murdoch and his father, James Murdoch. For example, John's father was born about 1786 in the small village of Commondyke in the Auchinleck estate of Ayr. John's paternal grandfather, also named James Murdoch, was born in 1752, also in Commondyke. Boswell rented a piece of land to a James Murdoch of Commondyke in 1787, and again in 1797. At the time of the first lease, John's father would have been one year of age and his grandfather would have been thirty-five. By the time of the second lease, John's father would have been eleven years of age and his grandfather would have been forty-five. It is quite possible and perhaps likely that this particular tenant James Murdoch could have been John's paternal grandfather. Another interesting similarity involves the tiny village of Gasswater (also spelled Gaswater), a place that features prominently in John Murdoch's immediate family history. John was born in Gaswater in 1820, and his father, James Murdoch, died in Gaswater in 1831 of gas poisoning ("the black damp") in a coal mine while trying to rescue a young man who had collapsed from the poisonous gas while exploring in a new mine shaft. Although most present-day maps of Scotland do not include any references to Gasswater, Gaswater, or Gas, these places are all found on certain eighteenth-century maps of the Auchinleck estate and parish. The village of Gass is shown on these maps as being only a short walk from Commondyke. Gasswater Coal and Lime (apparently an extraction-industrial area with an adjacent small village) is a very short distance farther east of Gass, just across a small stream that is also called Gass Water. Again, the close proximity of these locations to Commondyke also argues in favor of this particular Murdoch family being tenants on James Boswell's Auchinleck estate, and that the James Murdoch who leased land from Boswell near Commondyke in 1787 and 1797 was quite possibly John Murdoch's paternal grandfather.

If the upper lowlands of Scotland in general, the regions encompassed by Ayr, Dumfries, and Galloway, are the closest thing to an ancestral homeland for most Murdochs of Scottish descent, then the descendants of John Murdoch, his parents, James and Mary, and his paternal grandparents should probably look to the Auchinleck parish in Ayr as the closest thing to their Scottish ancestral homeland in particular. The village of Commondyke and the areas near the Gass Water stream should be areas of particular interest for present-day descendants of John Murdoch, and of his parents, James and Mary Murdoch.

An interesting footnote to the prominence of the Auchinleck Parish region as the primary Murdoch ancestral homeland is the existence of the Murdoch Stave. In the early 1900s, John Murdoch's nephew, David Lennox Murdoch, returned to his native Scotland and traveled extensively in the Auchinleck Parish area, where he visited with many known relatives and other Murdochs who were likely distant relatives. While on this trip, David learned of the Murdoch Stave. This object was created in former years as a tribute to the Murdoch heritage and name in Scotland, and it was kept in the homes of many Murdochs in the region, passed down from one to another from generation to generation, usually to the next oldest Murdoch descendant in the parish. David was photographed holding the stave, and he wrote about its origins and meaning after his return to Utah.

The stave is somewhat like a cane or walking stick with a brass handle or head. It is said to date back to the mid-1700s, and it was created by

John Murdoch of Bellowmill, father of the famous Scottish inventor William Murdoch. David described the features of the stave as follows:

> In examining it I found that it is a manufactured article, and not a native grown cut stick, but is made out of some smooth even-grained wood of foreign growth. It is a strong, well-made stave, with the head or handle projecting about halfway on either side of it. In other words the handle is fastened somewhat in the relative position that a handle is to a hammer. At the head of the stave is a wide brass ferrule containing the following original inscription, which is here given just as it appears on the brass ferrule:

THIS STAVE I LEAVE

IN LEAGSIE TO THE

OLDEST MURDOCH

AFTER ME

IN AUCHINLECK, 1743.[9]

PROMINENT MURDOCHS

Inventor William Murdoch, who has been called "the Scottish Edison," made a huge impact on modern society with the invention of coal-gas lighting, a development that began a revolution in human living habits after dark. He was also known for his improvements to the steam engine, and he built one of the first "cars," a three-wheeled steam powered contraption that looked much like a large tricycle. William is unique among the Murdochs, having been declared a deity by Nassred-din, Shah of Persia, who was so impressed by his invention of gas lighting that he believed he was the reincarnation of Marduk the god of light. William is not the only Scottish Murdoch to have achieved notoriety. Another William Murdoch (born 1873 in Dalbeattie, Scotland) served as the First Officer on the massive and ill-fated ship *Titanic*. He is remembered as a hero who organized the lifeboat rescue and gave his own life to save the lives of others. Official enquiries after the *Titanic* disaster cleared William's name and highlighted his brave actions, yet the 1997 Hollywood movie of the *Titanic* disaster by Producer/Director James Cameron portrayed William in an unfavorable and cowardly light, causing his descendants to protest his celluloid treatment. These protests resulted in a formal apology to the family by a Twentieth Century Fox film executive, as well as a donation of money in William McMaster Murdoch's name to the public high school in Dalbeattie.[10]

Yet another John Murdoch, this one born in 1748, achieved later fame as a teacher of the young Robert Burns. John worked for several families in

Alloway, Ayrshire, educating their children. He was only eighteen when seven-year-old Robert Burns became his pupil, and he was known for his strict methods of teaching. Many years later, after Burns's fame had spread, John Murdoch admitted that he had failed to see the full potential of his young pupil.

In addition to these somewhat well known Murdochs, numerous other Murdochs of other nations (but with Scottish roots) achieved fame, including Dame Jean Iris Murdoch, a prominent twentieth-century novelist who was born in Ireland and raised in England; James Edward Murdoch, one of the most famous American actors of the nineteenth century; and modern-day international media magnate Rupert Murdoch of Australia, one of the highest profile and most controversial businessmen of the early twenty-first century. Although the vast majority of members of the extended Murdoch surname clan have been and are average, ordinary citizens, and despite the fact that this surname is not particularly common, many Murdochs have distinguished themselves for their contributions to the arts, education, business, and other endeavors. For the most part they have distinguished themselves through their contributions in their local communities, the same way that John Murray Murdoch distinguished himself in his adopted home in Utah after leaving Scotland for America.

THE LIFE OF A SCOT: OTHER FAMILY LINES

Efforts to trace the family roots of John Murdoch's parents have not resulted in much information besides birth, death, and marriage dates and places. Other details of the lives of John's ancestors beyond his parents have been lost. Although some general information has been accumulated regarding individuals with the Murdoch surname line, less is known regarding the family lines leading past John's mother (the Murrays), or the other direct names two generations back, the Osbornes and McCalls. Based on the places these forebears lived and the lands from which they descended, we can assume that for at least two or three generations back, and probably more, John Murdoch's ancestors generally lived in the southwest Scotland region, most prominently in the adjoining counties of Ayr and Dumfries.

John's maternal surname line—the Murrays—is the most prominent of these family names in terms of Scottish influence. Various histories of Scottish clans and surnames indicate that the Murrays were predominantly highlanders who were centered in northeast Scotland, but by the thirteenth century a group of Murrays emerged prominently in the lowland region, in the area now known as Lanark or Lanarkshire. This region adjoins Ayr and Dumfries from the north and is thus very close to the

Murdoch home region. The Murrays of Bothwell in Lanarkshire became particularly prominent. Sir Andrew Murray of Bothwell, although scarcely more than a boy, was an associate of William Wallace in the late-thirteenth-century guerilla resistance wars with the English. This Murray is considered to have been a brilliant military strategist and is thought to have been largely responsible for Wallace's heroic victory over the English at Stirling Bridge in 1297.[11] After Sir Andrew died in that battle Wallace never again won a pitched battle. Bothwell castle in Lanarkshire, which was once the seat of the senior Murray clan chiefs, still stands, and it is considered the best remaining example of a thirteenth-century Scottish castle.

As we have already noted, these areas of ancestral homelands in southwest Scotland are considered to be in the lowlands, yet the farther south reaches are a hilly region that is part of the southern uplands. The people from whom John Murdoch descended most likely made their living the same way most people of this area did: through small-scale farming (especially oats, dairy, and some vegetables), sheep and cattle herding, limited trade, and, as the region became more industrialized, through the extractive industries (coal, lime, and gas), ironworking, and through limited small manufacturing enterprises such as textiles. Coal extraction in Scotland had existed at least since the fourteenth century, but it increased dramatically with the advent of the ironworking industry (which required coal fires to smelt the iron) that became somewhat prominent in Aryshire, particularly in the northern regions of the county.[12] Those few of John Murdoch's ancestors who may have lived in the coastal areas of Ayr or southward in the coastal shires of Wigtown and Kirkcudbright may have also figured out ways to extract a living through fishing and related coastal enterprises such as shipbuilding.

The Dark Side: Superstitution and Fear

An interesting final note on the ancestral homelands of the Murdochs and Murrays is that this southern Scotland region is also known for something far more striking (and disturbing) than mining, farming, or livestock herding: the infamous Scottish witch hunts of the mid-sixteenth through early eighteenth centuries. During this era Scotland was a medieval hotbed of superstition and the hideous practice of hunting out and investigating individuals accused of practicing witchcraft and sorcery. Confessions and corroborations were extracted by leaders of the church-state, usually under torture or the threat of it, and executions of those who were found "guilty" followed. The methods of torture that were used were so gruesome and creative that they have become part of a macabre legend.

The best estimates are that between one thousand and three thousand individuals (about 90 percent of them women), were executed in Scotland for the crime of witchcraft during this period.[13] Although these numbers pale in comparison with the estimated one hundred thousand executed for witchcraft or sorcery during that period in Germany, they eclipse by far the number killed in either neighboring England or the American colonies (i.e., Salem, Massachusetts). The legacy of the Scottish witch hunts and the common terms they produced was so well known that it influenced later popular literature, such as Shakespeare's *MacBeth*, and some of Robert Burns's poems, including *Tam O'Shanter* and *A Lass Wi' a Tocher*.

The European practice of witch hunting stemmed from a biblical exhortation in Exodus 22:18, "Thou shalt not suffer a witch to live," and a later Roman directive that sorcerers must be put to death. The ancient Christian church apparently did not advocate a belief in witches or witchcraft (despite some New Testament verses regarding the evils of sorcery). The religious focus on witchcraft and persecuting those thought to be witches was apparently a practice started by two fifteenth-century Dominican priests, Kramer and Sprenger, who persuaded church and political leaders that sorcery was part of a conspiracy against the church-state by Satan, and that it should be rooted out. When in 1484 the Pope enjoined the church to pursue the practice, it spread like wildfire. In 1563, three years after the Scottish reformation, the parliament of Scotland passed a law making the practices of witchcraft or consulting with witches a capital crime. This law is evidence that the witch-hunting craze was not limited to those who practiced strict Roman Catholicism.

Most of those who were accused and punished for the crime of witchcraft were women who did not fit the social norm. These women were often elderly, poor, disabled, or physically deformed, or were social misfits in some other way. They were often from isolated rural areas, particularly the small villages near seaports. Some of the recorded cases of witch persecution and execution in south Scotland involved girls as young as eleven years.

Because the Scots of this era (including their leaders, most notably King James VI) were deeply superstitious, it became convenient to scapegoat such women for things such as a poor harvest, natural disasters, accidents, and various supernatural omens. In fact, King James VI personally supervised a series of witch trials in Scotland after his wife, Anne of Denmark, was nearly shipwrecked in a storm in the North Sea, an event that was considered to be part of a supernatural conspiracy of evil. Accusations of witchcraft against women were sometimes the result of other women trying to settle scores with them. Women were not targeted for witchcraft simply as a result of the lower status and power they had as a group in European society. Part of the cause can be attributed to the common Catholic and Protestant biblical interpretations at that time that women were naturally more prone to temptation, the influence of Satan, and a poorer ability to reason, as evidenced by Eve's partaking of the forbidden fruit in the Garden of Eden, which led to the Fall of Man.[14] When fundamentalist zealots of the Kirk (church) and state targeted women for witchcraft investigations, they believed they were merely pursuing the natural order of things.

Disgusted with the Whole Lot

Although the Scottish witch hunts declined by the early eighteenth century and had effectively ended by the time of John Murdoch's birth in 1820, the attitudes and superstitions that led to and resulted from these abuses undoubtedly persisted in Scottish culture. In John Murdoch's later life he recounted that as a young man he believed in God, but much of what he was taught in the churches of his youth in Scotland simply did not make sense to him. "I had at this time been a member of the different churches and was acquainted more or less with the creeds of the Catholic and Protestant churches; but all were so different from the religion of Jesus and the Apostles that I could read of in the Testament that I had become disgusted with the whole lot...."[15] When John Murdoch heard the doctrines of Mormonism, much of what appealed to him went against the traditional teachings of Catholicism and Scottish Protestantism to which he had been exposed. For example, Joseph Smith and Brigham Young taught that Eve was actually perceptive in understanding God's plan by eating of the forbidden fruit in Eden, rather than being a simpleminded dupe of Satan and thus of lower moral status because of this act. Although he loved his native land and appreciated his ancestral home and its teachings, he was obviously striving for something he felt he could not attain by staying with the traditions to which he was born.

Notes

1. George F. Black, *The Surnames of Scotland: Their Origin and Meaning* (New York: New York Public Library, 1999).

2. "Linguistics of the Murdoch Surname," Murdoch Surname Website, http://www.strathearn.com/clan-murdoch/mu_history2.html (accessed November 19, 2004).

3. "Memorial Service," James and Mary Murray Murdoch Family Website, http://murdochfamily.net/jmmprogram.htm (accessed November 19, 2004). Note that the name

Murdoch is used exclusively in this volume, although John Murdoch himself and some of his descendants did adopt the Americanized *k* ending to the surname.

4. "100 Most Common Surnames," General Register Office for Scotland, http://www.groscotland.gov.uk/grosweb/grosweb.nsf/pages/surnames (accessed November 18, 2004).

5. "Historical Roots of the Murdoch Surname," Murdoch Surname Website, http://www.strathearn.com/clan-murdoch/mu_history7.html (accessed November 19, 2004).

6. "The Ravens and Cumloden, Newton Stewart," Murdoch Surname Website, http://www.strathearn.com/clan-murdoch/mu_history8.html (accessed November 20, 2004).

7. Nelli Potle Hankins and John Strawthorne, *The Correspondence of James Boswell with James Bruce and Andrew Gibb, Overseers of the Auchinleck Estate* (Edinburgh, Scotland: Edinburgh University Press, 1998).

8. William Murdoch, inventor of the gas lamp, is one of the most famous Scottish inventors. He is particularly known for inventing a mechanism for burning coal gas through a jetted iron tube, and he has been described as "the Scottish Edison." A short profile of William is found at The William Murdoch Archives, http://www.trainingscotland.i12.com/murdoch/profile.htm (accessed November 20, 2004).

9. John Murray Nicol, ed., *The James and Mary Murray Murdoch Family History* (Provo, UT: James and Mary Murray Murdoch Family Organization, 1982), 650.

10. A description of the controversy surrounding the 1997 film portrayal of William McMaster Murdoch in *Titanic*, including details about the formal apology by the film studio, can be found on the official Dalbeattie, Scotland, town website at http://www.dalbeattie.com (accessed November 21, 2004).

11. Neil Grant, *Scottish Clans and Tartans* (New York: Octopus Publishing, 2000), 231.

12. James Edward Shaw, *Ayrshire, 1745–1950: A Social and Industrial History* (Edinburgh, Scotland: Oliver and Boyd, 1953), 51.

13. The Dumfries and Galloway Musuem, www.dumfriesmuseum.demon.co.uk/frames.html (accessed November 26, 2004), lists the estimated number of people executed during the Scottish witch hunts at more than one thousand, whereas H. M. Flemings in *Scottish Witches and Wizards: True Accounts* (2002) estimates the number executed at about three thousand.

14. "Witch Hunting," Dumfries and Galloway Museums and Galleries On-Line, http://www.dumfriesmuseum.demon.co.uk/frames.html (accessed November 26, 2004).

15. John Murray Murdoch, Early History of John Murray Murdoch, written by himself at Heber, Utah, 5 Sept. 1898 (document in author's possession).

3

◆ ◆ ◆

EARLY YEARS

The parishes which formerly contained 1,000 souls contain now a population
of 20,000 or 30,000, and those who formerly had the oversight of the people
have been compelled in despair to give up the work, as a task which is utterly
beyond the power of human energy to accomplish.

— *Glasgow Herald*, February 5, 1849

I dreamt that I went out into the garden at the back of our house and my eye
caught site of a beautiful little bushy tree that my brother-in-law had planted
only a day or two before, and for his sake I very gently took hold of it with my
right hand and to my great surprise found that it had already taken root and
was actually showing signs of bearing fruit.

— JOHN MURRAY MURDOCH, recalling a dream from 1850

John Murray Murdoch was born on December 28, 1820, in the community of Gaswater, Auchinleck Parish, Ayrshire, Scotland. At the time of
his birth, his mother, Mary Murray Murdoch, was forty years of age, and
his father, James Murdoch, was about thirty-six years old. Some records
indicate that John was born in December 1821, but the 1820 date better
matches his own later descriptions regarding his age at key events during his life. John's parents had been married on January 10, 1811, in the
Auchinleck Parish, when Mary was twenty-eight and James about twenty-
five. John was the sixth of eight children born to the Murdochs. Of their
eight children, six lived into adulthood—three males (James, born 1814;
John, born 1820; and William, born 1825) and three females (Janet, born
1811; Veronica, born 1816; and Mary, born 1819). The couple's second child,
a girl they named Mary, was born in 1813 and died eleven days later. Their
seventh child, a girl they named Margaret, also died as an infant.

The Murdoch children were born during an era of unprecedented
population growth in Scotland. In fact, these children were all born during the first three decades of the nineteenth century, a period known for
the most rapid expansion of Scotland's population during modern times.[1]
But unlike many other western lowland and borders region Scots families
of their day, James and Mary eschewed moving to the urbanized industrial

cities such as Edinburgh, Glasgow, and Aberdeen, where many rural Scots landed during this period of population expansion and increasing industrialization; instead, they stayed in rural Ayrshire.[2]

We Work the Black Seam: The Death of James

Little is known regarding the first few years of John's life, or the circumstances of the Murdoch family during this period. It is known that John and his siblings attended school during their early years, and that their father worked as a coal miner, perhaps among other occupations as well. Some accounts of the Scottish coal mining industry indicate that it was common for miners of that era to work seasonally extracting coal and to pursue other interests (most commonly small-scale farming) when they were not working in the mines.[3] This situation was likely true for James, given the economy of that time. It is known that much of the farming in the area involved raising sheep and other livestock, so this endeavor is a likely candidate for James Murdoch's economic interests. By most accounts the Murdochs were a typical lowland Scottish family of that region and time: they were a close family, poor, had a large number of children, were literate, and sustained themselves by making use of the prevailing economic opportunities of their region.

Everything changed for the Murdoch family on October 20, 1831. On that date, when John was not quite eleven years old, his father was killed in a coal mine where he worked, the Lime Works near Gaswater. At that time, the Murdoch family was living nearby in a rented house, and James was earning approximately one dollar per day for his labor. The accounts of this accident that have been handed down through family records indicate that James died of the "black damp" (a miners' name for a poisonous mixture of nitrogen and carbon dioxide that seeps from underground coal seams and can cause suffocation) while trying to rescue a young man by the name of George Baird, who lived in the nearby village of Dalford. This young man had come to the Gaswater Lime Works to see a new twenty-five-foot-deep mine shaft that had just been dug. After Baird had ridden a "bucket" down the windlass, some observers noted that something was wrong with him, and the alarm was sounded. Baird had fallen victim to the foul air at the bottom of a new mine shaft that was being sunk. Black damp (also called "chokedamp") is essentially "air without oxygen." It can overcome a victim without warning and can result in death rather quickly. James Murdoch immediately went down the shaft to try to rescue Baird, but he was also quickly overcome by the poisonous gas. By the time that the foul air was dispersed and the two bodies were brought back up to ground level, both were dead.[4]

Coal mining has always been a hazardous occupation, and during the coal boom of the 1800s it was particularly dangerous. Miners of this era were continually exposed to lethal gases such as black damp and firedamp (a highly explosive methane-based gas) without any greater technology than canaries in cages to help detect these noxious substances. Poisonous gases were but one danger among many, including explosions, fires, collapse of mine shafts, falling down mine shafts, drowning, being crushed by falling equipment or rock, breathing coal dust, and continual exposure to cold, wet, and dirty environmental conditions. An 1842 report by the British government on the dangerous and often exploitive conditions in the nation's coal mines shocked the public and provided harrowing details of the underbelly of this industry, such as children younger than five years of age laboring for up to twelve hours per day in the mines doing back-breaking work.[5] One anecdote from this report specified that of the 348 deaths in one year at a particular coal mine, fifty-eight were children. Given these dangerous circumstances, James Murdoch's death in this occupation was not particularly unusual. Scottish men of that era—particularly those of the working and poorest classes—tended to eke out their living in occupations that were so dangerous as to make adult males somewhat of an endangered population with a short life expectancy. Records from various Scottish censuses of the nineteenth century indicate that females made up anywhere from 62 percent to 92 percent of the population during the first six decades of that century, in part because of the extremely high mortality rates for men.[6]

Life without a Father: Eking Out a Living

James's death left Mary Murdoch a widow with six children, ranging in age from six to twenty years. In addition, she was left with the care of a previously orphaned niece by the name of Margaret. Once the initial shock and trauma of James's death began to subside, Mary was left with a most pressing reality: how would she provide for her family? The solution to this painful dilemma came in the form of Mary and everyone else in the family pitching in to make ends meet. For an extended period of time, the family lived primarily on potatoes and salt.[7] Mary took in what work was available, such as sewing, taught her younger children to work, and occasionally helped out with milking cows and other tasks on farms in their community.

The eldest child, Janet, was twenty at the time of her father's death. She worked for other people in whatever capacity she could, such as sewing and working in farmers' fields. James Junior, the eldest son, was seventeen when his father died. As such, he became the "man of the family," and he worked in the mines. Veronica, fifteen at the time of her father's death, worked in a variety of situations including field work and making butter and cheese. The younger children also worked to help support the struggling family in whatever way they could. For John, this new set of circumstances meant that he quit attending school and began to work. The following spring, when he was barely eleven years old, John went to work herding sheep in the nearby hills. Although this work often took him away from his mother at a tender age, it proved to be a vocation that would be a lifetime pursuit and that would eventually be his ticket to America.[8]

As the family continued to mature and adapt, some of the older children married and moved away. John continued to work as a professional sheepherder for the next ten years, until he was about twenty, when he began to work in the coal mines, an occupation more dangerous but also more lucrative than tending flocks owned by other people. Although John's own history is somewhat unclear on this issue, there is a strong likelihood that during his youthful years as a shepherd he may have lived away from home—at least for much of the time—and boarded elsewhere, because he later recollected "I was about twenty *when I came home* and went into the mines...boarding with my mother until I was about 27 years old."[9] During this time period, John's mother continued to get by with the assistance of her children, and eventually she was able to move from her rented house into her own home, a small cottage with a thatched roof that was built with the assistance of some of her children and a few neighbors.[10] This type of dwelling was typical of homes of the time in rural areas of Scotland. Most of these homes were built of either stone or straw bale wall construction and had either thatched or shake roofs.[11] A few of the structures of that era are still standing nearly two hundred years later.

MARRIAGE AND A NEW RELIGION

As John moved into manhood he experienced other changes and responsibilities in addition to his new occupation working in the mines. When he was about twenty-seven years of age, he met Ann Steele, daughter and one of two children of James and Elizabeth Kerr Steele of Kirkconnel, from the nearby adjoining Dumfrieshire region (approximately thirty miles from Gaswater, Ayrshire). No details remain of their first meeting or their courtship, but we know they were married on February 24, 1848, in Ann's home community of Kirkconnel. Ann was nearly seven years John's junior, having been born October 27, 1828, in Kirkconnel. At the time of their marriage, John was twenty-seven and Ann was nineteen. The couple made their home in Kirkconnel, possibly living with Ann's parents for a time on their small farm. John went to work in a nearby coal mine. It is also quite likely that he continued to a lesser extent his profession of sheepherding, perhaps seasonally or on a limited time basis. The Murdochs quickly started their family. The first child, Elizabeth, was born November 21, 1848, not quite nine months after their marriage. Their second child, James, was born about eighteen months later, in June of 1850.

Ann's older brother, James Steele, was two years her senior. At the time of Ann's marriage to John Murdoch, James had recently married and was living in England, but it is clear that he was already well acquainted with his future brother-in-law. John later recalled of James Steele during this time period "We had worked together for years and respected each other very much. The only fault I had with him, if a fault it was, was that he did not care for religion, and I was rather religiously inclined."[12] Within a few months after John and Ann's marriage, James Steele re-emerged into their lives with a new perspective and a great zeal, bringing with him a message that would change their lives. In John's own words:

> In 1850 he [James Steele] paid us a visit at Kirkconnel and preached the gospel to us, in a way very much like that...I could read in the testament. I very soon found out that little as I thought he knew of the Bible before he went away, that man he could, with the greatest ease corner me on every point, and I wondered how this wonderful change had been brought about. He told me that the young lady that he intended to marry when he went back to England had been a Latter-day Saint from her youth, that she had converted him, and that he had received a testimony from God, that he had received the only true Gospel on earth. I do not believe that the same words spoken by anyone else could have come to me with the same force as coming from that young man at that time. I had been a member of two different churches before this time and had made myself acquainted with the creeds of the different sects and parties. Witnessing for myself the spite and bitter feeling manifested towards each other I became so disgusted that I was on the verge of giving up on religion altogether. But the words of that young man sank so deep into my heart that I began to investigate very seriously. His business called him back to England and I never saw him again."[13]

John felt quite lonely after James returned to England. He had apparently formed a very strong bond with his old friend turned brother-in-law during their short visit, and he found the spirit and enthusiasm of James's religious message to be powerfully attractive. He pondered the message of Mormonism day and night, deliberating regarding what course of action to take. One night John had a dream in which he went into a garden and saw an attractive small tree that his brother-in-law James Steele had planted just a few days earlier. It appeared to be green and vibrant, and as he examined it he realized that it had already taken root. He later understood the interpretation of this dream to mean that the gospel message he had received from James Steele had taken root with him.[14] John Murdoch and Ann Steele Murdoch were baptized members of the Church of Jesus Christ of Latter-day Saints on November 29, 1850. A small branch of the church was organized in their community, consisting of the Murdochs and two to four other recent converts. They held their meetings at John and Ann's home in Kirkconnel. They made their new faith the center of their lives. Although they were young in this new religion, they immersed themselves in it fully, and participated in every aspect available to them. John had heard that the ancient Christian gift of tongues was one of the manifestations among new converts to the church, and he desired and prayed fervently to receive this gift. He did not immediately receive any such manifestation, and he felt bad about that and for perhaps being presumptuous in asking God to grant him this gift. Spiritual manifestations soon came to John in other ways.

> I had also heard of some young girls that had got the gift of poetry and could sing it in tongues very beautifully, and thinking that I had asked for something too great for me and that I had been presumptuous in asking for the gift of tongues, I besought the Lord very anxiously to forgive me, and prayed that he would give me the gift of poetry; that if ever so simple I might be able to compose one little piece, and I would receive it as an answer to my prayer and as a testimony of the truth of the gospel that I had received. This time my prayer was answered just as I had asked.[15]

The answer to John's prayers came in the form of a poem he felt inspired to write in February 1851 to help him in his attempts to proselytize an old acquaintance from his village by the name of Thomas Scot, who had thus far rejected John's invitations to attend their branch meetings and learn of the Latter-day Saints. John delivered him a handwritten note containing a four-verse poem entreating him to come to a worship service and learn of the gospel, wherein the first verse stated:

> *Dear Thomas my friend*
> *These few lines I send.*
> *I truly abhor strife and schism,*
> *But I humbly pray that you make no delay*
> *Till you taste the sweet fruits of baptism.*[16]

Although this invitation was not accepted by his friend, the poetry that John was able to produce satisfied him of God's answer for him at that time.

THE RESTORATION: JOINING THE SAINTS

To understand the conversion of John and Ann Murdoch to Mormonism, it is important to understand the times and context in which it occurred. John considered himself to be religiously inclined, and noted that he had previously affiliated himself with two churches (the Presbyterian and Catholic faiths), but was keenly disappointed by the confusing nature of some of their teachings and found the frequent strife and disagreement among the churches to be nearly intolerable. In one sense, John's confusion regarding church dogma and the combative strife among the various sects paralleled the experience twenty years earlier in Palmyra, New York, of Joseph Smith, who later recalled, "In the midst of this war of words and tumult of opinions, I often said to myself: What is to be done? Who of all these parties are right; or, are they all wrong together? If any one of them be right, which is it, and how shall I know it?"[17] John Murdoch's report of religious confusion and dissension in Scotland in the mid-nineteenth century is corroborated by substantial contemporary evidence. The largest religions in Scotland at that time included several factions of the Presbyterian Church, the Catholic Church, and the Scottish Episcopal Church. There were several smaller independent churches as well. The eighteenth and nineteenth centuries were a time of significant religious strife in Scotland both within and between these denominations. For example, the period of 1833 to 1843 (when John Murdoch was a teen and young adult) is referred to as the *Ten Years Conflict* within the Scottish Presbyterian Church, a time of considerable controversy regarding the rights of lay parishioners and church governance, and which ultimately led to a schism that created the Free Church of Scotland.[18]

By the time John and Ann heard the message of the Church of Jesus Christ of Latter-day Saints in 1850 in Scotland, the church had been established for twenty years, and the founding prophet, Joseph Smith, had been dead for six years, having been made a martyr by an armed mob in Carthage, Illinois, in June 1844. From the church's small beginnings in western New York, Smith gathered around him a gradually increasing number of converts, and the center of the young church moved from New York to Ohio, then to the lawless western frontier of Missouri, before finding several years of refuge along the banks of the Mississippi River in Nauvoo, Illinois, all the while encountering fierce opposition and religious persecution unparalleled in U.S. history. The Mormons of that era were primarily Yankees from the New England and Mid-Atlantic states who shared little culturally with their frontier neighbors in Ohio, Missouri, and Illinois. The Saints frequently alienated and antagonized the "gentiles" by their unusual beliefs, their clannishness, their sense of being chosen and special, and their loyal adherence to Joseph Smith as a living prophet in the mold of Moses and Noah. These tensions were greatly inflamed during the Missouri period after the prophet Joseph announced that the Lord had revealed to him that parts of western Missouri had been given to the Saints by God as a land of their inheritance, despite the fact that there were many already suspicious non-Mormons living in those lands.

By the late 1830s, the Mormons had mounted a highly successful missionary effort in Europe, at first primarily in the British Isles, which garnered thousands of converts, many of whom immigrated to America to gather with their fellow Saints. Ultimately, a combination of internal dissension that accompanied the evolution of new religious practices introduced by Smith (such as plural marriages by men in the church hierarchy, formation of a shadow theocratic government, and the introduction of secret temple rites) and mounting external political pressure threatened to bring down Joseph's city-state of Nauvoo. Shortly after Smith's death, his successor Brigham Young began to make plans to take the Saints to a new refuge or Zion in the Rocky Mountains as Joseph had previously prophesied. By the time that John and Ann Murdoch became Latter-day Saints in 1850, the main body of church members had been in the valley of the Great Salt Lake in Utah for two years, and Brigham proceeded to speed the gathering of new converts from Europe to Utah, to increase the economic and political security of the church, and to create a powerful religious kingdom where the Saints would be free to practice their religion separated from mainstream American society.

Scottish Saints: Mormonism in Scotland

The first Mormon missionaries came to Scotland in 1839. The timing of
their arrival coincided with conditions and events in Scotland that served
to maximize the receptivity of many Scots to the message of the restored
gospel of the latter days. By 1839 Scotland's eighteenth-century preemi-
nence in intellectual, economic, and industrial innovation had subsided
and was giving way to the emergence of urban slums, overcrowding in
many cities and villages, decaying social conditions, and a general sense
for most Scots that the future held little or no promise for a better life.[19]
Thus the fresh message of hope and possibility for common people offered
by the Mormon missionaries was tremendously appealing to many Scots.
Furthermore, religious conditions in Scotland—including substantial internal dissension within the Scottish churches and the disenchantment
of many common Scots because of their lack of meaningful participation in the church—created an environment where Mormon claims of
the restoration of the authority, practices, and power of the ancient Christian church were unique and attractive. Some of the groundwork for the
possibility of public acceptance of the message of Mormonism had been
established by Edward Irving, a charismatic young Presbyterian preacher
from Dumfries. Irving advocated a need to return to primitive Christianity or a restoration of the ancient order, stating that the church had drifted
into apostasy and that a reliance on the gifts of the spirit was necessary to
prepare for the second coming of Jesus.[20] Irving—whose followers were
later dubbed "Irvingites"—was ultimately expelled from the Church of
Scotland for his outspoken and unorthodox views, but the impact of his
message undoubtedly prepared some Scots for the Mormon message of
the restoration. Joseph Smith was aware of Irving's views, and although he
said that the Irvingites possessed a counterfeit version of the truth, he also
recognized the similarity of their views to his own message and stated that
they were "perhaps the nearest of any modern sectarians" to the message
of the restored gospel.[21]

◆ ◆ ◆

Although the spread of the message of the restoration in Scotland was
inauspicious at first, it moved rapidly, and the decade beginning in 1840
saw the Mormon church grow from no branches and less than two dozen
members to more than three thousand members and fifty-seven branches
by 1851.[22] Most of the growth of the church in Scotland was in the industrialized urban areas and in the coal mining areas of the Scottish low-

lands. Paralleling the patterns of growth of the church in both America and England, the Scottish converts to Mormonism were primarily from the working class, as was John Murdoch. The "working poor" were as a group far more receptive to the message of the restoration than individuals from other social strata. They tended to be less comfortable and more restless for bettering their lot in life than those of the wealthy and bourgeois classes, but not so beaten down by life and incapable of making change as those from the lowest rungs of society. The year of John Murdoch's baptism, 1850, was the pinnacle of Mormonism's nineteenth-century growth in Scotland. That year saw the largest total number of church members (over 3,200) and convert baptisms (approximately eight hundred) of any year of that century.[23] Because of the emigration of members of the church to America and due to the increasing indifference of the Scottish people to the message of the restoration, the number of convert baptisms and total church members in Scotland began to decline by the end of 1851, and it followed a steady trajectory downward until there were fewer than five hundred members of the church in Scotland by 1880. It would be decades into the twentieth century before the number of Latter-day Saints there again reached and then surpassed the 1850 figures.

John and Ann Murdoch found great joy in their new faith, and they soon spread the message to other members of their family. John's widowed mother, Mary Murray Murdoch, was baptized a member of the church by John on December 22, 1851, barely a year after he had been baptized. John also introduced the church to other members of his family. His older sisters, Veronica and Mary, and his younger brother, William, all eventually embraced Mormonism, and like John eventually made their way to gather with the Saints in Utah. Despite the common religious bond they now shared, and notwithstanding the fulfillment they found in their new faith, there were also many obstacles and challenges connected to their embrace of Mormonism. The story of John's older sister, Mary Murdoch Mair, is one of the more heart-wrenching examples of the hard choices that sometimes fall upon those who commit all to their faith. Baptized the same year as her mother, 1851, Mary had a great desire to "gather to Zion" and raise her younger children among the Saints. Being married to a man (Allan Mair) who did not share her faith and wanted nothing to do with it resulted in great frustration for her. In 1866 she secretly abandoned her husband of twenty-five years, as well as her twenty-one-year-old son, Allan F. Mair. She took her three youngest children with her and left Scotland for Utah. Her husband and son were thus left to themselves, and they missed Mary and the younger children terribly. Twenty-nine years later her son Allan wrote to her, asking why she had abandoned them in Scotland. In trying to understand her religious zeal that he did not share, Allan asked her "is not Scotland as near to heaven as America?"[24] For Mary, the answer was clearly "no."

PERSECUTION'S HAIRY HEAD

John and Ann experienced trials of a different sort as a result of their new faith. Soon after their baptism, they experienced persecution and bitterness regarding their new faith from members of their community. In John's words:

> Some of the farmers around came unto the little village in the evenings to help to lay plans and scheme how to put us down and stop our damnable delusion that we had brought in amongst them and was sure to corrupt the morals of the good Christian gospel-loving people like unto themselves. They at last came to the conclusion that the proper way would be to withhold their labor from us and starve us out.... All manner of evil was said about us, and many false reports went abroad concerning us. One that I will just mention was that at our little meetings we dressed my wife in white and set her on the table to be worshipped as the Holy Ghost. Many such foolish things were said of us, too silly to mention.[25]

In the spring of 1851, due to their poor prospects in Kirkconnel, they moved to the village of Birnie Know, about eighteen miles away. John's leadership abilities and willingness to take on weighty commitments was becoming increasingly evident as they once again helped to anchor a small branch of the church that met in their home. They soon baptized more members into this branch (including John's mother and his sister Mary), but "persecution again began to show his hairy head. Times became very hard, work scarce, and wages very low."[26]

It is important to consider that the contention and persecution aimed at John and his family was not uncommon for Mormon converts of that era, in Europe and America alike. It is also worthwhile to consider that not all of the difficulties the young church in Scotland was experiencing were from outside sources. In fact, the quick growth and lack of maturity of leadership of the church in that area in the 1840s and 1850s created circumstances that occasionally resulted in great internal strife and challenges. The notes from a report of the Glasgow Conference of the church from 1849 illustrate some of the challenges. In a conference that was held

March 24–25, 1849, in Glasgow, it was reported that the branches of that conference numbered twenty-six and that the total number of members in that conference was 1,700 (over half the total members in Scotland at that time). The notes of the conference also show evidence of significant internal turmoil within one of the branches:

> It was resolved by this council, at last conference, that unless the president, council, and members of the Girvan branch would come out from their filth, drunkenness, quarreling, backbiting &c., that we would disfellowship the whole branch. From what he could learn, he believed that they were in the same state now that they were at the last conference, and he would move that we disfellowship the Girvan Branch. It was seconded by Elder Douglas and unanimously carried [President Kelsy's words]."[27]

The situation in the Girvan branch stands out because it involved an entire congregation, but it reflects a problem of that period that was not particularly unusual. In fact, between 1850 and 1859, there were nearly as many excommunications per year as there were convert baptisms in Scotland, and some years (1855 and 1856) saw even more members being "cut off" than entering the fold.[28] New members of the church in Scotland often faced heavy pressures from family and community members related to their church membership, and these pressures sometimes resulted in decisions to put aside their new faith. In addition, because there were so many new members and few or no experienced leaders, members were often in a situation of having minimal guidance and internal support within the church, which sometimes led to poor modeling and a lack of appropriate understanding regarding the behavior and level of commitment expected of a Latter-day Saint. The harassment and other persecution experienced by John Murdoch because of his conversion to Mormonism did not diminish his commitment to his new faith. If anything, the evidence is convincing that he only increased in his resolve and allegiance to the church during this period of difficulty. It is also likely that the problems he was experiencing in connection with being a Mormon in Scotland made John begin to ponder seriously for the first time the possibility of leaving his native land for America, so that he could be part of "the gathering" in Zion.

GET UP AND LEAVE THIS PLACE

As the year 1851 progressed, John Murdoch found himself in even greater turmoil, and under increasing pressure, both financially and with respect to how he would honor his commitment to the church. After moving from Kirkconnel to Birnie Know, John found himself with little money and an increasing financial burden in supporting the branch of the church there. His work opportunities were sporadic, and he was given the promise of steady work several miles away in Garrallan. However, he hesitated to take the new work opportunity because it would require another move, and because he felt it was his responsibility to provide a home in which the branch could meet and where the traveling elders could stay when visiting the members. He did not want to be responsible for the branch breaking up, and he did not receive clear direction from the elders of the church regarding what course of action to take. One day John was given a day's work by his brother James, to assist in working in a mine doing repairs when other workers were idle. As he descended deeper into the mine and out of the light, he felt troubled regarding what course of action to take, and he also once more felt a need to receive the gift of tongues, wondering why it had thus far been withheld from him. As he was pondering his troubles he recalled one of the elders telling him that if he had faith to open his mouth, the Lord would give him the words to speak.

> Those words seemed to come to my mind more forcibly than ever before. I immediately spoke in tongues, but being all alone no interpreter was there and I was no wiser than I was before, but still more depressed in spirit. Soon a ray of light came to my mind and I reasoned that if the tongue was of God and I believed it was, he would give me the interpretation. And if not I would conclude the tongue was not of God ... at that critical moment that was to decide whether I would go or stay and whether I was under the influence of a good or bad spirit, my fate was soon decided. The interpretation came with power in those simple words, that I never can forget while memory lasts: GET UP AND LEAVE THIS PLACE FOR IN LESS THAN SIX MONTHS THERE WILL NOT BE A BLOWING FURNACE IN LUGAR, a very unlikely prediction at the time, but [it] was literally fulfilled as hundreds can testify...."[29]

Within a few days after this experience, John moved his family to Garrallan, where he had been promised steady work. Although the move was only a few miles away, he was concerned it would break up the branch of the church that had met at his house, because it increased the distance some members would need to travel (presumably on foot) to fifteen or twenty miles for some. The members voted to meet at John's new place of residence, and although this meant that John would continue to have to provide the means for this very poor branch of church members to continue as a group, he was more confident about it because he was again earning better wages. He felt right about this situation, later stating, "We soon baptized a few more at this place. We had good meetings. The Lord was with us by his spirit and we rejoiced in the society of each other, although many were very poor but very faithful. My moving to this place in obedience to the interpretation of the tongues proved to be alright and for the good of the cause."[30]

SEEKING A NEW JERUSALEM: THE GATHERING

As the weeks and months passed on in Garrallan, John Murdoch's thoughts continued to focus on the possibility of emigrating with his family to Utah, to be part of the gathering of Saints. He had previously begun to save money for this purpose, but it was now all gone due to his responsibility to shoulder the financial burdens of the branch, and because of his previous intermittent work opportunities. Although emigration of Scottish Mormons to Utah was well under way, John did not see any immediate possibility of this opportunity happening for him. Not only did he now lack the funds for passage, but he was a relatively new member of the church (less than one year had passed since his baptism), and he believed that members who had demonstrated their faithfulness for a longer period of time would have a better claim for the opportunity to emigrate. Like most of the more zealous converts to Mormonism in Europe, John wanted by this time nothing more than to gather with the Saints in the New Jerusalem, where he would not only enjoy the sociability of living with other Latter-day Saints and being taught by prophets and apostles, but would also experience the opportunity for a better economic life as he saw it, freed from the constraints of a rigid class system, a decaying economic and industrial machine, and a society whose time of prominence was quickly vanishing.

At a time when emigration to Zion seemed impossible to John Murdoch, events were transpiring thousands of miles from Scotland that would ultimately lead to his opportunity. By the summer of 1851 the main body of Latter-day Saints in America had been in the Salt Lake valley for three years or longer, and the gathering of Saints from Europe and elsewhere was adding to the numbers at an impressive clip. The Mormons had struggled through the trek west, made it through the first harsh winters and lean harvests, learned how to harness the power of water to irrigate an arid region, and had begun to take increasing steps toward full economic independence. To a great extent, self-sufficiency for the Mormons in Utah was a necessity, because they were separated by great distances from any major center of trade, industry, or agriculture. But the Mormon emphasis on economic self-sufficiency was as much theological and ideological as it was pragmatic. Church president Brigham Young, having survived the church's disastrous political and economic encounters with non-Mormons in Ohio, Missouri, and Illinois, was determined that the Saints should become independent in every respect and develop a true theocratic kingdom of God on earth.

> We do not intend to have any trade or commerce with the gentile [non-Mormon] world, for so long as we buy of them we are in a degree dependent on them. The Kingdom of God cannot rise independent of the gentile nations until we produce manufacture, and make every article of use, convenience, or necessity among our own people. We shall have Elders abroad among all nations, and until we can obtain and collect the raw material for our manufactures it will be their business to gather in such things as are, or may be, needed. So we shall need to commerce with the nations. I am determined to cut every threat of this kind and live free and independent, untrammeled by any of their detestable customs and practices.[31]

One of the many ways in which Brigham Young hoped to pursue Mormon economic independence was through the development of a sheep industry. Although sheep were not native to the Great Basin region, they were highly adaptable to its arid climate, rocky terrain, and cold winters, with the ability to go long periods of time without water and to receive nourishment from native shrubs and woody plants. Furthermore, sheep could provide for a variety of needs: wool for clothing, blankets, and rugs; meat for human sustenance, and by-products that could be used for candles, soap, lamp oil, and other things. Furthermore, they could graze during the summers in the nearby Wasatch Mountains. It was reported that Brigham purchased some sheep from an immigrant who was going to California, which were thought to be the only sheep in Utah at that time. Because there was no one who had the training and skills to properly care for them, the sheep soon became prey to wolves and coyotes. Brigham saw potential in establishing a Mormon sheep industry and began to consider how it might be done. He corresponded with Franklin D. Richards, president of the Mormon mission to the British Isles, and asked him to immediately send two Scotch shepherds and their dogs.

John Murdoch was overjoyed to receive a letter from the church headquarters in Liverpool, England, notifying him that he had been selected to go to Zion in response to President Young's request. He was instructed to prepare for a January 1852 departure from Liverpool, and to sell all of his household effects, sending any money he could spare to the church office at Liverpool. Church officers would then make arrangements for the passage of his family, using these funds. If the funds were not sufficient, he would be assisted by the church. This arrangement proved satisfactory to John, who later commented that it "was strictly tended to in good style."[32] He received a subsequent communication informing him that the man who had been selected to be the other sheepherder had purchased two excellent sheep dogs, but was short on funds. Once again, John was asked to please send more money to the office in Liverpool to assist in this situation. Although he was very short on funds at this point, he was determined to do whatever it took, and he found a way to send three sovereigns to Liverpool. He thus found himself almost without funds at the onset of his journey, a situation that would prove to result in much hardship for him and his family.

YES, MY NATIVE LAND, I LOVE THEE

It is not clear when the Murdochs received their invitation to prepare for the January 1852 trip from Scotland to America, but it may have been as little as two or three months prior to the scheduled departure date, because of the obvious rush that was required to prepare for the journey. Although they were thrilled at their opportunity to make this journey and start a new life, it was also a time of reflection, as they knew they would never return to Scotland, and that they might never again see their extended family members. As the final weeks and days arrived prior to their departure, John and Ann and their two young children (Elizabeth, now three years of age, and James, now eighteen months old), began to make the rounds to family and friends for a bittersweet series of good-byes. In December, a farewell party was held for them in the home of a fellow Latter-day Saint, a Brother Gallaghar, who was a baker and confectioner in the town of New Cumnock. Their good wishes and good-byes extended into the wee hours of the morning. Ann sang a song for the occasion that John referred to as "Yes My Native Land I Leave Thee." This song was most likely "Yes My Native Land I Love Thee," a tune that was written by the Reverend Samuel F. Smith in 1832, and that was included in the first hymnal of the Church of Jesus Christ of Latter-day Saints, and also included in a popular Protestant songbook by the title of "Southern Harmony." By 1851 it had become traditional for many emigrants from the British Isles to sing this song prior to leaving for America. The first verse is as follows:

Yes, my native land, I love thee,
All thy scenes I love them well;
Friends, connections, happy country;
Can I bid you all farewell;
Can I leave you, Can I leave you,
Far in heathen lands to dwell?

John also participated in the festivities by reciting a composition he had prepared especially for the occasion:

O Scotland my country, my dear native home
Thou land of the brave and theme of my song.
O why should I leave thee and cross the deep sea,
To far foreign lands lovely Scotland from thee.

How pleasant to me thy mountains and hills
The sweet blooming heather and far-famed blue bells,
The haunts of my childhood where oft I have strayed
With my faithful companions, my dog, crook, and plaid.

O Scotland my country and land of my birth,
In fondness I'll remember thy worth.
For wrapped in thy bosom my forefathers sleep,
O why should I leave thee and cross the wide deep.

But why should I linger or wish for to stay?
The voice of the prophet is haste flee away.
Lest judgments o'ertake you and lay Scotland low,
To the faithful in Zion O then let me go.

Farewell then loved Scotland, my home and my all,
When duty requires it we bow to the call.
We brave every danger, we conquer each foe.
To the voice of the prophet, O then let me bow.

Farewell then dear kindred, one last fond adieu.
Farewell my dear brethren so faithful and true.
May angels watch o'er you till warfares are o'er,
And in safety we all meet on Zion's fair shore.[33]

On New Year's Eve 1851, John and Ann attended another good-bye reception held for them in Kirkconnel, in the home of Ann's parents. "We had a very friendly gathering of kindred, friends, and neighbors. Many had come a great distance to bid us the last sorrowful goodbye. Many bitter tears and heartfelt sorrow was manifested for us all on account of the foolish step that those outside of the Church thought we were taking, more especially for the two innocent little children that they said would never see land on the other side of the ocean."[34] Early the next morning, New Year's Day 1852, the Murdochs said a final goodbye to family and boarded a train for Glasgow, where they arrived that evening. That night, they were the guests of the evening at a gathering held in a meeting hall that served as home to the Glasgow conference of the church (most likely the Mechanics Institution on Canning Street, in the Calton section of Glasgow). John was introduced to the group as "President Young's shepherd," and he received many congratulations from fellow Saints who likely wished that they too were leaving for Zion. "Many said they wished they had been shepherds. Two nice young ladies stepped up in front and very modestly said, "We wish we had been your wives and going with you," which made a hearty laugh from the crowd. I noticed the crimson blush on the lovely cheek of the young lady that spoke to me while the other gave a pleasant smile that almost captivated me."[35]

It was at the New Year's gathering in Glasgow that John met for the first time the man who was to be his partner in the sheepherding enterprise, this man's wife, and the two dogs that had been purchased. None of them particularly impressed John: "He looked rather sickly and limped along with a bad foot that afterward caused his death in Salt Lake City. His wife was rather a large woman, had rather a sour look about her under lip, and gave unmistakable signs that she would need baby clothes before we reached the other side of the big water. The shepherd Aleut [dog] was much in the same fix, but I was told that it was so planned that the dog race might increase on the journey as they would bring a big price in Utah."[36]

The day soon arrived for them to leave Scotland. The Murdochs and their companions boarded a steamer bound for Liverpool, where they would secure their passage to America. The gangway was lifted and they rushed aboard, amidst cheers and waving handkerchiefs. Fittingly, as they went down the River Clyde into the firth, it began to rain. A thick Scotch mist engulfed them, soon ushering in darkness, slowly obscuring their final views of their homeland. "The last glimpse we had of dear old Scotland was as we passed Elza Crag [Ailsa Craig]. Aaron [Arran] hills on the other side were completely hid from our view."[37] It was a bittersweet feeling as John and Ann Murdoch caught the last few glimpses of the mist covered mountains of Scotland. The sadness of leaving home never to return was tempered by their buoyant optimism about what lay ahead of them in the new world. As they clutched their two precious young children and began to think of the journey ahead of them, they likely realized that there would be challenges and trials along the way. They had no way of knowing that the price they would pay for their deliverance to Zion would be greater than they could have ever imagined.

Notes

1. Michael Finn, ed., *Scottish Population History* (Cambridge, England: Cambridge University Press, 1977), 301.

2. Ibid., 313.

3. James Edward Shaw, *Ayrshire, 1745–1950: A Social and Industrial History* (Edinburgh, Scotland: Oliver and Boyd, 1953), 234–35.

4. Dallas Earl Murdoch, *The Brigham and Thomas Todd Murdoch Family Histories* (The Brigham and Thomas Todd Family Organization, 1998), 51.

5. "The Dangers of Coal Mining," The Lanarkshire Mining Industry History of Mining, http://www.sorbie.net/lanarkshire_mining_industry.htm (accessed February 13, 2005).

6. Finn, *Scottish Population History,* 317.

7. John Murray Nicol, ed., *The James and Mary Murray Murdoch Family History* (Provo, UT: James and Mary Murray Murdoch Family Organization, 1982), 204.

8. Dallas Earl Murdoch, *Family Histories,* 6–7.

9. John Murray Murdoch, Early History of John Murray Murdoch, written by himself at Heber, Utah, 5 Sept. 1898 (document in author's possession).

10. Ibid.

11. Alexander Fenton, *Country life in Scotland: Our Rural Past* (Edinburgh, Scotland: John Donald Publishing, 1987), 71–81.

12. John Murray Murdoch, Early History.

13. Ibid.

14. Nicol, *Family History,* 205.

15. John Murray Murdoch, Early History.

16. Ibid.

17. Joseph Smith Jr., *The Pearl of Great Price* 2:10 (Salt Lake City: The Church of Jesus Christ of Latter-day Saints, 1981).

18. Shaw, *Ayrshire, 1745–1950,* 96–131.

19. Frederick S. Buchanan, "The Ebb and Flow of Mormonism in Scotland, 1840–1900," *Brigham Young University Studies* 27 (1987): 28.

20. Ibid., 29.

21. Joseph Smith Jr., *Teachings of the Prophet Joseph Smith,* comp. Joseph Fielding Smith (Salt Lake City: Deseret Book, 1951), 210.

22. Buchanan, "Ebb and Flow," 30.

23. Ibid., 36.

24. Nicol, *Family History,* 87–91.

25. John Murray Murdoch, *Early History.*

26. Ibid.

27. *Report of the Glasgow Conference, 1849.*

28. Buchanan, "Ebb and Flow," 36.

29. John Murray Murdoch, *Early History.*

30. Ibid.

31. Leonard J. Arrington, *Brigham Young: American Moses* (Urbana: University of Illinois Press, 1986), 169.

32. John Murray Murdoch, *Early History.*

33. Ibid.

34. Ibid.

35. Ibid.

36. Ibid.

37. Ibid.

4

♦ ♦ ♦

THE JOURNEY

*Farewell, my friends! farewell, my foes! My peace with these, my love
with those: The bursting tears my heart declare—Farewell, the bonie
banks of Ayr!*

—Robert Burns, from *Farewell Song to the Banks of Ayr* (1786)

For we cannot tarry here,
We must march my darlings, we must bear the brunt of danger,
We the youthful sinewy races, all the rest on us depend,
Pioneers! O pioneers!

—Walt Whitman, from *Pioneers! O Pioneers!*, (1900)

When John and Ann Murdoch boarded a steamer in Glasgow bound
for Liverpool in early January 1852, not only did they have their two
young children (Elizabeth, age three, and James, age eighteen months) with
them, but Ann was also about four months pregnant. A mid-nineteenth-
century passage across the Atlantic may have proven difficult under most
circumstances, but the particular conditions in which the Murdochs began
their journey intensified the challenges that lay ahead. The combination
of having two young children, Ann's late first trimester or early second
trimester pregnancy, the mid-winter timing of the voyage, being essentially penniless, and traveling in crowded conditions conspired to create "a
perfect storm" of difficulty for them. The severe weather (gale-force winds
and torrents of rain were reported) on the short trip between Glasgow and
Liverpool heightened the symbolism of their great challenge and proved to
portend great problems ahead for the Murdochs.

Pukings and Filth: On to Liverpool

John apparently spent the night of this short trip on the deck of the
steamer, having spent his last money so that Ann and the children could
be in a cabin rather than in the miserable hold of the vessel. Because of
the severe storm they encountered, the trip to Liverpool was slowed, and
they arrived much later than scheduled. When they did arrive, John was

soaked and freezing, while Ann and the children were suffering from severe seasickness.

> We landed in Liverpool very much behind time. The captain said it was the worst storm he had ever seen and how the steamer kept afloat during the night he could not tell.... I got a thorough soaking, being on deck all night, choosing rather to share the unpleasantness of the severe storm with my two solitary companions rather than to be crowded down in the hold, flooded with pukings and filth coming from a crowd of poor, helpless seasick emigrants of both sexes.... My wife and children were in the cabin very seasick and thought they would never see father again...when I looked into the hold at daybreak the sight was appalling and the stench unbearable, and though drenched to the skin and almost shivering with cold, I thought my condition much better than theirs. I was not the least seasick. I went into the cabin to find how my wife and family had braved the storm. They too were very seasick and looked more like raised ghosts then human beings, though their condition was much better than that of the poor emigrants in the hold, though it cost me the last ten dollars I had left.[1]

CROSSING THE ATLANTIC: THE KENNEBEC

After they arrived in Liverpool, the Murdochs waited for ten days while their American-bound ship, the *Kennebec*, was loaded with cargo. They were part of a group of 333 Zion-bound Saints—mostly English and Scots—who would sail from Liverpool to New Orleans, venture up the Mississippi River from New Orleans to St. Louis and Iowa on smaller boats, and then trek on to the Salt Lake valley by wagon and foot. This group has been referred to as the fifty-sixth company, and it was under the direction of John S. Higbee, who was appointed president and sometimes referred to as "captain" of the company. Higbee, a veteran church operative who had been imprisoned with Joseph Smith in a wretched jail in Liberty, Missouri, in 1838–39, was assisted by three counselors, Elders John Spiers, Thomas Smith, and William C. Dunbar. Included among the 333 Saints were sixty-nine whose travel was funded entirely or in part by the church's Perpetual Emigrating Fund (P.E.F.), a scheme of Brigham Young to provide the poorest of European Saints with the opportunity to borrow church funds for their travel to Utah, and then pay back into the fund so that it would remain stable. This was the first group to include P.E.F. immigrants. On board with the Scottish and English Saints were another sixty-six extremely poor non-Mormon Irish immigrants, bringing the total number of passengers on the *Kennebec* to 399.[2]

The original plan was for this voyage to be a charter comprised entirely of immigrating Mormons. However, the poor condition of the vessel that was first anticipated for this journey—the smaller *Devonshire*—caused a change of plans, and the larger, newer, stronger, and more commodious *Kennebec* was contracted. To make this upgrade more economically feasible, the leaders of the company decided to open up additional space for the sixty-six Irish immigrants, whose fares helped to defray the cost for the Saints. This move helped with the costs of the trip for the Saints, but it also led to more crowded conditions. Because the Irish immigrants were woefully short of provisions for the trip, this move led to other problems as well. John and Ann's family were listed in the *Kennebec*'s manifest records, with John's occupation being noted as "shepherd."[3] Three other men on this list also noted their occupation as shepherds, including George May, Henry Ballard, and John Calvin (incorrectly listed as "John Colvin" on the manifest). Although John never mentioned by name the man who was to be his partner in the sheepherding enterprise, it is most likely that it was Calvin, because he was the only one of these three men who was from Scotland (Renfrew), and because there was evidence that he had sheep dogs with him on the overland journey to Utah. It is unclear whether the Americanized "Murdock" spelling of their last name (rather than the traditional Scottish "Murdoch") on the *Kennebec*'s manifest was entered by John, a ship's clerk, or the leader of the group, but this was apparently the earliest recorded time in which their name was spelled in that manner.

The *Kennebec* left the Bramley-Moore dock in Liverpool, bound for America, on a cold and wet day, January 10, 1852. The anticipated length of the voyage was to be about eight weeks. Just before the gangway was lifted and the vessel sealed off for its crossing of the Atlantic, John ran off the ship "with the last three halfpence I had on earth and bought one-half ounce of tobacco, thinking it was the last I would ever use." Although he was a zealous convert to Mormonism, and the Word of Wisdom (health code) of his new faith frowned on tobacco use, old ways die hard, and John wanted one last smoke before he departed, assuming that once he arrived in Zion, such allowances would not occur.

The *Kennebec*'s destination was New Orleans and the Mississippi River delta, but there is some evidence that a stop in New York was made at six weeks, and the journey to New Orleans then took another two weeks.[4] Although a January passage across the Atlantic could prove to be a dangerous challenge even under favorable conditions, the *Kennebec* was an excellent choice for the job. Built in 1851 in Maine, this vessel was nearly new, a sailing ship considered to be "not a clipper but a fair specimen of freighting ships which belong to this port" (the port of Bath, Maine).[5] With a total tonnage of 925, the *Kennebec* was over 170 feet long and thirty-four feet wide. These dimensions may sound impressive, but one must consider that the area encompassed within them would be home to approximately four hundred people and their supplies for over two months, and that such crowded conditions would ultimately prove to be oppressive for many of the passengers.

The two month passage to New Orleans was considered to be a relatively smooth one, with the only notable difficulty being the encountering of a "terrible hurricane, which swept the deck clean of cook houses, water barrels, and everything else that could be washed overboard."[6] The key word in describing the relative smoothness of this journey is "relative," as many of the passengers, including John Murdoch, had never before been on an ocean-going freighter, and they were likely troubled by many of the conditions and events that the ship's crew took for granted. In fact, John's own recollection of this leg of the journey was that it was "rather a rough passage."[7] Whatever difficulties with seasickness, crowded accommodations, bad winter weather, and similar physical circumstances the group experienced were compounded further by social and economic problems encountered aboard this floating community. The combination of the non-Mormon Irish immigrants and the English and Scottish Saints created some tensions. John's description of these Irish passengers as being "Irish emigrants of the lowest grade"[8] may seem harsh and condescending, but there are independent accounts of the voyage that support the notion that the extreme poverty in which the Irish passengers lived created notable conflict at times, particularly during the latter part of the journey:

> Besides the Saints there were a number of Irish emigrants on board, who were not supplied with sufficient provisions to last them till the end of the voyage; but in order to lay in a sufficient supply, they stole all they possibly could from the Mormon emigrants, who consequently had to go short themselves, and were compelled to subsist on half rations the last four or five days before landing.[9]

One of the interesting aspects of cultural differences among the crowded passengers of the *Kennebec* was between the Scottish and English Mormons, and this actually proved to be of value to both groups. All of the Saints on this voyage were provisioned by their leaders for the two month journey with clean water and various foodstuffs, most particularly including pork and oatmeal. Cultural differences in food preferences proved to be the fuel for satisfactory bartering, "as the English did not like

oatmeal and the Scotch could not relish pork, they exchanged these articles of food with each other, to the great satisfaction of both parties."[10]

The Irish emigrants apparently fared much worse than the Saints,
because they had little or no provisions, which helps explain the pilfering.
Although John referred to the Irish as being a low-class lot, he charitably
did not accuse them of stealing food in his own recollection, but instead
placed the blame on the ship's captain, who he said "had not furnished
provisions for his Irish emigrants, only oatmeal, but supplied them from
our stores."[11]

As the *Kennebec* entered the Gulf of Mexico and neared New Orleans
in early March 1852, the insufficient provisions proved to be an increasing
challenge for many aboard. When the ship became stuck for ten days in
the mud of the Mississippi delta just south of New Orleans, the problems
worsened and reached a crisis point for some families. John's own family
was one of those who were particularly impacted by these circumstances.
Those passengers with money or goods valuable enough to barter for food
fared better than those without. The Murdochs had neither at this point.
John's own later recollection serves to describe the gradual wasting away
that his two young children began to experience, which must have been
particularly frustrating to him and Ann because they were so close to New
Orleans that food was being obtained by those who had the means:

> ... many of the steerage passengers suffered much privation for want of food
> and fresh water, there being none on board for steerage passengers at least, or
> any fuel to cook with. I think the cabin passengers and those who had money
> fared better as they could buy some provisions from boats that came to our ship
> from land. For myself I fared well, being healthy and strong and not the least bit
> seasick. I could put a handful or two into a bowl and dip a cupful of water from
> the side of the ship, pour it on the oatmeal, and make breakfast, dinner, and
> supper on it and get fat. But such food was not good for little sickly children.
> Shortly thereafter it carried off both of our little children with dysentery. But
> our troubles did not end here.[12]

CONSUMED WITH GRIEF: UP THE MISSISSIPPI

The *Kennebec* arrived in New Orleans in mid-March, 1852, several days
later than anticipated because of the ten days stuck in the mud, and perhaps because of conditions encountered at other points during the voyage.
The exact date of the arrival in New Orleans is somewhat of a mystery.
Logs and diaries of passengers that have been uncovered have listed at least
three different dates: March 11, March 14, and March 19. Because of tragic

events that would soon unfold, the specific date of arrival for the *Kennebec* is an important issue in better understanding some of the pivotal experiences in John Murdoch's life.

As the Murdochs reached their next point of embarkation, they likely did not fully realize that the dysentery little Elizabeth and James Murdoch were suffering was sapping the life from them. By the time they arrived in New Orleans, the condition of their children was obviously of great concern to them, but it is likely that they were not aware of the unimaginable losses that would soon be theirs.

After the *Kennebec* arrived in New Orleans, the Murdochs and their traveling companions were moved to a Mississippi steamboat, *Pride of the West*, which would take them them from New Orleans to St. Louis—a distance of about seven hundred miles—and to different travel arrangements for the overland journey to Utah. By this point in its lifespan, the name *Pride of the West* was a pitiful title, as this steamer had become a veritable moving scrap heap. Some reports indicate that *Pride* was in such bad shape by 1852 that it was literally held together with chains wrapped tightly around its girth.[13]

For most of the passengers on this leg of the journey, the trip north up the Mississippi delta region from New Orleans to St. Louis may have been simply a few days' diversion on their journey to Zion. Despite crowded conditions on the steamer, they may have welcomed the new scenery and lack of oceanic turbulence. The Murdochs were not so fortunate, for they were about to face the nightmare of every parent. By the beginning of this leg of the journey, Elizabeth and James were becoming increasingly frail and sickly from the dysentery that was draining their strength. It is likely that John's attribution of the cause of their illness—their subsisting solely on a diet of oatmeal—is not fully explanatory. Although their oatmeal diet may have worsened or complicated their symptoms, it is likely that the primary culprits of their illness were invisible to them and thus unrecognized. Although the field of microbiology was in its infancy and the role of bacteria, viruses, and amoebae was not well understood at this time, one can be almost certain that the condition of the two children was worsened by one or more of these culprits. Bacterial and amoebic dysentery were common and sometimes deadly ailments in the mid-nineteenth century. Looking back in time it seems likely that one or both of these forms of disease may have been the etiology of James's and Elizabeth's symptoms. They could have encountered these infections by drinking unclean water, by living in the crowded environment and poor sanitation conditions aboard the *Kennebec* and *Pride of the West*. Perhaps these miniature deadly life forms were carried aboard the *Kennebec* by flies or other insects that they encountered as they moved into the Gulf of Mexico, and particularly during the time that they were stuck in the mud. The immature immune systems of the two young children would simply not have been able to cope with these conditions as well as could those of a healthy adult.

Because *Pride* was very crowded, the Murdochs could not obtain a covered berth at first, and they lay on the deck in a cold rain for some time. John was able to persuade an engineman to allow him to rig a makeshift bed with some boards and rope under a steam pipe to provide some shelter for the children. At this point, John S. Higbee, ecclesiastical leader, president, and captain of their emigrating group, ordered John to remove these items and clear out, stating with no intended irony, "Brother Murdoch, we want this place for the sick."[14] John, who was likely torn between his desire to be obedient to his ecclesiastical leaders and to do whatever he could to aid the comfort of his family, later recalled, "I made no reply but thought within myself—if it is for the sick, it is already occupied to its utmost capacity. I think that the kind engineman persuaded him that there might be danger of the pipe bursting, and we had the use of it as long as we needed it."[15] This incident between Captain Higbee and John Murdoch was one of several that would lead to John's low esteem and resentment of Higbee, for the rest of his life. As his two children became weaker and their condition deteriorated further, John begged Higbee "...for some nourishment [but] he said he had no money given him to provide for us. My wife once begged of him with tears in her eyes to give her a little taste of pie for her sick boy. He said if he is sick he wants medicine, I will get some. But neither the medicine nor the pie ever came."[16]

James Murdoch died on March 20, 1852, when he was twenty months old, as the *Pride of the West* ventured north up the Mississippi. A short time before James's death, John tearfully pleaded with a stranger for a morsel of bread to give to his dying son. The scrap of bread he ultimately obtained was the last thing his child ever ate, and it was not sufficient to change the course of malnutrition and disease that had been set in motion. James's death verified the fears of his maternal grandparents and some non-Latter-day Saint friends in Scotland, who had worried that the children would never make it to Utah alive.

Grief-stricken, John took the body of little James from Ann and made arrangements with the captain for the steamer to stop so he could bury his son on land. Late in his life, John recalled that he buried his son "in a wood yard on the bank of the Mississippi, 12 miles from Columbia."[17] It is

unclear where this spot was, or even which state it was in. Trying to deter-
mine the specifics of James's burial place requires an understanding of the
approximate date on which the *Pride* left New Orleans and headed up the
Mississippi, the estimated daily progress of the ship, and the geography of
the Mississippi delta region. Because the *Pride* had definitely not reached
St. Louis by James's death date of March 20, and because of John's report
that his son was buried along the banks of the Mississippi, we must rule
out Columbia, Missouri (which is 120 miles west of St. Louis, and along
the Missouri—not the Mississippi) as the burial spot. Assuming that there
was not another mid-nineteenth century community by the name of Columbia that no longer exists, the most likely possibility of what John meant by
Columbia was the small community of Columbia, Louisiana, which is
about forty miles west of the Mississippi, between Natchez and Vicksburg,
Mississippi, and was an active community in the mid-nineteenth century.
If we accept the March 20 death date as being accurate, then it seems possible that the March 19 departure of *Pride of the West* from New Orleans
could be the most correct date, because this point along the river is about
120 miles north of New Orleans, and *Pride* would have averaged about
sixty miles per day. John's recollection that the burial spot was "12 miles
from Columbia" was most likely an error brought on by the passage of
many years between James's death and John's committing this information
to paper late in his life. In addition, family records (and the information
listed in Family Search of the LDS Church) that have for several years
listed the death place of James Murdoch as being in Kansas City, Wyndt
(Wyandotte?) County, Kansas, appear to be obviously in error. After considering carefully all the available evidence, the best explanation is that
James Murdoch died on March 20, 1852, probably in the afternoon or
otherwise later in the day, and that he was buried along the Louisiana
side of the Mississippi River, perhaps about forty miles east of Columbia,
Louisiana.

Although John and Ann Murdoch were consumed with grief over the
loss of their youngest child, they had little time to dwell on it, because
they were also struggling by this time to keep alive three-year-old Elizabeth, who was suffering from the same malady as James. In addition, Ann
was by then in the last two months of a pregnancy, and they must have
feared for her health and the life of their unborn child, as Ann was nearly
overcome with exhaustion and grief. *Pride of the West* arrived in St. Louis
in late March—probably March 28 or 29, as Elizabeth's condition was
worsening.

St. Louis: Unspeakable Sorrow

When they arrived in St. Louis, the Latter-day Saint emigrants who had come from the British Isles to New Orleans on the *Kennebec*, and then up-river on the steamer, split into smaller groups and took somewhat differing routes and departure dates for the overland trip to Utah. The Murdochs were no longer under the direction of John S. Higbee, which must have been a relief to them, as they obviously felt that he had been insensitive and uncaring toward them and their plight. They were now assigned to a group led by Abraham O. Smoot, a respected veteran leader of emigrating groups, and a man who would later become mayor of Salt Lake City. Those emigrants under Smoot's charge apparently stayed in St. Louis for several days while he attended to the business of preparing for their overland journey west to Kansas City, and while there he had the difficult task of attending to another tragedy that struck a group of emigrating Saints that had left St. Louis on March 30, as they were heading north to Council Bluffs (Kanesville), Iowa, on the steamboat *Saluda*. On April 9, the overworked boilers of the *Saluda* exploded in a great fury as the vessel was stopped near Lexington, Missouri, to avoid large chunks of early spring ice that were floating downriver from Minnesota and Iowa. The explosion was so fierce that the bodies of several passengers were observed to be blown up a steep embankment or bluff. The citizens of Lexington heroically came to the aid of the survivors, but in the end, seventy-five of the total 175 passengers were killed in the explosion (including twenty of the Mormon emigrants), and many others were seriously injured.[18]

While the Murdochs were in St. Louis awaiting the return of Captain Smoot and their departure up the Missouri to Kansas City, Elizabeth's condition continued to worsen. Very little is known about her last days or the circumstances of her death, but John recorded that she died on April 4, 1852. It is likely that by the time of Elizabeth's death, no change in her diet would have been sufficient to spare her life. Dysentery was a common cause of death among young children during the nineteenth century, a condition that resulted in a slow and painful death by dehydration, toxic shock from infection, and ultimately shutting down the vital organs. By the last few days of her life, the inflammation and infection of Elizabeth's bowels would not have responded to the various cures of the day. Years later, total bowel rest with intravenous liquid nutrition and sulfa drugs was a common and effective treatment, but this method was unknown and unavailable in 1852.

Elizabeth was four months shy of her fourth birthday when she died. Some family and LDS church records indicate Elizabeth's burial and death place as being Kansas City. However, as is true in the case of the death and burial place of her brother, James, this information is entirely inconsistent with all of the other available information and known sequences of events. In the space of barely two weeks, John and Ann Murdoch had experienced the death of both of their two young children and were forced by circumstances to bury them in places they would never again see. For most of the remainder of his life, John's report to others of the circumstances of Elizabeth's burial was simply that she was buried at St. Louis, and that they were treated very kindly by strangers: "...she passed away and was buried in a strange land among strangers. The people were very kind to us."[19] This simple report is what he repeated to others and what he wrote in his personal history in 1901, when he was eighty years old. Apparently, the true circumstances regarding Elizabeth's final resting place were too horrific and disturbing for John to repeat to another soul until near the end of his life. Some accounts of this alternate story indicate that John wrote it in his own history later in his life, whereas other accounts state that he told the grisly facts to a family member—perhaps his nephew David Lennox Murdoch—who later updated John's history with these additional details. Regardless of the way in which this story was transmitted, there is general consistency in family records regarding the essential facts of John's addendum:

After the little girl's body was prepared for burial and placed in a substantial box a strange man came along and apparently sympathized with us in our bereavement. He told us that a short distance away was a cemetery and said he would send a wagon to convey the casket to the place of burial free of charge. We gladly accepted the profer. When all was ready he said, "Now, the wagon road goes around that large building you see but there is a trail leading direct to the cemetery which you and I can take and we will be at the burial place when the wagon comes". The wagon came and we deposited the box in the grave and I carefully covered it over the earth. Again I was very sad and lonely and instead of going back to camp the way I came I decided to go by the wagon road. Going into the building I saw a large vat of boiling water and as I watched it a human form came to the surface. Surprised I stood gazing and to my horror saw the head of my own little girl with her yellow curly hair rise to the surface and disappear. It is impossible for me to express my feelings, but went to camp and kept this sorrow to myself until the present time. We learned that this was a dissecting establishment.[20]

Although modern-day readers might be tempted to question whether American citizens and businessmen could engage in such a revolting practice as John Murdoch witnessed his daughter's body being used for, or whether they might take such evil advantage over someone as grief-worn and burdened as was this Scottish immigrant, we must face the disturbing fact that the practice of using human remains in dissecting plants to make soap and fertilizer has happened on a large scale as recently as the twentieth century. It has been widely reported that this practice was engaged in by the Nazis in some of the Jewish concentration camps of Poland during the Holocaust of the 1940s, and by the Khmer Rouge regime in Cambodia in their "killing fields" of the 1970s. Despite the fact that most states prohibited the dissection of human remains in the mid-nineteenth century, there are compelling reasons to believe the second-hand account of John Murdoch's experience.[21] Modern-day Americans might be surprised to learn that during the early to mid-nineteenth century, the problem of grave robbing was not uncommon. Although it was widely considered to be a sacrilegious act, stolen corpses would be sold to medical students and schools, and in some cases they were used for making fertilizer and soap. The problem was bad enough that it spawned the practice of placing iron cages over graves to protect interred bodies, a peculiar strategy that apparently originated in Scotland.[22] In 1852 Missouri was still in many respects a frontier region, full of a variety of unprincipled opportunists who could have certainly done this and worse. Although it is difficult to identify specific practices of this sort in Missouri, there are plenty of reasons to accept John Murdoch's account.

Modern psychological science has verified that when humans are confronted with a situation that is so far outside the bounds of normal human experience as to be unrecognizable in the daily routines of life, it is not uncommon for us to "dissociate," or enter into a state of seeming unreality or altered consciousness, regarding the horrific circumstance with which they are faced. John Murdoch's report of his experience in observing the body of young Elizabeth is not inconsistent with such a state of altered consciousness. The fact that he did not speak of this event again until nearly half a century later suggests that he did his best to remove the thought of it into the deeper regions of his consciousness so that he did not have to think about it on a daily basis, much like many combat veterans who have experienced the horrors of war but do not talk about them, even to their most intimate friends and family. We can only imagine the burden that this experience was to him throughout the remainder of his life.

MY SCOTCH JOHNNIE: A BIRTH, CHOLERA, AND CAPTAIN SMOOT

In mid-April, Abraham Smoot returned to St. Louis from the *Saluda* disaster upriver at Lexington, and the Saints who were waiting for him for their departure west were joined by another immigration group from the British Isles who had departed Liverpool on the *Ellen Maria* on February 10. Basic supplies for the overland trek had been purchased, and the Murdochs and their compatriots were ready to begin the journey west. Although most of the Mormon immigrants from the British Isles were very inexperienced in any skills related to pioneering, this particular group was considered to be particularly unseasoned: "Few companies had been as green as this group of...immigrants."[23] They followed the Missouri River to Kansas City, a distance of about 275 miles. The group stayed in Kansas City for several days while they awaited the arrival of their wagons, which had been ordered and constructed in St. Louis according to Smoot's specifications. These wagons proved to be of such fine quality that Brigham Young advised those emigrating in 1853 to obtain wagons of the same kind from the same firm that had been used by Captain Smoot.[24]

On May 20, somewhere near the Missouri River near Kansas City, Ann Murdoch was delivered of a baby, a girl they named Mary Murray Murdoch, after her paternal grandmother in Scotland. John wrote that their daughter was "born in a small tent in the midst of the most terrific thunderstorm I have ever witnessed."[25] Mary was born two months to the day after her older brother, James, died, and about six weeks after the death of her older sister, Elizabeth. Based on records left by many pioneer women of the nineteenth century, it is likely that Ann's delivery of their baby was not accompanied by any extended period of rest or any relaxation of her responsibilities. Many pioneer women gave birth to their children along the Mormon and Oregon trails during the mid-nineteenth century, and the accounts that some of them left behind indicate a reality much different from that experienced by modern American women. Commenting on this aspect of pioneer life, historian Lillian Hissell has written:

> Childbearing did not in any degree alter the determination to emigrate. The decision to make the journey rested with the men, and farm men of the early nineteenth century were not inclined to excuse women from their daily responsibilities to prepare for the occasion of childbirth. Women were expected to be strong enough to serve the common needs of the day, and strong enough to meet the uncommon demands as well. The society of emigrants yielded little comfort to frailty or timidity—or for that matter motherhood.[26]

As the Smoot Company was laying over in Kansas City in late May, the group was stricken with cholera. About forty of the company became afflicted with the disease, and more than fifteen died from it. Cholera is caused by a bacterial infection that may be contracted through drinking water or eating food containing the cholera bacterium. It is typically spread through unclean sanitary conditions, through the feces of infected persons. The symptoms usually include profuse watery diarrhea, severe vomiting, and painful leg cramps. Rapid weight loss is typical. Because it can result in quick dehydration and kidney failure, cholera can be fatal within a matter of hours. This localized epidemic soon reached a crisis stage and threatened not only the health of these emigrants, but their safety from local citizens as well. Isaac Brockbank, a member of the Smoot Company, recorded in his journal that the local citizens—including many who had been bitter enemies of the church during the Saints' time in western Missouri two decades earlier—considered forcing them from the area once they received news of the cholera outbreak: "... as the scourge in the camp increased, and the brethren and sisters dying off, alarm spread thro the surrounding country and the result was that Indignation Meetings were held, and propositions made to have the Saints removed. But as the scourge continued, they were afraid to go near the camp.... Rude boxes of any kind were made use of and dead laid away without ceremony."[27]

On June 1, apparently about one to two weeks after the start of the outbreak, enough of the afflicted persons had recovered sufficiently that Captain Smoot deemed it necessary to get the group moving westward. The Smoot Company left Kansas City with about 250 individuals and thirty-three wagons, the first group to start the trek to Utah under the auspices of the Perpetual Emigrating Fund support. It is quite likely that Smoot's concern regarding possible hostile treatment by the local citizenry pressured him to mobilize his party before all were healed. As soon as the last of his company who survived the outbreak was fully healed, Smoot himself became afflicted with cholera, and it nearly took his life. The entire camp stopped for two days during the worst of his symptoms, fasting and praying for him. His condition became so bad that he actually wrote out his will and made preparations for dying.[28] John was appointed Smoot's day nurse, and he did his best to provide comfort and support for him during the day, until he was relieved by the night nurses in the evening. The entire camp had great reason to be fearful of losing Captain Smoot. Not only was he a beloved and respected leader, he was the only man among the company with significant pioneering skills and experienced in the trek to Utah. Later in his life, John affectionately recalled his concern and care for Abraham Smoot, and his tender feelings for him:

> Being very weak he was always very anxious to be taken from his carriage and laid on his bed on the ground the first thing when we camped. I had made his bed in a hurry to get him on to it, but he was soon covered with little black ants, and thinking that we must move it, I said, "Brother Smoot, I have made your bed among the ants. What shall we do? He replied with a sweet smile on his face, Brother John, if they will let us alone, we can well afford to let them alone. This noble saying of a free born American relieved my mind very much. He sometimes called me his little Johnny. I once was very much delighted to hear him say that his little Scotch Johnny had gained a place in his heart that would not soon be forgotten. He thought I did not hear him which made it so much better.[29]

John's affection and respect for Abraham O. Smoot was echoed by most of the emigrating party, a testament to Smoot's leadership, personal traits, and fair treatment of his charges. James Thomas Wilson, a young member of the emigrating party from England, stated:

> Everybody loved our Captain. He was both thoughtful, polite, considerate and although our wagons were loaded to the bows, when he would see any of the company lagging as they trudged wearily along with stick in hand to aid them in their locomotive powers and he was convinced they were not putting it on, he would tell them to ride. The rule was that all able bodied men, women, and youth should walk. There was to be no favourites who rode just when they pleased, while some who were more deserving had to trudge on.[30]

The crisis created by Smoot's bout with cholera passed after the worst of the symptoms ended, and the captain, who was greatly weakened by the illness, gradually resumed his leadership responsibilities. Later in life, he reflected on his near-death experience:

> The train was stopped and the whole company fasted and prayed for two days for my recovery, but I continued growing worse until my limbs and the lower part of my body were apparently dead, but then the faith of the Saints and the power of the Almighty prevailed in my behalf and I recovered. I had, however, lost seventy-five pounds in weight within a few days.[31]

From Kansas City, the Smoot Company followed the Missouri River north to the point where the Platte River joined it near Council Bluffs,

Iowa. At this point, the Mormon trail followed the Platte and North Platte rivers through the length of Nebraska, moving into present-day Wyoming a few miles past Chimney Rock and present-day Scottsbluff, Nebraska. John Murdoch's personal history includes few details of the trek to Utah after the Kansas City layover and the cholera outbreak. He did note that Captain Smoot assigned him to go back from the main company on a large mule to retrieve a cow they had seen a day earlier. Smoot gave John strict instructions regarding the route to take. Ultimately, despite following the captain's instructions to the letter, John became separated from his party by as many as ninety miles, became lost, and was in a perilous situation for his own survival. Relying on his wits and faith, he barely survived the three day ordeal, and ultimately had to abandon the worn-out mule and stagger into camp on foot. The only other aspect of the trek that John mentioned in his recollections later in life was that he "got the mountain fever and became very sick" when they reached the Black Hills (probably somewhere adjacent to the current Nebraska-Wyoming border), and that Captain Smoot "had a good chance to pay me back which he did with interest. He did all that he could have done for me if I had been his own son. I have always had a good word for Captain Smoot."[32] It is easy to imagine that the trek to Utah was a long and difficult grind for John and Ann, given that they were still fresh from the trauma of losing two children, that Ann was making the journey while recovering from childbirth, and that they had a newborn daughter to care for.

Across the Plains and into the West

Several details of the Smoot Company's journey west are available from journals and recollections of members of this party. Ten persons were assigned to each wagon, and a captain was appointed over each of these subgroups. One cow (for milk) and one tent were assigned to each group of ten, and each group was allowed ten pounds of flour per day, and initially some sugar, coffee, bacon, and fish. After the party reached Fort Kearney (about a two week journey from Council Bluffs), the coffee, bacon, fish, and sugar began to disappear from the menu, and soon their provisions consisted mainly of milk and flour. Indians often approached the party to trade for bread or flour, but as supplies waned, little trading was done. Smoot's group traveled along the south side of the Platte, but there were other emigrating companies moving along the north side, and the captains of the companies would occasionally cross the river to inquire regarding the progress and well-being of the other groups.

During the Platte/North Platte leg of the trek, John's likely sheepherding partner, John Calvin, was at the center of a foolish incident that nearly proved disastrous to the company. After his shepherd dog had strayed behind the party, Calvin received permission from Smoot to ride one of the mules back to the previous camp spot to search for the dog. Calvin successfully retrieved the dog, and when he ventured back to the Smoot wagon train, he rode the mule at top speed in high spirits, moving into the center of the wagons yelling and whooping with his hat in his hand. Calvin's alarming behavior caused nine of the teams to run "helter skelter as if driven by a cyclone and it was with the greatest difficulty that all of the teams were kept from following suit."[33] James Wilson noted further that this incident caused a few wagon wheels and tongues to be broken and some of the cattle to lose their horns through crashing into other cattle or objects, but that none of the immigrants were seriously hurt. "There were some very narrow escapes in order to steer clear of the maddened bovines, and as far as I am concerned, I never want to see another stampede."[34]

After the Smoot party crossed the North Platte, they began to encounter large herds of buffalo, and some stray buffalo would occasionally wander through camp in the evening or early morning hours. As they moved farther west, the previously abundant supply of grass and other forage for their milk cows became scarce, partly because of the increasingly arid conditions, and in part because this section of the trail was heavily traveled and thus overgrazed during the summer of 1852. As a result, the milk supplies decreased, which proved to be an increasing hardship, especially for the children of the party, who relied primarily on milk for their nourishment. As they moved into the high plains of present-day Wyoming, two incidents brought more sorrow to the group. A young man drowned while bathing in a river, probably somewhere between Chimney Rock and Fort Laramie. Shortly after passing through Fort Laramie, a despondent woman disappeared from camp and was never seen again. This woman had apparently never wanted to leave England and was never enthusiastic about making the trek. She became increasingly depressed as the journey wore on, and when she disappeared, she left a baby without a mother's care.[35]

◆ ◆ ◆

The last major stretch of the Mormon trail went from the Green River (near present-day Rock Springs, Wyoming) to Fort Bridger (about thirty-five miles east of present-day Evanston, Wyoming), and then southwest across the Wasatch Mountains and into the valley of the Great Salt Lake. After crossing the Green River, there were heavy stretches of sand, which required that the milk cows be hitched along with oxen, for additional leveraging power with the wagons. From Fort Bridger to the valley, the Smoot party began to encounter increasing numbers of friends, many of whom came to bring them more supplies and to encourage them on their last stretch of the journey. Captain Smoot made an advance trip to the valley on August 30, and then returned to join the company and lead them to their new home. As they made their final descent down Emigration Canyon, the wagon wheels had to be locked and ropes were used to help ease the wagons down the steep slopes. When they camped that evening—their final night of the trek—the Smoot party was treated to a feast of fine beef that had been sent by Brigham Young. Many in the party danced until late in the night, in joyous anticipation of the conclusion of their long journey.[36]

A Very Hearty Welcome

John, Ann, and Mary Murdoch, along with the other members of the Abraham O. Smoot Company, arrived in Salt Lake City on a beautiful late summer day, September 3, 1852, eight months after leaving their homeland of Scotland, and about six months after arriving in New Orleans. For their final walk to Salt Lake, many in the party put on their best clothing. They were greeted at the mouth of Emigration Canyon by Pitt's Brass Band, and as they walked down Emigration Street, they were met by Brigham Young, his two counselors, and the members of the Quorum of the Twelve Apostles. Emigration Street was lined with large numbers of spectators, and the event turned into something of a parade. As they moved into the city, Captain Smoot directed the progress of the company from horseback, and led them into the public square, where there was a sumptuous banquet prepared for them, and where Abraham Smoot was publicly praised by members of the church hierarchy for his strong leadership on the successful trek. The members of the company and the church leaders made a gift to Captain Smoot of a number of stray cows that had been picked up along the trek, left behind by other immigrants.[37]

John Murdoch recalled that he and his fellow designated shepherd, John Calvin, were introduced by Captain Smoot to President Young, and that they received the surprising news that there would be no immediate need of their sheepherding skills.

> ...Brigham Young gave us a very hearty welcome, and gave us many words of encouragement. Captain Smoot introduced us to Brigham as his two shepherds with our dogs, and gave me a very good recommend. Brother Brigham informed us that he had rented what few sheep he had left to his Brother Lorenzo for five

years and would not need us at the present time for that purpose. He said we needed to rest and to remain at camp and the brethren would fund us something to eat and the way would be opened for us that we would get work.[38]

Individually and collectively, the members of the Smoot Company had endured many hardships to reach this new starting point in Zion. Company records indicate that there were twenty-four deaths and four births among the party. The Murdochs were the only family to be counted in both columns.[39] The loss of their two young children was still a fresh memory. For John, the circumstances in which he discovered the body of his daughter Elizabeth in the dissecting plant in St. Louis must have been a still fresh wound, a traumatic incident with no rational explanation or justification. As they savored the celebration of their arrival in Salt Lake and the prospects of their future in Zion, they were also weighed down with the heavy burden of their losses, and the uncertainty of what would now await them. It had been less than two years earlier that John and Ann were baptized as members of the Church of Jesus Christ of Latter-day Saints and joined their lives to this new cause. In that short period of time, the Murdochs had proven themselves to be committed to the church and its teaching without reservation. This intense commitment and the hardships they had experienced the previous two years would ultimately serve them in the path ahead and would provide a foundation for later generations of the Murdoch family.

Notes

1. John Murray Murdoch, *Early History of John Murray Murdoch, written by himself at Heber, Utah, 5 Sept. 1898* (document in author's possession).

2. "Sailing of the *Kennebec*," Immigrant Ships Transcribers Guild: Kennebec, http://www.immigrantships.net/v6/1800v6/kennebec_saluda18520319.html (accessed February 25, 2005).

3. "Sailing of the *Kennebec*."

4. "The Journey to Winter Quarters," The May Tragedy, http://homepage.ntlworld.com/john.boon/The%20May%20Tragedy/The%20Journey.htm (accessed March 8, 2005).

5. Notes on the *Kennebec* from the Maine Maritime Museum, Bath, Maine, March 4, 2005.

6. "Sailing of the *Kennebec*."

7. John Murray Murdoch, *Early History.*

8. Ibid.

9. "Sailing of the *Kennebec*."

10. Ibid.

11. John Murray Murdoch, *Early History.*

12. Ibid.

13. "Journey to Winter Quarters."

14. John Murray Murdoch, *Early History.*

15. Ibid.

16. Ibid.

17. Ibid.

18. Elliott C. Berlin, *Abraham Owen Smoot, Mormon Pioneer Leader* (Provo, UT: Brigham Young University, Master's Thesis), 57.

19. John Murray Murdoch, *Early History.*

20. Ibid.

21. "A Tribute to the Frontier Doctor," Frederick W. Bolling, http://www.fredrickboling.com/frontier%20medicine.html (accessed June 10, 2005).

22. Ann F. Diseroad, "Cages on Graves Explained: A Wee Bit of Old Scotland Right Here in Columbia County," *Columbia County Genealogical and Historical Society Newsletter,* http://www.colcohist-gensoc.org/Essays/Cages%20on%20Graves%20Explained.pdf (accessed June 10, 2005).

23. Berlin, *Abraham Owen Smoot,* 58.

24. Ibid.

25. John Murray Murdoch, *Early History.*

26. Lillian Schlissel, *Women's Diaries of the Westward Journey* (New York: Schocken Books, 1982), 123.

27. Berlin, *Abraham Owen Smoot,* 59.

28. Ibid.

29. John Murray Murdoch, *Early History.*

30. Thomas Wilson, *The Journal of Thomas Wilson* (microfilm copy in Brigham Young University Library, Provo, UT), 44–45.

31. Berlin, *Abraham Owen Smoot,* 59.

32. John Murray Murdoch, *Early History.*

33. Wilson, *Journal of Thomas Wilson,* 48.

34. Ibid.

35. Berlin, *Abraham Owen Smoot,* 61.

36. Wilson, *Journal of Thomas Wilson,* 54.

37. Berlin, *Abraham Owen Smoot,* 63.

38. Hiram McDonald and Anne Rasband McDonald, eds., *Our Generations: A Legacy of Faith* (Bountiful, UT: Hiram and Anne Rasband McDonald, 1996), 161.

39. "List of births and deaths of the Abraham O. Smoot Company," *Deseret News,* September 4, 1852, 3.

5

• • •

A NEW START

Israel, Israel, God is calling, Calling thee from lands of woe.
Babylon the great is falling; God shall all her tow'rs o'er-throw.
Come to Zion, come to Zion, Ere his floods of anger flow.
Come to Zion, come to Zion, Ere his floods of anger flow.

—LDS Hymn

Certainly most Mormon converts felt they had undergone a spiritual change.
But without the lure of a home in America would there have been fewer
of them? One must remember that in many ways Mormonism was the least
attractive of the several available means of emigration to a new country.
Demanding of the emigrant strict obedience and continuing economic
sacrifice, it offered in return a home in one of the least inviting regions of
the hemisphere. Clearly the Mormon religion itself, if not the sole factor
behind emigration, was the key to the process.

—LEONARD J. ARRINGTON, *The Mormon Experience:*
A History of the Latter-day Saints

After the triumphal entry of the Smoot Company into Salt Lake City
on September 3, 1852, a new reality began to emerge for the Murdochs. John and Ann were given the opportunity for their passage based
on Brigham Young's requisition for a Scottish shepherd to assist him in
getting the sheep industry started in Zion. It was assumed all along that
John would take on this responsibility upon his arrival in Utah, and that it
would provide the means for taking care of his family. But the announcement by President Young that he no longer had flocks and thus no longer
required John's services as a shepherd changed their plans, and it became
apparent that they would need to find new opportunities for work.

The Murdochs and many others of their party camped in the public
square that first night in Salt Lake. By the end of the second day, September 4, the crowd had dispersed and the square was nearly emptied. "There
was not a soul left in camp except the two shepherds (Murdoch and Calvin), their wives, the two children, and the two dogs."[1] In retrospect, it is
easy to imagine that at this point, John and Ann Murdoch were relieved to

finally be in Zion, having faith in the providence of their new circumstances, but they must have also had anxiety regarding their next steps and immediate needs.

The Greatest Man on Earth

Part of Brigham Young's carefully planned process for the success of Mormon immigration to Utah was to have established settlers assist the new arrivals in the steps toward becoming independent and helping to build the kingdom. "The already established Saints were under instructions to take the new arrivals into their homes, care for them, and provide employment until they could begin to farm or practice their own occupations."[2] These instructions were an extension of Brigham Young's teaching that "True charity to a poor family or person consists of placing them in a situation in which they can support themselves. In this country there is no person possessing an ordinary degree of health and strength, but can earn a support for himself and his family."[3] True to this ideal, the Murdochs' initial toehold in Zion came in the form of an invitation from a man named Dalton from Farmington (several miles north of Salt Lake), who took them and the Calvin family to his home to labor for one month. We have no record of what type of work was involved, but John did receive wages for his labors, which he noted made him feel "rich enough to divide with my poor companion," the hapless Calvin, who apparently had a sore foot, was unable to work, and had to return to Salt Lake.[4] John's next employment opportunity came from none other than Brigham Young, who hired him in early October to dig potatoes in his weedy city lot of one and a quarter acres. Although this work was hard and lonely, the perpetually optimistic and trusting John considered it a great privilege to work for President Young (whom he regarded as "the greatest man on Earth"), even as he was derided for doing so by other recent immigrants who had a lower opinion of the Great Colonizer:

> Some disaffected spirits came around me, some of them from my own country, which made their tale of woe the more plausible, telling me that they had worked some for Brigham but he had not paid them as he ought have done, and I would not get my pay either. They asked what share I was to get for digging such a hard lot as this. I replied I had not made any bargain, but I was sure that President Young would do right by me. Then they would turn away with derisive laughter, saying I would soon learn better.[5]

John's trust in Brigham Young proved to be warranted, as he found the president's dealings with him to be satisfactory in every respect. During this same time period, John also found work in public works projects such as digging drainage ditches, and he apparently worked for other church authorities as well. It is not known where exactly the Murdochs lived during their first several months in Utah, but several family records indicate that the Murdochs' initial period there proved to be a significant struggle in terms of maintaining satisfactory food and shelter. It is also apparent that Brigham Young had continued interactions with John and took a personal interest in him. John received a blessing under the hands of Brigham, and was promised that he "would live to have houses and lands and would prosper."[6]

LIFE IN ZION

There are precious few details regarding the circumstances of the Murdoch family from their arrival in Salt Lake in 1852 until they began to achieve some stability about three years later. To understand what those first years in Zion may have been like for them, it is useful to draw upon the broader historical record of Utah in the 1850s. The exodus of the Saints from Nauvoo, Illinois, to the valley of the Great Salt Lake began in early 1846, peaked in 1848, and was essentially completed by 1852. From that point forward for the next few years, the new arrivals in Utah were, like the Murdochs, primarily European converts to Mormonism who emigrated as part of the gathering of Zion. Brigham Young's grand plan for colonization involved the development of a "Mormon corridor," which extended from the hub in Salt Lake City to the spokes in outlying settlements as far-flung as San Bernardino, California, to the south, and the Cache valley and Bear Lake regions of northern Utah to the north. This corridor would extend the reach of the Saints and solidify their claims to the region. During the 1850s, Mormon merchants began to establish a system of trade from Salt Lake City up and down this corridor, while Brigham Young attempted to encourage the development of an independent near-nation, promoting the establishment of a diverse set of industries ranging from cotton farming to sugar production to ironworking.

The 1850s were a time of immense poverty in Utah. Although there were many tradesman registered in Salt Lake City, most families found it necessary to make at least a portion of their living from farming or ranching. The popularity of the emerging agricultural lifestyle in Utah was not necessarily because of inherently good farming conditions. On the contrary, the soil of most of the region was very poor in comparison with the dark rich soils of the Midwest, and the frost-free period was relatively short and unpredictable. Because rainfall was so scarce in this semi-arid climate, elaborate systems of irrigation needed to be developed in order for proper watering of animals and crops to occur. Because of these challenges, a life in farming or ranching was not naturally inviting in terms of imminent prosperity and ease. Rather, the lure of agriculture resided in the relative independence it promised, which seemed particularly inviting to many families when they realized that working in the emerging centrally orga- nized industries often involved payment "in chips and whetstones," which were often difficult to convert to consumer goods.[7] Although John Mur- doch might have potentially worked in any one of several emerging indus- tries and businesses, he ultimately followed this preference for an agricul- turally based lifestyle, which eventually provided security for his family.

The Murdochs' arrival in Utah coincided with an era of important political and theological developments. In 1849, shortly after the arrival of the first Saints in the region, Brigham Young promoted the establishment of the provisional State of Deseret, which operated essentially as a theoc- racy, being governed in part by the semi-secret Council of Fifty, with Young at the helm. After nearly two years of this provisional form of gov- ernment, the U.S. Congress rebuffed the effort, and Utah emerged as a territory, with U.S. President Millard Fillmore appointing Brigham Young as Territorial Governor and Superintendent of Indian Affairs, perhaps to lessen the sting of denying the Saints statehood at that time. Within a rel- atively short time, conflicts became apparent between the church-state hierarchy in Utah and the federal government in Washington. These con- flicts did not revolve around any single issue, but they were certainly com- pounded by the uniting of civil and religious authority in the hands of Brigham Young. Perhaps more important, in 1852, the year the Murdochs arrived in Utah, Brigham publicly acknowledged that the Latter-day Saints sanctioned the practice of polygamous or plural marriage. The public announcement regarding polygamy was necessary because the practice had gradually grown since Joseph Smith introduced it secretly among numerous members of the church hierarchy in Nauvoo. The practice was now becoming increasingly obvious to both insiders and outsiders, and it had become the grist for extremely strong negative reactions in the eastern United States. With these developments the stage had been set for a long era of increased tension and open conflict between Utah and the United States government. When John and Ann Murdoch entered Utah in the fall of 1852, they may not have been fully aware of the political tensions that were beginning to mount, and it is unlikely that they could have foreseen that the practice of plural marriage would ultimately become one of the major defining features of their lives.

Within a couple of years after their arrival in Salt Lake City, John and Ann had begun to establish themselves in the community and in the church. John purchased a yoke of oxen and used his animals and his own industry for various kinds of work, such as mowing, hauling, and moving goods and raw materials, working the land, and so forth. He mowed hay on shares with a hand scythe to feed the oxen during the winter. They also purchased a cow for milk. The Murdochs settled in the Third Ward area of Salt Lake and purchased a city lot, and John built a small house there. It is unclear exactly where their home was, but it would have been within the geographical boundary of the Third Ward, which at that time encompassed the area between 300 East and East Temple Street from east to west, and the area between 600 South and Roper Street from north to south. The Third Ward at this time contained nine ten-acre blocks and a farming district.[8] In present-day Salt Lake City, this area would be just south and east of the downtown business district.

In 1854 and early 1855, swarms of grasshoppers entered the valley, destroying most of the crops. This pestilence and related unfortunate events led to two consecutive years of extremely poor harvests, resulting in widespread hunger. Most of the settlers were forced to resort to unusual and even extreme means to sustain themselves during this period. Ann was one of many women who went into the surrounding hills outside of Salt Lake City to dig sego lily and thistle roots, which helped sustain them during this near-famine. On September 14, 1854—at the height of the grasshopper infestation—Ann gave birth to another child, a girl named after her, simply, Ann Murdoch. This girl was now their second living child and their first child born in Utah, having arrived about two and one-half years after the birth of her older sister, Mary, on the plains of Kansas.

A story that has been passed down through family histories regarding John's oxen illustrates some of his challenges and activities during this time, as well as his characteristic optimism and trusting nature:

John worked hard mowing hay to feed the animals during the coming winter. In the fall he turned the oxen into a big field thinking they could feed there until winter came. Then he could bring them home and feed them the hay. When winter came he spent days looking for them but no one seemed to have seen them. Of course he felt bad after working so hard to get the hay to feed them. After everything else failed, John sought the Lord in prayer and asked that he would assist him in finding them. As he prayed, a voice said "You will find your oxen." Still no word came of his oxen. Feed was scarce that year, and after John was offered a good price for it he decided to sell. He still had faith that he would find the oxen. Next spring he was notified by Apostle F. D. Richards that a large herd of cattle was being brought to a certain corral in the city, and John thought he could buy a yoke of oxen from that herd. He went to look at the cattle and behold, he saw his own oxen there. He informed the men in charge that two of the oxen belonged to him, and they said that was impossible. He immediately went to Apostle Richards, and together they returned to the corral. The man in charge was not satisfied, as there were no marks or brands on the oxen. He asked if there were any others besides himself who could identify them. John said "Yes, every man, woman and child in the Third Ward. We will not need them however. If I call the oxen they will come to me, and if they will not own me, I will not own them." "All right, try it," they said. He got off the fence and went to a place where the oxen could see and hear him and held out his hat and said, "Come, Bob." The ox came right up to him. He put his right arm over his neck and called, "Come under, Bright." The other ox came right up to him and stood as if under the yoke. The two men clapped their hands and said, "These are his oxen, and no one can dispute that kind of evidence." He then selected a well-matched yoke of young oxen and bought them, thus making two yoke.[9]

DEVOTION AND RESPONSIBILITY

As the Murdochs became increasingly established in Great Salt Lake City, John's devotion to his religion matured, and his capacity for leadership and service in the church was recognized. On March 28, 1856, John and Ann participated in the endowment ceremony and were "sealed" as husband and wife by priesthood authority. In Mormon theology participation in the endowment ceremony—either in life or by proxy after death—is a necessary precursor to entering into the Celestial Kingdom and enjoying the presence of God. As Brigham Young said, the purpose of the endowment is "to receive all those ordinances in the House of the Lord, which are necessary for you, after you have departed this life, to walk back into the presence of the Father, passing the angels who stand as sentinels, being enabled to give them the key words, the signs and tokens, pertaining to the holy Priesthood and gain your exaltation in spite of earth and hell."[10] In addition, having one's marriage solemnized or sealed by the power of the priesthood is considered essential to the Mormon doctrine that a marriage and family relationship may endure beyond mortality and into eternity. "Unless an eternal marriage covenant is sealed by this [priesthood] authority, it will not take the participating parties to an exaltation in the highest heaven within the celestial world."[11] These activities took place in the

Salt Lake Endowment House, a two story structure that was built on the northwest corner of Temple Square as a precursor to the Salt Lake Temple and used for sacred Mormon ordinances and instruction in the years prior to the completion of the temple.

Later that year John was ordained a high priest (a senior priesthood office within local congregations) by Presiding Bishop Edward Hunter, who set John apart as a counselor to the Third Ward Bishop Jacob Weiler, on October 21, 1856. John served as second counselor to Bishop Weiler until 1859, when he was promoted to the position of first counselor after the previous first counselor moved from the ward. John served in this capacity until the Murdochs moved out of the Third Ward in 1860. The ecclesiastical service and leadership John performed during these four years is best understood within the context of the importance and function of nineteenth-century Mormon wards in Utah's religious, political, and social life:

> In pioneer Utah the ward was more than the basic ecclesiastical unit—it was the most important political unit, and except for the family, the most important social unit as well. As the central and largest concentration of population, Salt Lake City was divided into many wards. The same organizational unit was used for colonizing the various outlying settlements.... The ward was the unit of welfare; the unit from which younger men (and later women) were called on missions to proselyte in "foreign" fields of labor; the unit where babies were christened or "blessed," younger men (and older men as well) ordained to the priesthood, funerals held, dances, musical festivals, and bazaars sponsored, young people taught, and group consciousness established.[12]

The predominant figure in nineteenth-century Mormon wards was the bishop, and "each ward was shaped to some extent by the character and personality of its bishop."[13] Bishops were responsible for a wide range of ecclesiastical, financial, social, and even political tasks in that era, and often they served in this lay office for two decades or longer. Although the office of bishop was a religious or ecclesiastical position, the specific responsibilities attached to the office during the pioneer era were overwhelmingly temporal in nature. The bishop might speak on doctrinal matters and counsel members regarding their spiritual needs, but might just as easily be involved in resolving irrigation disputes, assigning men to work projects such as road building and maintenance crews, construction of schools and meetinghouses, helping to assimilate and assign recent immigrants within the ward boundary, and ensuring that cattle were kept out of certain fields. A bishop's Sunday sermon could just as easily address the need to repair fences and clear irrigation ditches as any theological matter. Nineteenth-century Mormonism did not draw many distinctions between the temporal and religious, and all things were considered to be part of the overall spiritual purpose of life. Because of the all-encompassing nature of the bishop's responsibility, these Mormons relied heavily on their counselors for managing many of the day-to-day tasks that could be delegated, and John Murdoch most certainly would have been involved in every one of these examples of responsibilities, and likely many more, during his four year tenure as a member of the Third Ward Bishopric.

A BOILING HEAT: THE REFORMATION

One of the church-wide efforts during this era that John Murdoch would have undoubtedly been involved in as a member of a bishopric was the "Reformation" of the 1850s. Within a short time after the Saints entered the Salt Lake valley in the late 1840s, it became apparent to members of the church hierarchy that some of their members were becoming lax in their fidelity toward the teachings and expectations of the church and were waning in their devotion. As this concern became increasingly widespread by the mid-1850s, Brigham Young and his counselors developed a plan to revitalize the personal commitment of the Saints, with the aim of bringing "backsliders" fully back into the fold and keeping those Saints who were teetering in their commitment and zealousness from joining the ranks of the disaffected and disengaged. The 1850s reformation movement was spearheaded by Brigham's counselor Jedediah M. Grant. Extremely popular with the Mormon people, Jedediah Grant was known as "Jeddy, Brigham's sledge hammer."[14] Possessing a fiery and charismatic personality, he was undeterred in his zeal to shape up the Saints. Beginning in 1856—the year John Murdoch joined the Third Ward bishopric—Grant selected "reformation missionaries" who were assigned to visit individual wards and hold special conferences designed to make those in attendance aware of their shortcomings and reaffirm their commitment to the church. These conferences were popular, as those appointed by President Grant as missionaries were generally excellent preachers and motivators. They were also armed with a twenty-seven-item catechism or checklist to help ascertain the worthiness of individual church members, which asked questions such as "Have you ever committed murder or shed innocent blood?" "Have you betrayed your brethren?" "Have you ever committed adultery?" and "Do you wash your bodies once a week?"[15] The question regarding weekly bathing was a personal obsession with Grant, but it did not necessarily reflect common practice at that time. On one occasion at a presiding bishop's meeting in 1856, he asked those bishops in attendance who prayed alone and with their families, and who washed themselves at least once a week, to stand. When most of those in attendance remained seated, he intimated that he might send marshals out to wash them. He shouted that the bishops and their counselors must be the first to repent, and then they should go from house to house in their ward to ensure that their ward members and their homes were clean, as a precursor to a spiritual revitalization and preparation to receive the reformation missionaries.[16] Even Brigham Young had a difficult time living up to this particular evidence of personal cleanliness. When he was later asked if he washed once a week, he stated that "he did not [but] he had tried it. He was well aware that this practice was not for everybody."[17]

It is unknown whether or not John Murdoch was in attendance at this particular meeting, or what his specific responsibilities were in regard to the reformation directives, but given the close proximity of the Salt Lake Third Ward to the center of Salt Lake City and church governance, we can safely assume that John and his fellow bishopric members were closely scrutinized and were recruited to engage in many activities designed to revitalize the commitment and piousness of their ward members. Grant directed the reformation missionaries to promote outward manifestations of spiritual revitalization, such as confession of sins, rebaptism, visions, and speaking in tongues, and to not let up "until it had become a boiling heat." The outward evidence that the reformation activities were having their intended effect might be fences in good repair, clean and orderly streets, tithing receipts, and payment of debts. A more complex indicator of the success of these efforts would have been evidence of the biblical injunction of "separating of the wheat from the chaff," within the church.

TEARS FOR WEE GRANNY

As John Murdoch and his family were getting established in Salt Lake City, a great family drama was taking place back in Scotland, across the Atlantic Ocean, and over the plains of the American west. John and Ann were eager to assist John's mother, Mary Murray Murdoch, in coming to America and joining their family in Zion. Despite their poverty in the early 1850s, they saved earnestly to help provide her with funds to make the journey. At age seventy-three, the diminutive "Wee Granny" became one of over one thousand European converts to Mormonism who in 1856 crossed the Atlantic Ocean by ship, went from the east coast of the United States to Iowa by rail and steamer, and trekked west from Iowa City on foot as a member of one of several Mormon handcart companies. These pilgrims set out to join their fellow Saints in Zion as they traveled toward the valley of the Great Salt Lake in the Utah Territory. Assigned to the Martin handcart company, Mary Murdoch walked some seven hundred miles along the trail from Iowa City, over a period of slightly more than nine weeks. Like all of her fellow travelers, Mary Murdoch experienced the severe testing exacted by this journey. A few miles northeast of Chimney Rock, Nebraska, her exhausted and depleted body could take no more. She died there on the windswept high plains on a warm day in early October, 1856, and was buried in an anonymous shallow grave. Her famous final words—uttered to Ann's older brother, James Steele, who comforted her as she passed—were *"Tell John I died with my face toward Zion."* Wee Granny's story is one of the most often repeated regarding the members of the ill-fated Willie and Martin handcart companies. Among her numerous descendants, the story of Wee Granny's walk across the plains and her death is revered.

On October 4, 1856, two days after Wee Granny's death, Brigham Young received news from Apostle Franklin D. Richards regarding the dire circumstances of the Martin and Willie handcart companies. These pioneers were late in leaving Iowa City, lacking in provisions, and facing starvation and freezing in the coming weeks on the high plains and mountain passes of Wyoming. On October 5 and 6 a semi-annual conference of the church was held, only a few blocks from the Murdochs' home, with thousands of members in attendance. It is likely but not certain that John was present. Brigham Young quickly turned the theme of the conference into organizing a rescue, and many members of the church prepared immediately for a brave and often heroic rescue effort. A few weeks later, in early December 1856, the first survivors of the Willie and Martin companies began to reach Salt Lake City, and they straggled into the public square—many of them half dead or seriously injured—for the next several days.

Family stories indicate that when John Murdoch went to the public square to meet the Martin company to find his mother, he was met by his sister-in-law, Elizabeth Steele (the widow of his good friend and exemplar in the gospel, James Steele, who had assisted Mary Murdoch in her final hours of life, and who later himself died and was buried in the freezing ground in Wyoming). Elizabeth told John the crushing news of the deaths of her husband, James, and Wee Granny. As he returned to his home, Ann could see by his countenance that something was wrong. She waited motionless in the doorway for a while, and then John told her, "They have both given their lives for the gospel's sake." Ann was over eight months pregnant with their daughter Janett Osborne Murdoch when she received the crushing news. Janett was born December 20, 1856, a light in the midst of the grief John and Ann were experiencing at the loss of Wee Granny and James Steele. Janett later told her own children and grandchildren that her mother would always stroke her hair and say, "no wonder you cry so easily my little girl. For six weeks after you were born I cried every day and couldn't sleep at night for thinking of Dear Wee Granny."[18]

In the space of four years John and Ann Murdoch had experienced a lifetime's worth of difficulty, loss, and trauma. They had left their homeland of Scotland for good, crossed the Atlantic Ocean on a freighter powered by sails and wind, witnessed the deaths of their two young children as they attempted to move up the Mississippi River with insufficient provisions, experienced the birth of a baby girl during a thunderstorm on the plains, walked across the plains and Rocky Mountains, battled poverty and hunger as they attempted to establish themselves in Zion, experienced the loss of a brother and mother who were on their way to join them, and then experienced the births of two more girls during the very peak of their difficulties. In the face of such challenges, how did they survive? How did they move on? Part of the answer to these questions is that such travails were simply a fact of life in their place and time. Many other pioneers experienced similar difficulties, and there were simply few options but to keep going. Another part of the answer is that they were obviously motivated and buoyed by their faith, which helped put their suffering into the perspective of a larger plan and purpose, and which provided the means for spiritual and social support and nurturing during their times of anguish. Finally, there is ample evidence from the writings left by John Murdoch and the recollections of his descendants that he had a resilient constitution and a naturally optimistic disposition, which enabled him to eventually bounce back from even the most severe testing, despite any despair he may have experienced during the midst of the trials.

COURTING THE WRATH OF GOD: THE UTAH WAR

During 1857 and 1858, tensions worsened between the Latter-day Saints and the U.S. government, and a new zenith was reached with the invasion of Utah by a hostile army of American soldiers, "Johnston's Army." Like most Utahns of that time, John Murdoch ultimately played a role in this drama, and the Murdoch family was undoubtedly affected by it.

The "Utah War" was the complicated product of a number of factors. First, there was the indignation of many prominent American citizens and politicians regarding the Mormons' practice of polygamy, as well as the fact that the Utah territory was a semi-autonomous near-nation, with Brigham Young wielding an extraordinary amount of power and influence and federal authority there in disarray. The Republican Party made the "Mormon problem" a central target of their platform in the campaign of 1856, when they declared their opposition to polygamy and promised to eradicate it, referring to the practice as one of the "twin relics of barbarism," along with slavery. Republicans in particular were concerned about the amount of independence that the Utah territory enjoyed, and the perception that the Mormon hierarchy believed that they were above the laws of the land and sought a separatist kingdom. This perception was only strengthened when the territorial legislature sent a communication to Washington in March 1857, announcing that they would decide which federal laws they should obey, and that they would observe only acts of the U.S. Congress that they considered to be applicable to their condition. Reports of immigrants to California who had passed through Utah and had been harassed by Mormons and had their requests to purchase provisions refused also increased animosity.

Second, the Saints who had lived through the Missouri and Illinois periods during the 1830s and 1840s harbored great bitterness toward the U.S. government for failing to protect them during their severe persecutions in those states. The highest leaders of the church—almost all of whom were products of those years—were not hesitant to publicly discuss their resentment toward the United States, and they frequently made inflammatory statements in public talks, even prophesying the imminent overthrow and destruction of the federal government.[19]

Third, the federal officials who were sent by the American presidents and U.S. Congress to oversee public matters in the territory were often hostile, condescending, and insensitive toward the Saints and their leaders, which made matters worse. This particular problem was heightened after 1855, when three non-Mormons were appointed as federal judges in the territory. None of the three were favorably disposed toward the Saints, but one of them—W. W. Drummond—was particularly hated, as he represented all that the Saints resented in the "gentile" world. Drummond was highly effective in further inflaming anti-Mormon and anti-Utah sentiment nationally through his sensationalized reports. There was no federal official who was loathed more by the Saints and their leaders than Drummond, whom they regarded as a whoremonger, carpetbagger, and political hack.[20] Of course, the Utah War was caused by more than just these issues, and there were more immediate circumstances that led to the specifics of the invasion, but these general problems were the fuel that fed the fire.

Mormon leaders believed that a hostile federal action was possible and were not surprised when they heard the first reports of the impending invasion in July 1857. U.S. President James Buchanan had approved a show of military force in May of that year, as a way to suppress what were considered the intolerable and un-American actions of the Mormons in Utah. After several false starts and a change in leadership, Colonel Albert Sidney Johnston led 2,500 troops from Fort Leavenworth toward Utah, accompanied by the newly appointed territorial governor of Utah, Alfred Cumming, whom they were to install by force if necessary. As Johnston's army moved closer to Utah, Brigham Young and his associates declared martial law and planned their strategy. A number of different options for dealing with the invasion were considered, including guerilla resistance, direct confrontation with force, leaving the area, and a "scorched earth" policy that would destroy their own homes and businesses but leave the invaders with weakened supply lines.[21] As summer turned into fall and the region began to have the feel of a militarized zone, a great anxiety gripped the people, although many were confident that they would ultimately prevail.

In the fall of 1857, John Murdoch became one of 1,100 men of the Utah Nauvoo militia who were called upon to move into the mountain passes east of Salt Lake City, not far from the present-day Interstate 80 freeway, and fortify the region against the entry of Johnston's army. John served as a captain of fifty under the command of Major Daniel McArthur, a veteran of the Kirtland, Missouri, and Nauvoo periods of persecution who had successfully led a handcart company from Iowa City to Salt Lake City the previous year. McArthur's contingent guarded the Echo Canyon area of present-day Summit County, which was considered to be a strategic region because it was one of the most popular routes for westward expansion, having been used for the 1847 Mormon emigration. John and his fellow militia members created a dam by building a rock wall at the narrows of the creek and built several stone fortifications to deter the federal soldiers.[22] The stone fortifications they constructed remain visible to this day. Given that John Murdoch was a captain of fifty, it is likely that he spent at least part of his time supervising men on these construction efforts. We know nothing specific regarding his experience during this time of crisis, as he never left a written record of it, and there are no specific family stories that have been handed down other than the fact that he served.

It is both fortunate and miraculous that a direct military confrontation between the Utah militia and the federal troops never took place. Although the militia did engage in harassment and other guerilla activities—including the burning of Fort Bridger and three supply trains (consisting of more than seventy wagons of provisions)—a massed battle never occurred.

In the spring of 1858, as reports came in indicating that the federals would soon be upon Salt Lake City, and as Brigham Young was becoming more pessimistic regarding the potential outcomes, he had the citizens of the area prepare for an evacuation, leaving open the possibility of implementing his scorched earth policy of burning their homes and farms to make the area of little use to the army. In all, about thirty thousand people moved south from the Salt Lake City area into the Provo and central Utah areas, where they lived in improvised housing or with residents of that area and awaited further instructions. The Murdoch family—John, Ann, and their three little girls—were part of this exodus. Family records indicate that they evacuated to Goshen, a small community about sixty miles south of Salt Lake, and stayed there until the fall. Johnston's army marched through a deserted Salt Lake City in late June of 1858. There was a widespread belief among the Saints that this evacuation could be permanent. Although Brigham Young believed that forcing a showdown between the Saints and the federal army would bring the wrath of God down on the United States and serve to usher in a millennial era, he also tried to keep his options open, and considered an escape route to the north.[23]

Ultimately, a diplomatic solution was found, and the Utah War ended late in the summer of 1858. Although Brigham Young was forced to step down as territorial governor, the newly installed Alfred Cummings proved to be a popular governor for most Utah residents—Mormon and non-Mormon alike—as he took positions of tolerance toward the Utahns, often in opposition to the actions of the federal judges. In addition, the presence of the federal army provided the region with much-needed infusion of capital, as residents of the territory returned to the army's headquarters at Camp Floyd again and again to trade fresh farm products such as milk, butter, fish, eggs, and wheat for items that were difficult to come by in their isolated economy, such as clothing, utensils, tea, and cash.[24]

In many ways, the Utah War was a fiasco, but some of its effects were significant. Severe hardships and strains were faced by the displaced Salt Lake City residents such as the Murdochs who were evacuated south in early summer, and Johnston's army also suffered great deprivations during the winter of 1857–58. Probably the worst result of this conflict was that it, along with the residual of frenzy and fanaticism wrought by the Reformation, created an environment of intense panic, suspicion, fear, and vengeance that led in part to one of the bloodiest tragedies in the history of the American west, the September 1857 Mountain Meadows Massacre in southern Utah.[25]

As the 1850s came to a close the United States government found that there were larger problems to occupy the federal military than the conditions in the Utah territory. As the nation spiraled into the dissension over slavery and states' rights that would soon lead to the Civil War, the extinction of polygamy was put on hold as a national priority. The federal troops were soon withdrawn from Camp Floyd, leaving behind much needed supplies and provisions that proved to be of great worth to the residents of the territory. The Murdoch family maintained their domestic and business routines. John continued to serve in the Third Ward Bishopric and make a living through small-scale farming, the use of his oxen, and other related enterprises. On January 15, 1859, another girl, Sarah Jane, was born to John and Ann Murdoch. The Murdoch household now consisted of six individuals, including four young girls ranging in age from newborn to nearly seven.

A New Home: Settling the Upper Provo

By late 1859 John Murdoch was thirty-eight years old, in an era when the average life expectancy is thought to have ranged from the mid forties to the early fifties, and when as few as one out of ten persons lived to age sixty-five. The small home he had built in the Third Ward section of Salt Lake City was becoming too small for his growing family of six. Although he was slowly becoming established, his family was still relatively poor, and he longed for the American dream of more opportunity and prosperity. Not knowing how many years he had left, he must have also wanted to build more security for his children. Perhaps the promise that John had received in a blessing a few years earlier from Brigham Young that he "would live to have houses and lands and would prosper" weighed on his mind. In addition, he began to have a desire to help settle and build a new town as the first wave of Utah pioneers had done.[26] In any event, it is clear that about this time he began to look for new opportunities to get some land and make a new home for his family.

John's opportunity came in the form of a chance to be part of the settling of the Heber valley in present-day Wasatch County, a picturesque high mountain valley on the east side of the Wasatch Mountains and Mount Timpanogos. At that time, this region was referred to as the upper

Provo valley. In 1859, John learned that land could be purchased in this region for next to nothing by simply paying the surveying fees, that irrigation water was plentiful, and that it had been proven that wheat could be grown in the high mountain valley with a very short growing season. The first small band of Mormon settlers in the Heber valley had survived the severe winter of 1859–60, and more families were needed. In the spring of 1860 the Murdochs sold their home, property, and many of their belongings, purchased provisions, and left Salt Lake in the company of a small group of like-minded families and individuals, including William Foreman. Their belongings were loaded into wagons, and they also brought with them a pig, a cow, a few sheep, and some chickens. This small band of pioneers made the journey to the Heber valley in the space of three days.

Immediately after their arrival, the Murdochs and their companions moved temporarily into a log and dugout fort that had been established by the first small wave of settlers who had arrived the previous year. John immediately went to work securing land and building a dugout in the fort where his family could reside for a short time. This temporary structure was simply a large square room—about sixteen by sixteen feet, dug out of the earth, with walls about ten feet high. The roof was made of unhewn cottonwood log rafters with willow branches placed on top crosswise. To help keep out the elements, wheat straw and soil were placed on top of the structure.[27] He planted a small crop consisting of the basic staples—oats, wheat, and potatoes—and began to build a log house using cottonwood trees from the banks of the Provo River. A map of the locations of families who built homes in Fort Heber (named in honor of Brigham Young's counselor Heber C. Kimball) in 1859 and 1860 shows the location of the John Murdock (Murdoch) home as being near the southwest corner of the settlement, just north of the intersection of 200 North and 300 West.[28] The families near the Murdochs included several who would later be connected through kinship ties as their children and grandchildren were married and started their own families: the Todds, McDonalds, Rasbands, Dukes, Moultons, Giles, Carlyles, and others. A branch of the church was started, with William S. Wall as president. He selected John Murdoch as his first counselor and James Laird as his second counselor. Given that the settlers in the valley at this time were all Latter-day Saints and that a local civic government structure had not yet been established, the branch leaders also served as de-facto civic authorities, representing them with the territorial legislature and serving in a judicial capacity.[29]

◆ ◆ ◆

As the summer of 1860 progressed, the small band of Mormon settlers at Fort Heber desired to build a community structure. There was no meetinghouse at this point, and with the 24th of July Pioneer Day celebration approaching, it was suggested that a bowery (an unenclosed outdoor covered shelter) be constructed. John proposed that with a little more additional effort, they could build a more permanent meetinghouse that would be suitable for worship, dances, and community meetings during the long winter months. This suggestion was well received, and in a short time an eighteen-by-twenty-by-forty-foot log meetinghouse was constructed inside of the walls of the fort, in time for the July 24th celebration. The structure included a large open fireplace and chimney on each end, which could burn logs three to four feet in length. Deacons of the church were assigned to keep logs on the fire during cold weather, and families took turns providing candles for meetings. This structure was ultimately used for these purposes for the space of about six years.[30]

By the end of the summer of 1860 there were approximately two hundred persons living in sixty log homes and dugouts in the settlement. This initial group of residents comprised almost entirely persons from the British Isles—England and Scotland in particular—who had converted to Mormonism during the 1840s and early 1850s. That summer included a frenzy of activity to prepare the people for over-wintering and expansion. Crude roads were constructed, fences were built, crops and animals were tended. John Murdoch organized the first sheep cooperative in the area, and he personally cared for the sheep that summer, in preparation for moving them far enough south in the winter that they did not require hay. At this time most of the settlers had a few sheep that were used to provide wool for spinning and weaving in "jean" cloth.[31] John's experience as a shepherd in Scotland had made him expert in knitting, and he taught this skill to his family and others. The harvest of 1860 was plagued by early frosts, which caused wheat to shrink, but did not stop the settlers from installing the first threshing machine in the area, a horse-powered contraption that was operated primarily by hand. The slowness of the operation resulted in not all of the grain being harvested before winter arrived, but the prospects of the group for surviving the winter still looked more promising than they had the previous year.

On November 7, 1860, another daughter, Jacobina Wells Osborne Murdoch, was born to John and Ann. When the Murdochs made their journey from Salt Lake to the Heber valley the previous spring, Ann would have been in the early first trimester of this pregnancy. The addition of

Jacobina increased the family to seven: John, Ann, and their five daughters ranging in age from newborn to age eight.

The winter of 1860–61 again proved to be severe, with temperatures dipping as low as thirty to forty degrees below zero. At one point it was so cold that local journalist John Crook reported that people believed the mercury in their thermometer had frozen. Keeping buckets of water available was a constant problem at times, because they were often frozen solid.[32] During the long dark days and evenings indoors, lights consisted of homemade tallow candles fashioned from the tallow of beef. Despite the harsh circumstances, the residents of Fort Heber fared relatively well that winter. They occupied themselves with drama, dances, socializing, and worshipping together.

As Vivid as Lightning: A Mighty Faith

During the spring of 1861 church leaders from Salt Lake established a ward in Heber, owing to the growth of the region in the previous year. The branch presidency in which John Murdoch served was disbanded, and Joseph S. Murdock (no relation to John) of American Fork was called to serve as the bishop of the new Heber Ward. In addition, Brigham Young's brother, John Young, traveled to Heber that same year to organize the first High Priest's Quorum in the region. Elisha Averett was originally called as the leader, but he moved away less than a year later, and John Murdoch replaced him as Quorum President, choosing Thomas Todd and John Jordan as his counselors. John held this position for several decades, serving in that capacity until just a few years before his death.[33]

On August 19, 1861, John received a blessing from church patriarch Joseph Young. In Latter-day Saint doctrine, those who are ordained to the priesthood office of patriarch have special authority and a prophetic gift to bless the members of the church by discerning their spiritual lineage in one of the twelve tribes of Israel, speak of their potential, predict future activities, identify particular gifts they possess, and pronounce protections, warnings, or blessings upon them. These patriarchal blessings are recorded and hold special prominence in family collections as a sacred record. Among other things, John's blessing stated:

> You shall have wives and children and a numerous posterity upon the mountains of Israel... You shall hold important stations in the Church of Jesus Christ... Wicked men and devils shall tremble before you while the righteous shall rejoice at the sound of your voice... Your mind shall be as vivid as lightning and the gift of discernment shall rest upon your head: have power to detect all evil

and be a stay and a staff to the widow and a father to the fatherless... No evil nor accident shall befall thee. Not a hair of your head shall fall by the hands of your enemies. You shall have a mighty faith and power with the heavens. Your tongue shall be like the pen of a ready writer. You shall have that wisdom that your enemies cannot gainsay nor resist. You shall live to see the redemption of Zion and be gathered up with the pure in heart. Your eyes shall see the temple of the Lord....

By 1862, the settlements in the Heber valley had continued to grow. More roads were built, and a bridge was constructed over the Provo River. As it was becoming apparent that the region was beginning to flourish, it became necessary to formally restructure the political boundaries of the region and to install local civic leaders. In early 1862 the Heber valley area was partly in Utah County and partly in Salt Lake County. When the federal government created the Nevada territory out of the western part of the Utah territory, establishing new civic borders became even more important. A legislative act created the new Wasatch County in the Heber valley area, with boundaries of the summit of the Wasatch Mountains to the west, the Utah-Colorado territorial line to the east, the Summit County line to the north, and the Sanpete County line to the south. Territorial probate judge J. W. Witt organized the first county government, and John Murdoch was selected as the first county treasurer. Population of the new county was estimated to be approximately one thousand, and the first school districts were formed. The largest population center of the county was Heber, but other settlements were beginning to become established, including Center Creek, Charlston, and Wallsburg.

As the year 1862 continued, John Murdoch's dream of a new life and opportunity for his growing family was beginning to take shape. In the space of two years they had once again started over and had survived their first two years in the growing but still isolated and frontier Heber valley community. His family of seven was thriving, and he had his own land and the beginnings of a business and livelihood. In the space of ten years, he and Ann had first lost their only two children on the journey west, under the most taxing and stressful of circumstances, and made it to Salt Lake City in utter poverty. But they had pressed forward and now had a household of five young girls and the tangible hope of more prosperity in the years ahead. John's spiritual, leadership, and organizational abilities had continually been recognized, and he now held positions of responsibility, influence, and respect in the church and civic life of his community. John was now forty-one years of age, and the course of the rest of his life may have seemed to be well set. But a Robert Burns rhyme that John was quite fond of, "The best laid schemes of mice an men Gang aft aglee," would once again prove to be true in his life, for the year 1862 would soon bring a life-changing event into his family's world, and a fulfillment of his recent patriarchal blessing that he could have not even conceived of scarcely a decade earlier.

NOTES

1. Hiram McDonald and Anne Rasband McDonald, eds., *Our Generations: A Legacy of Faith* (Bountiful, UT: Hiram and Anne Rasband McDonald, 1996), 161.

2. Leonard J. Arrington and Davis Bitton, *The Mormon Experience: A History of the Latter-day Saints* (New York: Alfred A. Knopf, 1979), 135.

3. McDonald and McDonald, *Our Generations*, 162.

4. *Deseret News*, April 13, 1854.

5. Ibid.

6. John Murray Nicol, ed., *The James and Mary Murray Murdoch Family History* (Provo, UT: James and Mary Murray Murdoch Family Organization, 1982), 212.

7. Charles S. Peterson, *Utah: A History* (New York: W. W. Norton & Company, 1984), 57.

8. Nicol, *Family History*, 213.

9. Andrew Jensen, *Historical Record, volumes 5-8, Church Encyclopedia, Book 1* (Salt Lake City, UT: Church of Jesus Christ of Latter-day Saints), 309–10.

10. John A. Widtsoe, ed., *Discourses of Brigham Young* (Salt Lake City, UT: Deseret Book Company, 1971), 416.

11. Bruce R. McConkie, *Mormon Doctrine*, 2nd ed. (Salt Lake City, UT: Bookcraft, 1966), 683.

12. Leonard J. Arrington, *Brigham Young: American Moses* (Urbana: University of Illinois Press, 1986), 208–9.

13. Ibid.

14. Will Bagley, *Blood of the Prophets* (Norman: University of Oklahoma Press, 2002), 50.

15. Ibid. See also "Reformation (LDS) of 1856–1857," Paul H. Peterson, http://www.lightplanet.com/mormons/daily/history/1844_1877/reformation_eom.htm (accessed May 19, 2005).

16. Arrington, *Brigham Young*, 212–13.

17. Bagley, *Blood of the Prophets*, 50.

18. Anne Rasband McDonald, *History of James and Mary (Wee Granny) Murdoch* (document in author's possession).

19. Arrington, *Brigham Young*, 171; Bagley, *Blood of the Prophets*, 38.

20. Arrington, *Brigham Young*, 165; Bagley, *Blood of the Prophets*, 46.

21. Arrington, *Brigham Young*, 166–67.

22. "History of Summit County," Summit County Historical Society, http://www.co.summit.ut.us/history/summit/history.html (accessed May 23, 2005).

23. Bagley, *Blood of the Prophets*, 75; Allan Kent Powell, ed., *Utah History Encyclopedia* (Salt Lake City, UT: University of Utah Press, 1994), 607.

24. Arrington, *Brigham Young*, 168–70.

25. Ibid., 167–68, 170; Bagley, *Blood of the Prophets*, 83–87.

26. Nicol, *Family History*, 215.

27. Annie Janett McMullin, *Description of an Early Home in Wasatch County* (document in author's possession).

28. William James Mortimer, ed., *How Beautiful Upon the Mountains: A Centennial History of Wasatch County* (Heber City, UT: Wasatch County Chapter, Daughters of Utah Pioneers, 1963), 9.

29. Ibid., 12.

30. Ibid., 12–13; Nicol, *Family History*, 215.

31. Mortimer, *How Beautiful*, 15–16.

32. Embry, *History of Wasatch County*, 25–26.

33. Mortimer, *How Beautiful*, 16; Nicol, *Family History*, 215.

6

◆ ◆ ◆

WEE GRANNY

That I do not accept the faith that possessed them does not mean I doubt their frequent devotion and heroism in its service. Especially the women. Their women were incredible.

—WALLACE STEGNER, *The Gathering of Zion:*
The Story of the Mormon Trail

For some must push and some must pull
As we go marching up the hill,
As merrily on the way we go
Until we reach the Valley, oh.

—From "The Handcart Song"

No treatment of the life and times of John Murdoch would be complete without a thorough description of the final journey of his mother, Mary Murray Murdoch, a member of the ill-fated Martin Handcart Company of 1856. This amazing story has both saddened and inspired thousands, and has become a fixture in the tale of the Mormon immigration to Utah.

Some basic facts of Mary Murdoch's life are useful in setting the stage for the story of her final four months. She is known affectionately among her numerous posterity and students of Mormon history and Scottish emigration as "Wee Granny," because she is said to have stood four feet, seven inches tall, and to have weighed barely ninety pounds. She was born Mary Murray in 1782 at Glencairn, Dumfries, Scotland. On January 10, 1811, at age twenty-eight, she married James Murdoch, a man four years her junior. Together they had nearly twenty-one years of marriage and eight children. James lost his life in a mining accident, breathing poisonous gas as he tried to rescue a fellow worker who met the same demise. At age forty-nine, Wee Granny found herself a single mother, with the responsibility of raising several of her children (the youngest of whom was only five years of age) as well as an orphaned niece. In the midst of these very difficult circumstances, she made the best life she could for herself and her family, living in a small stone cottage with a thatched roof, which had been built with the help of her children and some neighbors, a few years after the death of her husband, James.[1]

Years later, at age sixty-seven, Mary Murdoch was introduced to the message of the Church of Jesus Christ of Latter-day Saints by her son John, who was himself a recent convert. Wee Granny was baptized on December 22, 1851, by John. Soon after her baptism, she began to experience some of the persecution and derision that was frequently directed at converts to this strange new faith. The fact that John and his wife, Ann, left for Utah only a few days after her baptism certainly may have heightened whatever difficulties she experienced related to her decision to join with the Mormons.[2]

THE HANDCART PLAN

During the first six years of emigration along the Mormon trail, most companies of Saints traveled by the proven method of wagon and ox. However, by the mid-1850s it was obvious to Brigham Young and other leaders of the church in Utah that this method would have to be improved. It was somewhat slow and required a huge investment in capital, livestock, equipment, and trained personnel, all of which were in short supply. Given that most of the European converts to Mormonism were very poor, most of these new Saints lacked the resources needed to undertake such an immense journey. Moreover, there were literally thousands of European converts who were highly motivated to make the journey but who lacked the means. In short, the processes currently available to help the new converts assemble in Utah were simply not sufficient.

Brigham Young was well aware of this problem and worked on ways to make the gathering a reality for all Saints who desired passage. In 1849, he proposed the creation of a revolving fund to be used for aiding the poorest Saints in their desire to reach Zion. This fund, which became known as the *Perpetual Emigrating Fund*, began with a few thousand dollars contributed by members of the church. From these funds, indigent Saints would be able to borrow the resources necessary to help get them to Zion. After their arrival, they would then repay their loan back into the fund, thus making additional resources available for others in their circumstances. For a while, this system worked very effectively. John Murdoch was a member of the 1852 emigration group led by Abraham O. Smoot, which has the distinction of being the first large PEF group to migrate to Utah. However, a combination of economic distress in Utah and burgeoning numbers of poor converts desiring passage to Zion put unbearable stresses on the system. By 1855, it was determined that emigration would need to be reduced, even at a time when increased numbers of Utah Saints were desperately needed as the church and kingdom were being built. It was clear that a less expensive mode of travel would need to be developed.[3]

For Brigham Young the answer to this significant set of problems came in the form of his plan to have new converts emigrate to Utah on foot, aided by handcarts for hauling their provisions. Although handcarts were not a totally new invention—they had been used for years by peddlers on America's east coast—and although many trappers and pioneers had trekked west on foot—including some gold seekers who pushed their belongings in a wheelbarrow—Brigham Young's marriage of these ideas was a unique plan that would afford economical and timely passage to large numbers of emigrants. Thus, the handcart plan was hatched, the Perpetual Emigrating Fund was revitalized, and in late 1855, the call went out from the church leadership to the European missions to renew the gathering.

The idea went forth to have the Saints travel from Europe to the east coast of the United States—New York, Philadelphia, or Boston—by ship, and then by steamer and train to Iowa City, Iowa, the westward railroad terminus in the United States at that time. At Iowa City, provisions would be gathered, handcarts and tents would be constructed, and a well-organized trek some thirteen hundred miles to Zion in the space of an estimated seventy to ninety days would ensue. The leaders of the church in Europe promoted the new plan with optimism and zeal, and the membership of the church there responded en masse. Thus, one of the most unique forms of immigration in American history was born. Mary Murdoch was eager to join her son John and his family in Utah, and would be among the first wave of Saints to test this new means of travel.

ABOARD THE HORIZON

Mary Murdoch left Liverpool, England, for Boston on May 25, 1856, aboard the *Horizon*. This was the last of four ships that carried handcart emigrants to Boston or New York that year, and it was by far the largest vessel, a monster that carried 856 passengers this particular voyage. This vast group was placed in the charge of Edward G. Martin ("Captain Martin"), a returning missionary. By contrast, the other three ships, the *Enoch Train*, *S. Curling*, and *Thornton*, which left Liverpool between March 23 and May 4, carried between 534 and 764 passengers each.[4]

Most of the passengers on these ships were from the British Isles—primarily from England, where missionaries had encountered phenomenal success; but also from Wales, Scotland, and Ireland. In addition, there were also a fair number of Danes, Swedes, Norwegians, and a few Swiss and Italians who made these trips. The majority of the handcart pioneers that year, 68 percent to be exact, had their travel expenses paid for at least in part through the church's Perpetual Emigrating Fund. By and large, this was a poor group of immigrants. Historian Wallace Stegner has written poignantly of the desperate financial straits in which many of these people found themselves, and the great hopes for a better life that they had found in Mormonism: "Mainly Englishmen from the depressed collieries and mill towns, with some Scots and a handful from the Cape of Good Hope and the East Indian Mission, they were the casualties of the industrial revolution, life's discards, to whom Mormonism had brought its irresistible double promise of a new start on earth and a guaranteed Hereafter."[5]

Many previous emigrants to Utah had stayed for a time in the eastern United States to work and earn money for the remainder of the trip to Zion; however, Brigham Young committed the resources of the Perpetual Emigrating Fund to get these Saints to Utah as soon as possible. He was well aware of the high rate of apostasy among those who had attempted the gradual move west, and he did not want to lose members. He also did not want the fund to be used as a means to simply escape the terrible economic trap that existed in Europe at that time. Rather, Brigham wanted the fund to be used to support "the honest poor," as he put it. He planned for these groups of travelers to get from Europe to Utah as soon as possible, where they would find strength in numbers and provide additional strength to the vast melting pot of pilgrims who had gathered in the mountain west.

As an elderly widow living in difficult economic times, Wee Granny was undoubtedly in a financially difficult situation. However, she did not have to rely on the Perpetual Emigrating Fund to pay the cost of her trip. Her son John and his wife, Ann, desperately wanted Wee Granny to join them. They worked hard to save every cent they could until they had enough to get her there.

Although Wee Granny traveled alone in terms of family, there were at least some other Scottish Saints in this immigrating group to whom she had a connection. Traveling with her on the *Horizon*, and later in the Martin Handcart Company, was James Steele, age twenty-nine, brother to Mary's daughter-in-law in Utah, Ann Steele Murdoch. James had played a pivotal role in introducing the message of the restoration to Wee Granny, by first spreading the word to John, who looked to him as an exemplar. With James was his family: his wife, Elizabeth (age twenty-eight), and their two children, James (age three) and George (age one). In addition,

Elizabeth Steele's mother, Mary Ann George Wylie, widow of Oliver Wylie Jr., traveled with the Steele family. Mary Wylie's age is not listed in the official Fifth Company roster, but various family sources have indicated that she was sixty-six, only a few years younger than Wee Granny.

The specific details regarding Mary Murdoch's relationship with the Steeles and Mary Wylie are not documented, but family lore is that she interacted closely with them, perhaps sharing a handcart and being assigned to the same tent. Because Mary Murdoch and Mary Wylie were indirectly connected through their children, and because they were of a similar age and in a similar situation in many respects, it seems likely that they may have relied on each other to some extent, and perhaps even developed a friendship. Given the challenge that James and Elizabeth Steele must have had in making this journey with two small children, it is also quite possible that the two older women assisted with their care.

The trip across the Atlantic on the *Horizon* took slightly more than one month, ending in Boston on June 28. Because this trip was long and rough in spots, with modest accommodations and crowded quarters, we can assume that Wee Granny experienced a fair amount of discomfort during the voyage. However, it would be a mistake to think that the voyage was a terrible situation. On the contrary, most of the Saints who kept journals or later wrote of their experience reported enjoying the voyage across the Atlantic. For most of them, it was their first trip away from their homelands, an exciting adventure.[6] Because the ships were chartered by the church, the passengers enjoyed a commonality of purpose, as well as a communal spirit among them. "A Mormon charter ship differed as sharply from the usual emigrant vessel as a Mormon village on wheels differed from the usual Missouri wagon train. It was ordered to the smallest corner and to the ultimate quarter-hour."[7]

The ships were divided into wards with bishops to head them. Each day consisted of a sequence of orderly activities, ranging from the temporal (eating meals, cleaning quarters, disposing waste over the side of the ship) to the spiritual (prayer meetings, instructive talks by leaders, and occasional baptisms, weddings, and funerals) to the social (music, dance, or group singing). In Mormonism, unlike many other faiths of the day, there was no great disconnect between these activities, because all things were believed to be spiritual in their own realm.

Because it is known that many of the women in the emigrating companies spent a considerable amount of time during these voyages sewing tents and cart covers from heavy rolls of drilling fabric that were issued to them in Liverpool, it is likely that Wee Granny spent much of her days thus occupied, and possibly teaching some of the younger women some of the intricacies of sewing.

The Launching Point: Iowa City

On a bitterly cold New Year's Eve 1855, just a few months before the first handcart pioneers began their trek westward, the last rail of the Mississippi and Missouri railroad was laid in Iowa City, Iowa.[8] With this event Iowa City became the western terminus for railway travel in this sector of the United States, as well as the outfitting and embarkation point for travel on foot for the handcart pioneers of 1856 and 1857.

Most of the handcart pioneers from the seven companies who started their journey from Iowa City during those two years arrived by railroad from New York or Boston, by way of Chicago. Because Wee Granny arrived in Boston on the *Horizon*, her railroad journey from Boston to Chicago would have taken her through New York, Pennsylvania, Ohio, and Indiana, on to northern Illinois, a total distance of just over one thousand miles. In Chicago, she and her traveling companions would have changed trains for the additional 250-mile trip to Iowa City.

Wee Granny and most of her traveling companions from the *Horizon*, many of whom would become members of the Martin Handcart Company, arrived by rail in Iowa City on July 8, 1856. The rail portion of the trip took approximately ten days. It is unclear how many of those days were actually spent traveling and how many were spent transferring, dealing with U.S. immigration officials, and so forth. It was not a matter of getting on a train in Boston and getting off in Iowa City. Rather, there were at least a couple of occasions when the group had to be shuttled across large bodies of water (including the Mississippi River) on steamships to make connections, and they also would have been required to make a connection in Chicago.

Because most of these immigrants were financially destitute and were being supported by Perpetual Emigrating Funds, they would have purchased the lowest price fares for their trip. Typically, the least expensive berths on U.S. trains were in "emigrant cars"—converted freight cars— roughly forty feet long, with tiers of wooden benches on all four sides. As many as eighty passengers would have been in each of these cars, crowded conditions by any standard. They likely had little access to sanitary facilities and probably slept sitting or leaning as best they could. Although the rigors of this part of the journey paled in comparison with what they would experience once they began their trek on foot, this portion was likely an uncomfortable segment of the journey.

In addition to Wee Granny's introduction to the vast American landscape—the eastern hardwood forest turning into the tallgrass prairie—she and her fellow travelers undoubtedly were introduced to oppressive heat and humidity, something that would have been foreign to their experience in the British Isles. British Saints, and particularly the Scots, were used to temperate conditions and mild levels of humidity. Given the cramped quarters she had experienced by ship and rail, by the time Wee Granny and the rest of her company reached Iowa City on July 8, she and her companions may have welcomed the prospect of camping out on the prairie and cooking meals in the outdoors, although it is unlikely that many in this camp had any experience in either endeavor. "Most of them, until they were herded from their crowded immigrant ship and loaded into the cars and rushed to the end of the Rock Island Line and dumped here at the brink of the West, had never pitched a tent, slept on the group, cooked outdoors, built a campfire. They had not even the rudimentary skills that make frontiersmen. But as it turned out, they had some of the stuff that makes heroes."[9]

After arriving in Iowa City, the first task for Mary Murdoch and her fellow travelers was to get from the railroad terminal in downtown Iowa City to the Mormon encampment site approximately three miles away. There, they expected to be organized, assigned to handcart companies, provided with equipment, and to be on their way in short order. Although it has since been rebuilt, the railroad terminal building (which now houses office space) still sits on the same spot that it did in 1856, off of South Dubuque Street. In 1856 Iowa City was the capital of the state of Iowa, and one of its largest cities. The Iowa City railroad terminal was only a few blocks from the recently completed capitol building, a large and elegant domed limestone structure on a hill that served as the headquarters for Iowa government until Des Moines became the permanent capital in 1857. Today, the "Old Capitol" is surrounded by the University of Iowa campus and is unquestionably the most prominent and beloved building in the cityscape. This structure was likely one of the first landmarks that Wee Granny would have seen in this growing prairie-city.

The walk to the Mormon encampment site was likely the first opportunity Wee Granny and her companions had to stretch their legs in nearly six weeks. The encampment site was in an area of tallgrass prairie along the banks of Clear Creek, where a few hardwood trees lined the creek banks and provided shade from the hot summer sun for the weary emigrants.

Today, the Mormon handcart encampment site looks substantially differ-ent from the way it looked in 1856. The present "handcart park" is jointly managed by the University of Iowa and the Church of Jesus Christ of Latter-day Saints and is surrounded by student housing, soccer fields, and roads. The encampment area is now heavily wooded, whereas in 1856 it would have been mostly open prairie. A small parking lot and a half-mile trail with a few markers and commemorative plaques are all that serve to remind visitors of the amazing story of the more than two thousand hand-cart pioneers who passed through there in 1856 and 1857.

Under the best of circumstances, a July 8 arrival in Iowa City would have been precariously late for pilgrims intending to make it to the valley of the Great Salt Lake on foot before the cold-weather season. It was clearly Brigham Young's intent for the handcart pioneers to be approaching the Rocky Mountains by July. However, for the Mormon pioneers who crossed the Atlantic on the *Thornton* and *Horizon* in May of that year, most of whom became members of the Fourth (Willie) and Fifth (Martin) hand-cart companies, the circumstances were anything but optimal. For a vari-ety of complex reasons, the last two companies of the 1856 emigration were delayed substantially. Stormy spring weather in England, high prices, difficult economic times, tight finances, labor shortages, poor communi-cation, and a fervent desire by an overwhelming number of Saints to make the trip to Zion that year all conspired to delay all the charter ships from leaving England, and to keep the last two groups in Iowa City much lon-ger than was desirable.

At any given time, three to four church agents were assigned with the enormous task of getting the handcart pioneers outfitted and on their way. Under the leadership of Daniel Spencer and with the expertise of skilled wagonwright Chauncey Webb, these agents worked incessantly to move the emigrants from Iowa City to the handcart trail as quickly as possible. But the late arrival and enormous size of the groups from both the *Thorn-ton* and *Horizon*, coupled with a number of adverse conditions, made the task of a timely and well-equipped departure virtually impossible.

Historians who have pieced together the circumstances surrounding the late departures and ill-prepared outfitting of the Willie and Martin companies have noted a number of significant challenges facing these preparations. There were insufficient foodstuffs available for purchase, prices were higher than expected, and P.E.F. funds were short. There were not enough tents and insufficient fabric to construct more tents in a timely manner. In addition, many of the cast iron cooking pots and other imple-ments that had been ordered had not yet arrived in Iowa City. But most significantly, by late June and early July of 1856, there was not a sufficient supply of appropriate raw materials to construct enough handcarts in time, nor were there sufficient skilled workers to build these handcarts.[10] Despite these adverse circumstances, Chauncey Webb put every available man to work on the construction of the handcarts, while the women in the camp worked on making the tents.

Although it was a risky proposition, the movement of greenhorn immigrants across the plains and mountains on foot with handcarts, rather than with individual wagons and oxen, was actually an ingenious idea. The design of these handcarts was similar to that of the carts that were used by apple peddlers in the eastern United States. The handcarts were built mostly of native oak or hickory, were six or seven feet long and approximately four feet wide, and could carry four to five hundred pounds. They were built on-site near the encampment area. Five people (often a family) were assigned to each handcart, and each person was allowed seventeen pounds of possessions, mostly consisting of bedding, clothing, and cooking utensils. After the weigh-in process at the Iowa City encampment prior to departure, many of the pioneers had to leave behind treasured personal possessions because of the weight limit.

The process of assembling the handcarts had worked well for the first three companies, but the fourth and fifth groups (the Willie and Martin companies) experienced substantial difficulties because of the lateness of the season, the lack of seasoned wood, and the scarcity of other needed materials. Thus, the handcarts made for the company with whom Wee Granny traveled were done so in haste, were constructed with green (unseasoned) wood, and without the iron and leather needed to maximize the strength and stability of the axles and wheels.

Written records left by some individuals who were in the Iowa City encampment area during July of 1856 provide us with some clues regarding Wee Granny's life there.[11] The weather was often hot and oppressively humid. The incredible power of the midwestern thunderstorms that rolled through the camp with powerful lightning bolts on a regular basis (almost certainly including some severe storms with tornadoes nearby) must have astounded the European immigrants. There were ticks, chiggers, mosquitoes, prairie rattlers, and assorted other pests with which to contend. There were births and deaths and sickness in the camp. As was true on the voyage across the Atlantic, the encampment was highly organized. There were daily prayers, frequent devotionals, and motivational meetings. Above all, there was work and waiting. Wee Granny likely put her experience to good use, possibly helping to make tents and assist with outdoor cooking.

A LATE START: HITTING THE HANDCART TRAIL

Wee Granny's assigned group, the Martin Handcart Company, was the fifth and last to leave Iowa City in 1856. They departed on July 28, a full twenty days after reaching Iowa City. Although there was concern regarding the lateness of the departure and their state of preparedness for the journey, most of these pioneers were eager to leave, putting their full trust in the Lord and in the men assigned to be their leaders. The Martin company included 576 persons, with a total of 146 carts, seven wagons with thirty oxen for carrying foodstuffs and group supplies, and fifty cows and beef cattle. Each company was further divided into groups of one hundred each, with sub-captains over them. Although the trip across the Atlantic to America, and from Boston to Iowa City, had indeed included hardships for Wee Granny and her companions, as had the twenty days in the hot humid encampment site, as the Fifth Handcart Company left Iowa City, they undoubtedly had very little notion of the hardships that lay ahead during the next several weeks. Mary Murdoch was about to be tested beyond the very limits of her strength.

The Fifth Handcart Company is generally known as the Martin company. During the first stretch of the trip via handcart (from Iowa City to Florence, Nebraska), this group was actually divided into two companies of more than two hundred individuals each, one captained by Edward Martin, and the other by Jesse Haven. These two groups traveled separately, but they were generally within close distance of each other.

This first leg of the handcart journey, from Iowa City to Florence, Nebraska (near present-day Omaha), was 277 miles long. This stretch took the Fifth Handcart Company slightly less than four weeks (twenty-five days to be exact). Assuming that this large group of over five hundred did not travel on Sundays, of which there would have been three, and because it is known that they took a couple of days off for repairs, they averaged slightly over thirteen miles per day, quite an impressive feat under the circumstances. For seventy-three-year-old Mary Murdoch, this rate of travel was especially impressive, but it soon began to take a toll on her.

Most of the companies reported that the first few days out from Iowa City found the pioneers in good spirits and glad to be on their way. The road across Iowa was relatively good, and it had been well traveled that year. Although the Martin company coped with the usual heat, dust, thunderstorms, equipment problems, sickness, and sheer drudgery that would accompany such a journey, this stretch went remarkably well. A few travelers from the company dropped out because of sickness or discouragement, but the vast majority stayed with the trek.

Although these Zion-bound pilgrims must have been in awe of the long stretches of empty prairie that they encountered during this stretch, it is important to consider that Iowa was far from an empty wilderness in 1856. In fact, the state was home to approximately six-hundred-thousand residents at that time, most of them farmers who had settled there from eastern states or European nations because of the legendary richness of the dark and deep loess soil, which is still considered to be the best large stretch of agricultural land in the United States. The surrounding population became increasingly sparse as the company traveled west, and the frequent farms along the road gave way to vast stretches of tallgrass prairies. In this same vein, Samuel Openshaw of the Martin company noted in his journal on August 7:

> ...we could stand and gaze upon the prairies as far as the eye could see, even until the prairies themselves seemed to meet the sky on all sides, without being able to see a house. I thought, how many thousands of people there are in England who have scarce room to breathe and not enough to eat. Yet all this good land is lying dormant, except for the prairie grass to grow and decay.[12]

As Mary Murdoch and her 500-plus compatriots made their way across the state of Iowa, they passed prosperous farms, tallgrass prairie, and small outposts of towns. The terrain across Iowa is considered to be very flat by western standards or even Scottish conventions, but it is deceptive in that regard. The road these pioneers traveled continuously wound up and down slight inclines, which from a distance would have the appearance of small rolling hills. Although the task of walking and pushing or pulling a handcart up and down such stretches of elevation gain and loss would later seem slight in comparison with what would be faced in the Rocky Mountains, it nevertheless would have required a great deal of physical effort during this break-in period, especially considering that this leg of the journey was conducted during the very hottest period of the summer, when daytime highs often reach the upper 90-degree range or higher, and the humidity is often 80 percent or more. Under these conditions the low temperature at night likely seldom dipped below 70 degrees, and the dewpoint would have often been in the 65- to 75-degree range, resulting in wet prairie grass every morning and moldy warm dampness at night.

Based on reports from the five handcart companies that traveled across Iowa during the summer of 1856, the pioneers mainly kept to themselves along the road and at campsites, but there were occasional interactions with Iowa residents. In some cases, there were reports of the Iowans going out of their way to be hospitable and encouraging, providing assistance and support as they could. In other cases, there was jeering and disgust openly shown by some of the less hospitable residents of the Hawkeye State, many of whom certainly had formed negative opinions of the Mormons based on sensationalistic media reports and a general negative public sentiment toward separatist groups. One story is that one of the handcart companies traveling across Iowa was held up for two hours while the handcarts and equipment boxes were searched by a sheriff and his men, who were looking for hidden females who they feared were being taken to Utah against their will to be forced to enter into plural marriages with lecherous old men.[13] The 1852 public acknowledgment by the leadership of the church after their settlement in Utah that the practice of polygamy was embraced led to an increasingly fierce flurry of public opposition and distrust. It is likely that rumors of this practice and lifestyle were known and discussed among the Iowa settlers, some of whom likely made negative judgments against the pioneers as a result.

However, to Wee Granny and her traveling companions, such discussions, even among them, must have seemed somewhat abstract. Although polygamy was a known doctrine at that time, and the public knowledge of it likely was associated with the decline in convert baptisms in Europe after 1852, most of the European Saints had probably not observed much in the way of day-to-day evidence of the practice at this point in time. These Saints were likely more concerned with how they were going to get through their next mile on the trail than anything else. Any public sentiment they may have felt directed against them may have had the effect of galvanizing them together.

By the middle of this twenty-five-day stretch of the trip, it became increasingly obvious that there were significant problems with the construction of many of the handcarts. Breakdowns were frequent, and those assigned to be mechanics could not keep up with the needed repairs. Again, in almost every historical source on the Martin and Willie handcart companies, two primary problems with the construction of the handcarts are noted. Many of the axles were constructed of wood instead of iron, and the wood that was used was generally green.

Poor construction of the handcarts was only one of the challenges faced during this stretch of the journey. As Wee Granny and her companions moved west from central Iowa and closer to the Missouri River, they encountered numerous sand hills, which made traveling very difficult. In addition, water became increasingly scarce during the last several days into Florence. At times, the best they could do was to locate muddy and sandy puddles in lowlands along the way and try to extract drinking water, filtering it as best they could. Of course, the result of relying on such poor water supplies was that many of the pioneers became sick. To make matters worse, food supplies were beginning to run short.

The first 277 miles of the handcart trail went relatively well and morale was still high, but by the time this vast collection of humans, animals, and equipment from the Fifth Handcart Company of 1856 crossed the mighty Missouri River and made their way into Florence, Nebraska, many were showing obvious signs of wear. Although we don't know the specifics of Mary Murdoch's experience, it is no stretch to think that given her age and lack of experience in frontier life, she suffered greatly as she trudged on mile after mile in the stifling heat and humidity. Given some of the family traits that have made their way through generations of her descendants, it is no stretch of the imagination to think that she suffered these deprivations quietly, without complaining or drawing attention to herself. She couldn't have known what new challenges were ahead, and she likely took each day as it presented itself. It rings true to think of her finding the will to endure the constant daily grind of this journey by focusing constantly on her desire to join her son John and his family in Zion.

A Fatal Decision: The Layover at Florence

On August 22, Mary Murdoch and the rest of the two groups of the Martin Handcart Company crossed the Missouri River at Kanesville, Iowa (Council Bluffs), and arrived at the fort in Florence, Nebraska, near present-day Omaha. This area held special significance for the Saints. It was here that the Nauvoo Saints erected a large village of forts and sod huts and spent the winter of 1847–48 after their forced exodus from Illinois. This was their Winter Quarters, and hundreds of empty buildings still stood. In the years since the quarters were constructed the brethren encouraged immigrating parties of Saints to stay there en route to Salt Lake. Because of the location and availability of shelter, Florence was a natural spot for rest, repairs, and resupplying.

The day before their arrival in Florence, the Martin company was greeted by Apostle Franklin D. Richards and his group of high-ranking elders of the church who overtook them as they made their way from Liverpool to Salt Lake. The Richards party was traveling by wagon and carriage. This visit certainly must have raised the spirits of the group, who were provided with assistance and encouragement. It was Elder Richards who had been primarily responsible for organizing and planning the emigration of the 1856 handcart companies. Many of these Saints knew some of these men personally, and most had probably heard some of them speak words of encouragement as they left Liverpool on the *Horizon*. Many individuals in the handcart company shook Elder Richards's hand and thanked him personally for the opportunity to come to Zion that year.

Even with the struggles and disappointments that had occurred by this point, the group had made good progress, and almost all appeared to be unanimous in their belief that they would be prospered and protected as they made the rest of the journey to the valley of the Great Salt Lake. One of the company, Cyrus Wheelock (author of the hymn *Ye Elders of Israel*), reported that "I have never seen more union among the Saints anywhere than is manifested in the handcart companies. Hundreds bear record of the truth of the words of President Young, wherein he promised them increasing strength by the way." [14]

One of the most significant events for the Martin Handcart Company had occurred in Florence a few days prior to their arrival. It was here in mid-August that a mass meeting of the Willie Handcart Company, who were continually one to two weeks ahead of the Martin company, took place. The purpose of the meeting was to discuss the feasibility of leaving Florence so late in the season and moving on to Salt Lake that fall. Several leaders in the Willie party were experienced in this route, and were obviously aware of the dangerous possibilities that such a late trek across the high plains and Rocky Mountains might have in store, particularly given the questionable status of many of the handcarts and supplies.

One idea that was proposed was to winter over along the Platte River in Nebraska, perhaps near Grand Island. Most of the public discussion among these leaders had the effect of convincing one and all that they should move on. After all, they had not come this far to sit out the winter in a dreary dugout or sod hut along the Platte. They were on a quest to join their fellow Saints in Zion and were confident in God's plan to get them there. At this meeting, one of the leaders, a seasoned frontiersman by the name of Levi Savage, broke ranks with the prevailing sentiment and bravely spoke out against trying to cross the plains and mountains so late. He argued that under the best of circumstances, they would reach Salt Lake at the end of October, and that there could be freezing cold and snow in the Rockies a full two months before that. He stated that they "could not cross the mountains with a mixed company of aged people, women, and little children, so late in the season without much suffering, sickness, and death." [15] His advice was to go into winter quarters immediately. But Savage was the lone dissenter when a vote was taken. To his credit, he made his famous statement, both ominous and prophetic:

"Brethren and sisters, what I have said I know to be true; but seeing you are to go forward, I will go with you, will help you all I can, will work with you, will rest with you, will suffer with you, and if necessary I will die with you."[16] Levi Savage did not die on this trek, but his experience, hard work, and courage clearly kept many more of the company from dying than otherwise would have. When Franklin D. Richards later heard of Savage's dissension, he scolded him most severely in a public meeting.[17]

The decision of the Willie company to move on was significant for the Martin company because it set a precedent for what they would do. There is no record of such a similar debate occurring at Florence among the Martin company. However, it is likely that they knew of this discussion and decision. Given their fresh enthusiasm that came from Franklin Richards's visit, and knowing that the company just ahead of them was pressing on, wintering over likely did not even seem to be an option to consider. And to be fair, wintering over on the plains of Nebraska was no guaranty of comfort and safety. Food and other supplies were short, equipment was questionable, and most of the immigrants had absolutely no experience dealing with severe winter weather. If Wee Granny's experience was anything like that of the several members of the Willie and Martin companies who then or later recorded their feelings, she trusted that the group would be seen through. This was God's plan for them, and their faith in the leadership of the brethren and the providence of their way was resolute.

During the short stay in Florence, some additional foodstuffs and other equipment were collected, and sore feet and tired backs were given a short reprieve. Perhaps the greatest challenge for the Martin company during this three to four day stop was to fix the many handcarts that were now obviously in need of repair. New axles were put in where possible, iron, leather, and tin reinforcing materials were added to the axles as they could be obtained, and other repairs were made. Still, there was not sufficient iron or time to do an adequate job of reinforcing the problem handcarts, and none of these repairs could change the fact that most of the handcarts were made of unseasoned wood that was subject to shrinkage, splitting, and warping. An additional problem with the handcarts, one for which there was not an apparent solution, was a severe shortage of lubricating materials for the axles. Although bacon grease was in short supply, some in the company used what they could of it to grease the axles of their handcarts, and others even used the little soap that they had, to help make the handcarts trundle more easily.

And They Walked and Walked and Walked...

When the Martin Handcart Company left Florence, they had just finished 277 miles of travel in slightly more than four weeks. The distance remaining from Florence to the valley of the Great Salt Lake was over nine hundred miles. In other words, they had thus far traveled slightly less than one-fourth of the 1,200 to 1,300 mile distance between Iowa City and Salt Lake City. At this rate, it would take them until about the end of November to reach their destination in Zion. Even under good weather conditions, late November would be unacceptably and dangerously late in the season.

Those individuals in leadership positions in the Willie and Martin companies knew that the pace of travel would have to be stepped up. Several among them figured that if they were able to average somewhat better daily mileage than they had during the first leg of the trek, they would reach Salt Lake by late October. Although late October would certainly be preferable to late November, those who had previously made the trek and were acquainted with the climate of the high plains and Rocky Mountains realized that even under the best circumstances they were in for a severe test. As he wrote from Florence on September 3 regarding the possible fortunes of the Willie and Martin companies, even Franklin D. Richards, usually effusive in his optimism regarding the migration, noted with characteristic understated caution and concern:

> From the beginning we have done all in our power to hasten matters pertaining to emigration, therefore we confidently look for the blessing of God to crown our humble efforts with success, and for the safe arrival of our brethren the poor Saints in Utah, *though they may experience some cold.*[18]

In comparison with the information available regarding the July through August and October through November time periods of that year, relatively little was recorded or has been later written of the journey of the Martin Handcart Company during the month of September. We know that the trail became progressively more difficult as these pioneers moved west from Florence and across Nebraska. There were numerous sand hills to contend with, and the trail was heavily rutted in many places. After re-provisioning in Florence, and after a redistribution of goods from some of the support wagons, the handcarts carried a substantially heavier load (as much as a hundred pounds) than they did during the Iowa portion of the trek. Not only did the increased weight require increased effort, perhaps just as important, it added additional stress to the already questionable handcarts, most of which were in constant need of attention.

As the Martin company continued to move west from Florence and across Nebraska, they generally followed the course of two rivers: first the Platte, then the North Platte. The range of travel per day was typically between ten and twenty miles, with an average distance of about fifteen miles. As they reached the Wood River (near present-day Grand Island, about one-third of the way west across Nebraska), there began to be increasing evidence of the vast herds of buffalo that still roamed the high plains in the mid-nineteenth century. The most obvious evidence of their presence were the heavy ruts they left in the shortgrass prairie of that area, along with the omnipresent "buffalo chips" that were scattered across the land, and which in their dried and hardened state provided fuel for the fires needed for cooking and warmth as trees became increasingly scarce. There were times when the buffalo were actually within visual distance, which must have been an impressive sight. At other times, the sound of moving herds of buffalo thundered across the plains, even when they were not in sight. John Chislett of the Willie company recorded in his extensive diary that the presence of buffalo caused their cattle to stampede, which resulted in the loss of milk cows and an end to their rations of beef.

Other signs of the changing geography included occasional sounds of wolves howling at night. Although we don't know the specifics of the Martin company's experience in this regard, some of the groups that had moved through earlier in 1856 built large fires near their equipment, cattle, and sleeping areas on several nights as a deterrent to the wolves, who had become increasingly noticeable and fearless.

As they pushed farther west, the party gradually began to notice a change in the level of humidity. Because of the combination of the changing seasons, higher altitude, and natural conditions of areas farther west in longitude, the oppressive humidity that had been experienced across Iowa in midsummer gave way to dryness. Although there may have been some relief associated with the increased dryness, it also had the effect of more rapidly reducing the moisture content in the unseasoned wood used to construct the handcarts. As a result, there were increased breakdowns of handcarts as wood pieces that were assembled in unseasoned state began to harden, shrink, split, and warp. Some of the handcarts continued to require extensive work to keep them patched together, and others became virtually useless.

Elder Franklin D. Richards and his party, with two wagons and three carriages, finished their business in Florence and overtook the Martin company on September 7, and then the Willie company on September 12. Many of the Saints were clearly inspired by the words of encouragement they received from their esteemed leader, who promised them in the name of God that if they would maintain their faith and obedience during the trek they would be upheld and strengthened, and that their path would be cleared of obstacles. It was at this point in the journey that Elder Richards also gave Levi Savage his severe public scolding for his prior dissent regarding the advisability of leaving Florence so late in the season. As they sang "All Is Well" around the campfire on so many occasions, that sentiment may have resonated deeply within these already weary pioneers, despite their challenges and trials.

However, Franklin Richards must have been increasingly worried as it became obvious that some of his letters had not reached the church leaders in Salt Lake as anticipated. He and his advisors must have wondered with some sense of terror if the supply wagons with much needed provisions would be waiting for the faithful but beleaguered members of the Martin and Willie companies, or if the leadership in Utah was even aware that there were still several hundred Saints on foot scattered across the Nebraska territory so late in the season.

REACHING HER LIMITS: CHIMNEY ROCK

As September progressed and Mary Murdoch and her compatriots in the Martin company moved across central Nebraska and into the increasingly barren, windy, and unforgiving high plains environment to the west, the journey began to take an ever increasing toll. Some who had started the trek in good health and spirits began to be worn down, and the daily tedium of their labor turned into a significant struggle. These struggles were particularly apparent in many of the elderly and sickly among the group. By this point in time, Wee Granny had walked over five hundred miles. Although she was obviously a tough and determined woman, and although her spirit was still willing, Mary Murdoch's seventy-three-year-old body had reached the limits of its capabilities. As the nights began to grow colder with the arrival of autumn, the ability of her small body to generate heat became compromised. Family stories refer to Wee Granny as a tiny, slight woman. She probably had little extra body fat to spare to begin with. But by the time the Martin company reached western Nebraska and was within visual distance of the great landmark of Chimney Rock, she clearly would have lost weight from the journey, an inevitable result of the insufficient food for fuel, as well as the tremendous physical challenge of walking an average of fifteen miles per day. As she reached the last several days of her life, Wee Granny's exhaustion, weakness, and pain must have been overwhelming. As she lay down in her makeshift bed during those last few nights, her joints must have ached immensely, and her body's struggle to provide heat at night must have resulted in long nights where she expended a great deal of badly needed energy through the involuntary act of shivering to produce body heat.

Despite the increasingly difficult circumstances in which they found themselves as they reached the western end of Nebraska, we know from many sources that the members of the Martin Handcart Company generally maintained a great deal of hope, optimism, and faith at this point in the trek. Despite their generally positive disposition, these were common people, who like anyone else had their share of faults and foibles. There was the usual amount of pettiness and bickering, and as they moved farther west and foodstuffs became increasingly scarce, there were some incidents of pilfering. At this point, the few incidents of stealing were motivated by an increasingly sharp hunger among members of the group. However, the spirit of cooperation among them was generally strong. Wee Granny and her fellow travelers were united in a common bond of purpose, and their faith in the divine destiny of their purpose sustained them in a very real way.

Tell John That I Died with My Face Toward Zion

Mary Murray Murdoch died on October 2, 1856, about ten miles northeast of Chimney Rock, Nebraska, just a few days short of her seventy-fourth birthday. Until recent years, her death date was considered to be October 3, because the company records indicate that she died near Chimney Rock, which the group passed on October 3. The revision of her death date has been based on statements from the diary of fellow traveler John Jacques, who recorded that Wee Granny died at approximately 4:00 p.m. on October 2, and that the day was hot and dry. Jacques also noted that she was suffering from diarrhea at the time of her death.[19] She was one of eighteen members of the Martin and Willie companies who died during the mid-September to early October period, before the severe winter weather hit. Several of these deaths were among elderly individuals, such as Mary Murdoch, and the rigors of the trip had obviously taken their toll on them. Some others who died during this time were noted to have been suffering from diarrhea or dysentery. It is quite likely that the combination of poor nutrition and exhaustion could have caused such a condition, and it is just as likely that the drinking water that was consumed contained various viruses, cysts, bacteria, and so forth.

At the time of her death, Wee Granny was attended by James Steele, brother of her daughter-in-law Ann Steele Murdoch, John's wife, and the man responsible for bringing the message of Mormonism and the restoration to the Murdoch family. In addition, it is likely that James Steele's wife, Elizabeth, her mother, Mary Wylie, and perhaps other individuals that she had become acquainted with during the long journey were with her during her final moments. As her death became imminent and she drew her last few breaths, she uttered, "Tell John that I died with my face toward Zion," a statement that is now immortalized as a symbol of her faith and sacrifice. As the life ebbed from her in those final minutes she obviously knew that she would not make it to Utah.

Weeks later, when word of her death reached the Murdochs in Salt Lake City, it had a crushing impact on them. Murdoch family stories indicate that when John Murdoch went to the public square to meet the Martin company and find his mother, Elizabeth Steele relayed the tragic news of the deaths of her husband, James, and of Wee Granny. It was Elizabeth Steele who reported Wee Granny's famous last words to John. As he returned to his home his wife Ann could see by his countenance that something was wrong. She waited motionless in the doorway for a while, and then John told her, "They have both given their lives for the gospel's sake." Ann was eight months pregnant with their daughter Janett Osborne Murdoch when she received the sad news. Janett later told her own children and grandchildren that her mother would always stroke her hair and say, "no wonder you cry so easily my little girl. For six weeks after you were born I cried every day and couldn't sleep at night for thinking of Dear Wee Granny."[20]

Mary Murray Murdoch's body was buried in a shallow grave in the high plains of western Nebraska, perhaps wrapped in the blankets that had provided her with some warmth on the cold nights that ominously crept in as that summer turned into fall. Her death on October 2 was oddly merciful in one respect. It is highly unlikely that she would have survived the awful circumstances that beset the Martin and Willie handcart companies in the next few weeks after her death, and her passing thus spared her the additional unimaginable suffering that fell upon her comrades. The bitter cold, wind, and snow that unceasingly assaulted them in the high plains and mountains of western Nebraska and Wyoming beginning in mid-October was merciless, and most of the approximately two hundred total deaths among the Mormon handcart pioneers occurred in those two companies during that horrendous period. It is estimated that approximately 20 percent of the combined total membership of the Martin and Willie companies died during those few ghastly weeks.[21]

Among those who died during this period was James Steele, who passed on November 10, 1856. One of the most famous works of art created as a memorial to those handcart pioneers who died on the high plains is of the burial of James Steele, by artist Clark Kelly Price, his great-great-grandson. This painting shows two men lowering a body-filled blanket into a shallow frozen grave, under what appear to be near-blizzard conditions. Standing in the background a few feet away are the figures of two women huddled together, wrapped in blankets and shawls, one holding a small child. It is assumed that the body was that of James Steele, and that the two women in the painting represented Elizabeth Steele and Mary Wylie.

The Great Tragedy

Although the story of Wee Granny's journey to Zion ends here, it is worth noting that the fate of the Martin and Willie handcart companies from mid-October until their arrival in Salt Lake several weeks later is one of the great tragedies of western U.S. history. As the years since 1856 have slipped away, various amateur and professional historians have attempted to analyze the circumstances that led to this tragedy, and some have gone so far as to place blame.

Blame is a difficult and elusive thing to assign correctly, especially when separated by many years from the actual events. Most of the efforts to try to make sense of this tragedy by assigning blame can be understood and accepted within the context of the years in which the actual events occurred. Others cannot, as some attempts to place blame seem remarkably insensitive and arrogant in retrospect. The comments of Brigham Young's counselor Jedediah M. Grant, who fanatically laid the blame on the victims, fall into this category. Grant swore from the pulpit of the Salt Lake Tabernacle that the handcart immigration would have been successful had it been carried out as directed by Brigham, and he blamed the death and suffering of those in the Martin and Willie handcart companies on the disobedience and sinfulness of those who suffered.[22]

Perhaps more than anyone else, Apostle Franklin D. Richards has been made out to bear a large share of the responsibility. Given his role as mission president in the British Isles and his responsibility for organizing and implementing the 1856 handcart migration, along with his effusive optimism and characteristic understatement of the risks of the trek west, such blame is understandable, particularly because he was in effect demoted and marginalized by Brigham Young in the aftermath of the tragedy. Following the late 1856 handcart tragedy, Richards retained his position as a member of the church's Quorum of the Twelve Apostles, but many sources indicate that he was in fact demoted in responsibility and prominence by Brigham Young, who on several occasions deflected blame from himself and put it squarely on Apostle Richards, as well as on Daniel Spencer.[23]

The blame on Apostle Richards also sticks because Brigham Young publicly and privately criticized him—most severely—for his handling of the situation, even to the point of making him a scapegoat. One of Brigham's best known public statements in this regard leaves little doubt, despite the carefully worded deflection at the beginning:

> Here is br. Franklin D. Richards who has but little knowledge of business, except what he has learned in the church...and here is br. Daniel Spencer...a man of age and experience, and I do not know that I will attach blame to either of them. But if, while at the Missouri River, they had received a hint from any person on this earth, or if even a bird had chirped it in the ears of brs. Richards and Spencer, they would have known better than to rush men, women and children on to the prairie in the autumn months, on the 3rd of September, to travel over a thousand miles...If any man, or woman complains of me or of my Counselors, in regard to the lateness of some of this season's immigration, let the curse of God be on them and blast their substance with mildew and destruction, until their names are forgotten from the earth.[24]

Despite the criticism, even his detractors have admitted that Franklin D. Richards was a good man who happened to be at the confluence of an unbelievable array of forces that resulted in as bad an outcome for the Willie and Martin handcart companies as could have been imagined, and that if blame is going to be assigned, a good share of it could rise in the chain to his superiors. In retrospect, this great calamity could have been avoided with better planning, timing, and communication. But under the circumstances they were in and based on the information that they had, most who were involved believed they were making the right decisions.

WE ARE THEIR TEMPORAL SAVIORS

If Brigham Young's deflection of any personal blame from the 1856 handcart tragedy and his harsh public criticism of Richards and Spencer make him look defensive and heartless to some, it cannot be emphasized enough that he was affected greatly by the tragedy of the Willie and Martin companies in a very personal way. Despite whatever failings he had, Brigham's response to learning of the plight of the desperate handcart pioneers on the freezing plains was swift and unequivocal in sending them aid as soon as possible when he learned of their situation in early October 1856. A month later, on Sunday, November 6, 1856, Brigham was presiding at a church service in the Salt Lake Tabernacle when word reached him that the survivors of the rescue were beginning to reach Salt Lake City, that they were in desperate circumstances, and that there had been many fatalities. He immediately changed the text of his talk, and began to mobilize the gathered Saints into action to comfort and nurture the beleaguered survivors.

> When those persons arrive I do not want to see them put into houses by themselves; I want to have them distributed in the city among the families that have good and comfortable houses; and I wish all the sisters now before me, and all who know how and can, to nurse and wait upon the new comers and prudently administer medicine and food to them. To speak upon these things is a part of my religion, for it pertains to taking care of the Saints... As soon as this meeting is dismissed I want the brethren and sisters to repair to their homes, where their Bishops will call on them to take in some of this company; the Bishops will distribute them as the people can receive them... The afternoon meeting will be omitted, for I wish the sisters to go home and prepare to give those who have just arrived a mouthful of something to eat, and to wash them and nurse them up. You know that I would give more for a dish of pudding and milk, or a baked potato and salt, were I in the situation of those persons who have just come, than I would for all your prayers, though you were to stay here all the afternoon and pray. Prayer is good, but when baked potatoes and pudding and milk are needed, prayer will not supply their place on this occasion; give every duty its proper time and place... Some you will find with their feet frozen to their ankles; some are froze to their knees and some have their hands frosted... we want you to receive them as your own children, and to have the same feeling for them. We are their temporal saviors, for we have saved them from death.[25]

To underscore Brigham Young's concern regarding the survivors and the deceased, it is useful to read the words of one of the survivors who encountered Brigham soon after arriving in the city in a state of starvation, frozen feet, and a newly deceased mother:

> We arrived in Salt Lake City nine o'clock at night on the 11th of December 1856. Three out of four that were living were frozen. My mother was dead in the wagon. Bishop Hardy had us taken to a home in his ward and the brethren and sisters brought us plenty of food. We had to be careful and not eat too much as it might kill us we were so hungry. Early next morning Bro. Brigham Young and a doctor came. The doctor's name was Williams. When Bro. Young came in he

shook hands with us all. When he saw our condition—our feet frozen and our mother dead—tears rolled down his cheeks.[26]

A hundred years after the 1856 handcart emigrations, Wallace Stegner, noted historian and author on the American west, ranked the fate of the Martin and Willie companies as the greatest tragedy in western U.S. history. He paid tribute to their sufferings by writing:

> Perhaps their suffering seems less dramatic because the handcart pioneers bore it meekly, praising God, instead of fighting for life with the ferocity of animals and eating their dead to keep their own life beating, as both the Fremont and Donner parties did.... But if courage and endurance make a story, if human kindness and helpfulness and brotherly love in the midst of raw horror are worth recording, this half-forgotten episode of the Mormon migration is one of the great tales of the West and of America."[27]

This story may have been "half-forgotten" when Wallace Stegner wrote these words in 1956, but recent years have witnessed an impressive resurgence of interest in trying to understand, rethink, and pay tribute to the unparalleled trek of the handcart pioneers. The tales of bravery, heroism, and faith of these remarkable individuals—ordinary people put in an extraordinary circumstance—continue to be kept alive in the minds and hearts of subsequent generations. The descendants of John Murray Murdoch and his mother Mary Murray Murdoch have kept her story alive throughout following generations. It is a tale of undaunted courage, remarkable resolve, and powerful faith.

NOTES

1. John Murray Nicol, ed., *The James and Mary Murray Murdoch Family History* (Provo, UT: James and Mary Murray Murdoch Family Organization, 1982), 52.

2. Ibid., 53.

3. Leroy R. Hafen and Ann W. Hafen, *Handcarts to Zion: The Story of a Unique Western Migration, 1856–1860* (Lincoln: University of Nebraska Press, 1960), 28.

4. Ibid., 91.

5. Wallace Stegner, *The Gathering of Zion: The Story of the Mormon Trail* (New York: McGraw-Hill, 1964), 222.

6. Ibid., 228.

7. Ibid.

8. Bob Hibbs, "Sunday Post Card: Railroads," *Iowa City Press-Citizen*, December 17, 2000.

9. Stegner, *Gathering of Zion*, 221.

10. Leonard J. Arrington and Davis Bitton, *The Mormon Experience: A History of the Latter-day Saints* (New York: Alfred A. Knopf, 1979), 133–34; Hafen and Hafen, *Handcarts to Zion*, 92; Stegner, *Gathering of Zion*, 229–31.

11. Lynn Slater Turner, *Emigrating Journals of the Willie and Martin Handcart Companies and the Hunt and Hodgett Wagon Trains* (Lynn Slater Turner, 1996).

12. Turner, *Emigrating Journals*.

13. Leland L. Sage, *A History of Iowa* (Ames: Iowa State University Press, 1974).

14. Hafen and Hafen, *Handcarts to Zion*, 97.

15. Ibid., 96.

16. Ibid., 96–97.

17. *BYU Studies* 37: 1: 31.

18. Stegner, *Gathering of Zion*, 240.

19. Stella Bell, *Life History and Writings of John Jacques* (Rexburg, ID: Ricks College Press, 1978).

20. Anne Rasband McDonald, History of James and Mary (Wee Granny) Murdoch (document in author's possession).

21. Hafen and Hafen, *Handcarts to Zion*, 140–41.

22. Will Bagley, *Blood of the Prophets* (Norman: University of Oklahoma Press, 2002), 52–53.

23. Stegner, *Gathering of Zion*, 258.

24. Ibid., 257–58.

25. Hafen and Hafen, *Handcarts to Zion*, 139.

26. Arrington and Bitton, *The Mormon Experience*, 134.

27. Wallace Stegner, "Ordeal by Handcart," *Collier's,* July 6, 1956, 85.

7

• • •

LIVING THE PRINCIPLE: ISABELLA

[This] doctrine, a small portion of the world is opposed to; but I can deliver a prophecy upon it...it will sail over, and ride triumphantly above all the prejudice and priest-craft of the day; it will be fostered and believed in by the more intelligent portions of the world, as one of the best doctrines ever proclaimed to any people.

— BRIGHAM YOUNG, *Deseret News, Extra*, September 14, 1852

We loved to hear mother laugh. It had such a pleasant ring and was so cheering that we wanted to laugh with her. She was very determined, too, and when she said 'no' we knew better than to ask her again. My mother had high ideals and a determination to carry on...She was devoted to the Church and held many responsible positions. She was blessed with the gift of tongues and we children wondered if she were an angel from heaven as we listened to her one day in Fast Meeting.

— ISABELLA CRAWFORD MURDOCH NICOL

Sometime in late 1861 or early 1862, John and Ann Murdoch became acquainted with a fellow Scottish immigrant by the name of Isabella Crawford, who was about twenty-six years of age at that time, while John was about forty and Ann was about thirty-two years old. Isabella was a close friend of Heber residents Catherine and William Foreman, in whose company the Murdochs had made the move from Salt Lake City to the Upper Provo valley in the spring of 1860, and who lived near them in their dugout in Fort Heber during their first months there. The Murdochs' acquaintance and friendship with Isabella was stimulated to some extent by a phrase in the patriarchal blessing John had received from church patriarch John Young, which stated he would have "wives and children and a numerous posterity upon the mountains of Israel." This comment, which they viewed as direct guidance from God regarding their lives, weighed heavily on their minds in the months immediately after the blessing. It was considered as a specific reference to the practice of plural marriage or polygamy, which was taught and promoted by Brigham Young and other leading church authorities at that time as a doctrine that was absolutely essential for proving one's faith and receiving the highest exaltation in the Celestial Kingdom of God.[1]

A Peculiar Institution

The practice of plural marriage was introduced secretly as early as 1831 by Joseph Smith, who regarded it as a revelation from God, an essential spiritual principle, and a prerequisite for attaining the highest blessings of heaven. Although Joseph never publicly acknowledged his endorsement of the practice, he taught it to his closest associates in the church hierarchy in the late 1830s and early 1840s in Nauvoo. He was also exceptionally zealous under extraordinarily difficult conditions in attempting to live the principle personally. Although he had hoped to introduce polygamy into the church on a more widespread basis and publicly acknowledge it as one of the most important doctrines, Joseph underestimated the severe opposition that he would encounter in doing so, including from his first wife, Emma, and, at least initially, from his older brother Hyrum. Despite the intensive opposition and need to keep the practice secret, it has been well documented that Joseph entered into at least thirty-three polygamous unions during a relatively short period of time, and that some children were born from these relationships.[2]

Even among many of Joseph's closest associates, the doctrine of plurality of wives was so radically different from their cultural worldview and Puritan New England mores that it often engendered shock, disgust, rejection, and dismay. Those who ultimately accepted the doctrine—such as several members of the Quorum of the Twelve Apostles—typically went through a period of great turbulence in coming to terms with it, and they accepted it only after deep soul-searching, and based on their ultimate conclusion that Joseph was God's prophet. This difficult set of circumstances often created a hostile environment in which the principle was initiated. Joseph was thus in a position of having to use extremely carefully chosen and veiled language in describing the practice to others, and in relying on the utmost secrecy and assistance from intermediary third parties in introducing the teaching to potential plural wives. One of the best examples of Joseph's attempts to explain and justify the doctrine to skeptics is from some phrases taken from a well-known letter to Nancy Rigdon (daughter of his counselor Sidney Rigdon) in 1842, soon after she had acted in revulsion toward him when he proposed to her, and rejected his invitation:

That which is wrong under one circumstance, may be, and often is, right under another...Whatever God requires is right, no matter what it is, although we may not see the reason thereof until long after the events transpire...so with Solomon: first he asked wisdom, and God gave it to him, and with it every desire of his heart, even things which might be considered abominable to all who understood the order of heaven only in part, but which in reality were right because God gave and sanctioned by special revelation...Our Heavenly Father is more liberal in his views, and boundless in his mercies and blessings, than we are ready to believe or receive.[3]

After Joseph's martyrdom in 1844, Brigham Young sought to institutionalize all of the teachings that the prophet had introduced as part of the restoration, including the practices that were more secretive, such as "celestial marriage," the secret theocratic Council of Fifty, and the temple endowment. Even during the intense pressure that Brigham faced during the dark period following Joseph's death and in the midst of the Saints' traumatic relocation west, he managed to introduce the practice on a more widespread basis among his closest associates. During a church conference on August 29, 1852, when the Murdochs were on the Mormon trail during the last stretch of their trek from St. Louis to Salt Lake City, Brigham and the church publicly acknowledged the practice through a presentation by Apostle Orson Pratt, who was selected for the task because of his keen theological insight and the respect that he had from the people.[4] Despite the extreme sensitivity of the subject and the risk that was involved in a public acknowledgment, it had become necessary to make such an acknowledgment because the practice was becoming more widespread, difficult to conceal, and the subject of an increasing number of rumors.

By the time the Murdochs had made their move to Heber in 1860, the doctrine of plural or celestial marriage was well established within the church, and they had the benefit of several years to have become spiritually and intellectually comfortable with a practice that was so far removed from the culture and teaching in which they had been raised, and so far discrepant from mainstream American culture. During the Mormon Reformation of 1856 and 1857 plural marriage was one of the key points of doctrine that was emphasized and promoted by church leaders and reformation missionaries. There is no question that John and Ann Murdoch would have sat through numerous doctrinal expositions at church meetings by 1862 in which plural marriage was taught with zeal and fervor.

The Murdochs' acquaintance with Isabella Crawford developed during this time, through their mutual friends William and Catherine Foreman, whom Isabella frequently visited. She apparently had many suitors who were interested in the possibility of marriage, and undoubtedly some of these suitors were, like John Murdoch, married men who felt a religious obligation to enter into the principle of plural marriage. It is unclear whether Isabella became acquainted with the Murdochs during visits from Salt Lake City to Heber with the Foremans, or whether she relocated to the upper valley before her marriage, but it was the friendship that she developed with the Murdochs, who lived in close proximity to the Foremans, that led to her marriage to John. One of the few surviving family recollections regarding their courtship reads as follows:

> John M. Murdoch, and his wife Ann Steele, were continually striving to keep the commandments of God, and the principle of plural marriage was taught and practiced in the church. They made up their minds that if the way were opened up and the time came favorable they would obey this principle. John in a patriarchal blessing he received in 1861 was told he would be blessed with wives and children. So being close neighbors, they became well acquainted with this young girl and it was made known to all of them that this union was right.[5]

Family traditions indicate that Ann Murdoch may have "chosen" Isabella for her husband or, at the very least, Ann approved of and consented to the union. Although the rules for such courtships were not well defined, the consent of the first wife was usually required (the "law of Sarah"), and interest could be initiated by the man, the potential plural wife, or the first wife if she believed it was her religious duty to do so.[6] John and Ann apparently shared the same religious conviction and desire on this matter.

On August 9, 1862, John Murdoch and Isabella Crawford were "sealed" together for time and eternity, through a Mormon priesthood ordinance that they considered to be essential to their spiritual progression and ultimate exaltation with God. The ceremony was performed at the Endowment House in Salt Lake City, a two-story structure that sat on the northwest corner of Temple Square prior to the completion and dedication of the Salt Lake Temple. Here, in a sealing room in the upper level of the building, the blessings of the *New and Everlasting Covenant of Marriage* were pronounced upon them in a special religious ceremony that could be performed only in that building (and later in temples) by a small number of Mormon priesthood authorities. Family traditions maintain that Ann accompanied them on their trip to Salt Lake from Heber and that she was present at the sealing ceremony. As faithful Latter-day Saints who had given everything they had for the sake of the gospel and the building up of the kingdom of God on earth, John Murdoch, Ann Steele, and Isabella Crawford all desired to obey every commandment of God given to them by the prophets. Their move into a plural marriage relationship was a natural progression of their faithful desires.

Her Early Years: Independent and Resolute

Although there are relatively few specifics that have been preserved regarding her life, Isabella Crawford is a singular and beloved figure in the history of the Murdoch family. The few details that have survived—and some of them are contradictory—are found in biographical sketches provided by some of her children, which have made their way into family history compilations, as well as a formal history of Wasatch County, Utah. She was born April 12, 1836, in Blantyre, Lanarkshire, Scotland, in the southwest region of the nation. The Lanarkshire area is not only the most heavily populated region of Scotland—containing about a quarter of the entire population of the nation—but has been considered as the most important area economically and politically.[7] Lanarkshire includes the industrial city of Glasgow, which is a few miles northwest of Blantyre. The Blantyre Parish is one of the smallest in Lanarkshire, forming a narrow strip about one or two miles wide and about eight miles long, in the northwest sector of that county. The name Blantyre comes from a Gaelic word meaning "the warm retreat." This region was historically rich in coal mining, the iron industry, and a cotton-based textile industry, of which Blantyre Mills was perhaps the largest interest. Blantyre is the birthplace and youthful home of famed Scottish explorer David Livingstone, who was born about twenty-three years before Isabella, and who worked in the local cotton mill as a lad—perhaps the same mill in which Isabella later worked.[8]

Isabella was the daughter of Andrew Crawford and Margaret McClure. When Isabella was about six years old, her father enlisted in the British army and was sent to Canada. The family never heard of him again until they learned of his death, which was thought to have occurred about 1844 while he was in Canada. Her mother was thus left a single parent with three young girls to support and very little means, and she went to work in the famous Blantyre Cotton Mills. Given the practical and economic circumstances her family was in, Isabella did not have the opportunity to attend school, although one family recollection indicates that she attended school for six days as a child but was dismissed because she refused to "curtsey" to the teacher several times a day, as was expected, thinking that once a day was sufficient.[9] She was said to frequently attend Sunday School, which likely nourished her spirituality and helped set the stage for her acceptance of the teachings of the Church of Jesus Christ of Latter-day Saints in her late teen years. Although we do not know the specifics of the Crawford family's faith, Isabella most likely as a child attended one of the three-cornered factions of Presbyterianism that had emerged in Scotland by the early 1840s: the official Church of Scotland, the Free Church of Scotland, or the United Presbyterian Church. She learned to read and write and was known as a good letter writer. At some point Isabella also went to work in the textile mills and became a skilled weaver.

The American-based Church of Jesus Christ of Latter-day Saints first sent missionaries seeking converts to Great Britain in the late 1830s, with the first of these missionaries arriving in Scotland in 1839. This event precipitated a short period of rapid growth of the Mormon church in Scotland. The heavily populated and industrialized areas of Scotland's upper lowlands—including Lanarkshire—became particular strongholds for the budding church. In 1855, Isabella Crawford's life changed forever when she embraced the doctrines and fellowship of this new religion, into which she was baptized on August 16 at the age of nineteen. Although Mormonism represented only a tiny fraction of religious affiliations in Scotland, Isabella was not alone in embracing this new faith and lifestyle. Church records indicate that although Scottish membership was on a decline by 1855 from the peak period of 1850–52, that year was still one of the top five years of Scottish membership in the church in the nineteenth century, with a total of over two thousand members.[10]

We cannot know Isabella Crawford's exact desires and motives in adopting Mormonism, but it is likely she was influenced by both spiritual and practical considerations, as were John Murdoch and Ann Steele, who had embraced the faith four years earlier. The spiritual aspects of the allure of Mormonism—the claims of a restoration of ancient Christianity with the accompanying charismatic manifestations and prophetic authority—were in stark contrast to the mainstream Scottish churches, which were in a period of internal squabbling and were becoming increasingly secularized and detached from the charismatic roots of primitive Christianity. The practical appeal of Mormonism to a young person from the working class of Scotland was also undeniable. Here was a faith that promoted both temporal and spiritual salvation, and that encouraged European converts to join the gathering of the elect in the American Zion—land of the New Jerusalem—offering a promise of a better life and escape from the

Joseph Smith, Jr., founding Mormon prophet. Used by permission, Utah State Historical Society, all rights reserved.

Brigham Young, circa 1860s. In John Murdoch's estimation, the church president and colonizer was "the greatest man on earth." Used by permission, Utah State Historical Society, all rights reserved.

"Our beloved Captain." Abraham Owen Smoot, leader of the Murdoch's emigrating company, nurse to John Murdoch, and future mayor of Salt Lake City. Smoot referred affectionately to John as "my Scotch Johnnie." Used by permission, Utah State Historical Society, all rights reserved.

John Murdoch's last view of his homeland as he departed on a steamer in January 1852 was of Ailsa Craig and the Arran Hills, just before they were enveloped in the darkness of a thick mist. Photo of Ailsa Craig used by permission, copyright 1994 by Ilan Kelman (www.ilankelman.org).

The dugout in Fort Heber that the Murdoch family lived in during the summer of 1860, drawn from memory by John and Ann's son Joseph A. Murdoch in the 1930s. Used by permission, James and Mary Murdoch Family Organization.

A rare photo of the old Iowa State Capitol Building in Iowa City, 1853. Note the wagons, oxen, and dirt roads. Mormon handcart pioneers would have seen this building from a short distance as they walked from the railroad terminus to the encampment site. This building still stands on the University of Iowa campus. Used by permission, University of Iowa Photographic Service.

Edward G. Martin, captain of the ill-fated Sixth Handcart Company, 1856. Portrait by Dan Weggeland. Courtesy International Society Daughters of Utah Pioneers.

Chimney Rock, Nebraska, approximately seven miles west of the spot where Mary Murray Murdoch died on October 2, 1856. Photograph by Tim Frodsham, Portland, Oregon, used by permission.

"Tell John I Died With My Face Toward Zion: The Passing of Mary Murray Murdoch (Wee Granny) Near Chimney Rock, Nebraska on October 2, 1856," by Clark Kelly Price. Image by permission of the artist.

John Murray Murdoch flanked by his wives Ann Steele (left) and Isabella Crawford (right), circa 1870s or 1880s. This is the earliest known photograph of the three of them together. Used by permission, James and Mary Murdoch Family Organization.

The LDS Endowment House in Salt Lake City, where Isabella Crawford was married to John Murdoch on August 9, 1862. Used by permission, Utah State Historical Society, all rights reserved.

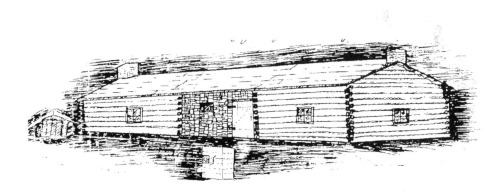

Drawing of log home in Heber, built by John Murdoch in 1865. This representation was drawn from memory by Joseph A. Murdoch in the 1930s. Nine of the Murdoch children were born in this home. Used by permission, James and Mary Murdoch Family Organization.

The large frame Murdoch family home built in 1880, which replaced the 1865 rectangular log home. This home, which has undergone several renovations in the 125-plus years since it was built, still stands in Heber City at 161 West 400 North. Photograph by Kenneth W. Merrell.

Looking southwest toward Mount Timpanogos and the Wasatch Mountains from the area about six miles north of Heber, near where the Murdoch sheep ranch was located. Photograph by Kenneth W. Merrell.

Sheep grazing north of Mount Timpanogos, late 1800s or early 1900s. Used by permission, Utah State Historical Society, all rights reserved.

Machinery and work area inside the Provo Woolen Mills, completed in 1872. Used by permission, Utah State Historical Society, all rights reserved.

Main Street, Heber City, Utah, circa late 1800s. Note the mud streets. Used by permission, Utah State Historical Society, all rights reserved.

John Taylor, successor to Brigham Young, third president of the Church of Jesus Christ of Latter-day Saints, and "living martyr" from the Carthage jail massacre. A fierce defender of the faith, the refined and articulate Taylor spent the last few years of his life directing the church from the "underground," during the darkest days of persecution in the 1880s. Used by permission, Utah State Historical Society, all rights reserved.

John Murray Murdoch, circa 1870s. Used by permission, James and Mary Murdoch Family Organization.

Portrait of John Murray Murdoch in his later years. A likeness of this image was placed on his new headstone memorial at the Heber cemetery in August 2002 by members of the Murdoch family. Used by permission, James and Mary Murdoch Family Organization.

Wilford Woodruff, avid fly fisherman, diarist, farmer and rancher, and fourth president of the Church of Jesus Christ of Latter-day Saints. Woodruff released the 1890 Manifesto announcing the church's intention to abandon the practice of plural marriage. Used by permission, Utah State Historical Society, all rights reserved.

Isabella Crawford Murdoch, John Murdoch, Ann Steele Murdoch,
circa 1890s. Used by permission, James and Mary Murdoch Family
Organization.

The Murdoch house built in the early 1890s after the law required separated households. Ann Steele Murdoch lived in this home. This structure is located at 118 South 500 West in Heber City. Photograph by Kenneth W. Merrell.

A working sheep ranch in Wasatch County, early 1900s. Courtesy U. S Forest Service. Used by permission, Utah State Historical Society, all rights reserved.

The Wasatch Stake Tabernacle, in Heber City, completed in 1889. The funerals of John Murdoch, Ann Steele Murdoch, and Isabella Crawford Murdoch were all held in this building. Used by permission, Utah State Historical Society, all rights reserved.

Downtown Salt Lake City, July, 1910, approximately two months after John Murdoch's death. Note the American flag banners posted for the annual Independence Day celebration. Used by permission, Utah State Historical Society, all rights reserved.

Memorial marker stone for Mary Murray Murdoch, "Wee Granny," dedicated by members of the Murdoch Family on June 24, 2001, in a private cemetery near Chimney Rock, Nebraska. Photograph by Kenneth W. Merrell.

The final resting place of John Murdoch, Ann Steele Murdoch, and Isabella Crawford Murdoch, in the Heber City Cemetery in Wasatch County, Utah. This memorial marker was dedicated by members of the Murdoch Family Organization on August 24, 2002, after the original small grave markers had fallen into disrepair. Note the spelling of the last name as "Murdock," as it appeared on the original headstone. Photograph by Kenneth W. Merrell.

Gravestone dedication and memorial service for John M. Murdoch, held August 22–23, 2002, in the Heber City cemetery. Used by permission, James and Mary Murdoch Family Organization.

oppression of grinding poverty, a rigid class system, and no prospects for a better future.[11]

Family stories indicate that Isabella may have been driven from her home, perhaps disowned by her mother, and terminated from her employment in the Blantyre Cotton Mills as a result of her new affiliation with the Mormons. As her daughter Catherine Crawford Murdoch Hicken later recalled:

> ...she lost her kind friends and companions. Her position in the mills was taken away from her, which was a great calamity. Her mother and sisters refused to speak to her. Mother, being a very sympathetic girl, this almost broke her heart, but she said, "I have a testimony and I can't help it if you turn me out." They did turn her out. Her mother told her to go, that she never wanted to see her face again and she never did. Mother took a few clothes and left her mother, never to see her again.[12]

Another recollection of Isabella's life by a Murdoch family member indicates the same tale of family tension over Isabella's conversion to Mormonism but includes a slightly different twist and some additional details that may have been handed down to family members as stories:

> Isabella's mother bitterly opposed her joining the Church and had no use for the Elders. She felt they were luring them to wild, unknown country. When Isabella made plans to come to America, it only widened the gap between them. Isabella had to make her decision against the wishes of her mother and family. They gave her no help or encouragement as she gathered up her meager clothing and what treasures she had and put them in a bag. Her mother was standing just outside the door when Isabella told her goodbye. When she got to the corner of the house she could hold up no longer. An adobe had fallen out of the corner of the house. She supported herself by putting her arm in the space with her head resting on it, and then gave vent to her feeling with sobs and tears. But her mother—after Isabella had released her pent-up feelings, she dried her eyes, picked up her bag and resolutely lifted her head and left her mother, never to see her or hear from her again.[13]

Isabella's story of family strife and banishment following her conversion to Mormonism was not unusual for that time and place. Many similar stories of her contemporary Latter-day Saint converts in Europe and North America indicate that many were shunned, disparaged, disowned, or otherwise persecuted for their newfound faith. The estrangement and persecution occurred not only at the hands of family members, but also by friends, community members, clergy, and employers. In this regard, Isabella shared a common fate with her future husband, John Murdoch, and her future sister wife, Ann Steele.

In the 1840s and 1850s, the British Isles—particularly England and Scotland—were the largest single focus of Mormon missionary efforts. These efforts met with great success for a period of time, and they also caused great resentment and friction among families and communities in the region. Many of the converts in that area—with the strong encouragement of church leaders in Nauvoo and later in Utah—immigrated to America to join their fellow Saints and to help establish Zion. This pattern was Isabella Crawford's destiny as well.

WOE TO ANYONE THAT WOULD HARM THOSE GIRLS

With a new religion, a new community of fellow believers, and the recent loss of important relationships in her life, Isabella left her homeland for America. The details of her voyage and immigration have been mostly lost, but her departure most likely occurred in 1855, shortly after her conversion and baptism, or it may have happened in 1856. Either way, she most likely traveled from Lanarkshire to Liverpool, England, prior to the oceanic voyage, as Liverpool was the chief point of departure from that region to America. Written family recollections indicate that Isabella traveled to America with three or four young female companions (including Catherine Campbell, who later became Catherine Campbell Foreman), with whom she was also working in the Blantyre Cotton Mills, and who all presumably had embraced the Latter-day Saint faith like Isabella and were desirous of emigrating to Zion. According to the brief anecdotal history compiled by Isabella's daughter, the burgeoning textile industry in the northeastern United States needed to employ skilled weavers, and these young women jumped at the opportunity to use the skills they had acquired in Blantyre to help secure their passage to America and their initial employment, so they could save money for the trek to Zion. The only written anecdote of her oceanic voyage was that it was a rough passage, twelve weeks on the water, and that "the ship was struck by lightning and eight sailors drowned." [14]

Their voyage from Great Britain most likely took them directly to Boston, near their new employment at the cotton mills in Holyoke, Massachusetts. There, they worked long hours in the mills and also formed a small branch of the church, over which Isabella's friend and traveling companion, Catherine Campbell, served as the group's leader. They saved money and planned for their eventual trek westward to Utah. They also needed to work in the mill to pay off the cost of their passage to America, which apparently had been fronted by their employer, the owners of the Holyoke Mill. This small group of friends and believers met regularly for religious services, paid tithes to church authorities, and testified to each other of the truth of the gospel and God's blessings in their lives. Sometimes their small services included the charismatic manifestation of speaking in tongues, which was a common occurrence in Mormon women's devotional meetings in the mid-nineteenth century. The names of the other three young women in this group have been listed as Jennet Chocharn, Jennie McKennredck, and Aggie Maggriar (note that the spelling of some of these three names provided from the record left by Isabella's daughter may not be correct).

Family lore indicates that Isabella became an expert weaver in fine linens while working in the Holyoke Mill. Based on many histories of the conditions in northeastern U.S. textile mills in the mid-1800s, the work Isabella and her companions did was undoubtedly physically strenuous, tedious, and boring, and it may have been dangerous at times as well. According to documents from the Lowell National Historic Park in Massachusetts, the average number of hours worked per week in the textile mills in that region during the mid-1800s was over seventy; most of the workers were girls and young women from poor families, many of them not even in their teenage years, and they typically lived in company-owned boarding houses.[15] Apparently, these working conditions also put Isabella in close proximity to some less than desirable co-workers. One anecdote states "[Isabella] had long black hair, which she wore in two braids. One day a girl who worked beside her in the mill asked her why she didn't cut her hair off. Isabella replied that she didn't want to. The girl said "well, it's too pretty," and with a pair of large scissors, cut off one of the braids."[16]

After two or three years of hard work in the mills, paying back the cost of their passage to America, and saving for the trip to Utah, Isabella and her companions (or most of them—the few written records are unclear on this point) prepared for the overland migration to Utah, to join their fellow Saints in the Latter-day gathering place. It is a terrible loss that the story of their trip was never recorded in detail. There are many gaps and some conflicting details, making it very hard to piece together the facts of this journey. The two or three brief available recollections from family records regarding their journey leave many questions unanswered, including the exact time period of their migration, their specific mode of travel, the specific persons who traveled in their group, and what experiences and hardships they encountered along the way. In addition, there are no official records in the LDS Historical Archives in Salt Lake City that verify this journey.[17]

To try to understand Isabella's trek to Utah, we must look at the available records, which include some apparent inconsistencies. The official James and Mary Murdoch Family History (known as the *Red Book* to family members) states only that Isabella "walked every step of the way across the plains and arrived with her friends in Salt Lake City in 1858." At first glance, this statement might seem to indicate that these young women traveled on foot with a handcart party, leaving from Iowa City, Iowa. However, the timing of their trip, the availability of handcart company rosters, and somewhat contradictory statements in other family documents make the possibility of a handcart migration seem unlikely. Assuming that the 1858 date is correct for Isabella's arrival in Salt Lake City, it could not have been with a handcart company, because there were no 1858 handcart companies. Church president Brigham Young cancelled all handcart emigration that year and tried to discourage formal emigration to Utah as well, due to continuing conflict with the occupation of Utah by Johnston's army, in 1857–58. If we assume that 1858 may have not been the correct year of her trek, the only other possible explanation for a handcart company journey to Utah would have been in 1857, with the Israel Evans Company (the Sixth Company). The reason this is the only other plausible explanation is that the names of Isabella Crawford, Catherine Campbell, or their two or three traveling companions do not appear on the rosters of any of the other handcart companies, but the Sixth Company rosters of 1857 have never been found, so it could be possible they were with this group. However, a handcart migration seems unlikely because of four sentences about Isabella's trip to Utah that are found in the recollection of her daughter, Catherine:

> ...they saved enough to buy a wagon, a yoke of oxen, and a well equipped outfit to cross the plains. A brother by the name of Bob was chosen for their teamster and a good brother he proved to be. Woe to any one that would harm one of those girls either by look or actions. When they landed in Salt Lake, the girls five (gave) Bob the outfit for his kindness to them.[18]

This notion of a wagon-assisted trek is also supported by a section from Annie McMullin Rasband's recollection, which states:

In time they heard of a train of Saints who were coming to Utah, so they made inquiries and found a good worthy brother who would help them with their preparations. They pooled their money, bought a light wagon and a team of horses. This brother would drive the team and care (for it) it in exchange for his transportation to Utah.[19]

Assuming these two recollections are based in fact, these young women did not travel with a Mormon handcart company in 1857, but most likely made a trek west with a hired wagon and teamster. For an 1858 teamster-led trip, they most likely would have outfitted from either Iowa City, Iowa (also the departure point for the handcart companies), or Florence (now Omaha), Nebraska, the most common departure point to the Mormon trail in 1858. The outfitting and departure to the Mormon/Oregon trail for Isabella and her companions would have occurred following train travel from Massachusetts, which likely took them first through Chicago, then south, and then further travel by wagon and foot to the outfitting point.

There are three fascinating and sometimes confusing aspects of the possibility of an 1858 overland trek. First they would have been one of only a handful of groups to make an 1858 overland migration. The LDS Historical Archives list only five overland migration companies for that year, the lowest annual number during the 1850s. Second, they would have made this trek against the advice and without the support of Brigham Young, who had discouraged emigration for 1858 because of increasing conflict in Utah as a result of the "Utah War" between the Saints and the U.S. government. Third, the most comprehensive list of all Mormon immigrants to Utah during the 1847 to 1869 pioneer period, which is found in the LDS Church History Archives, does not even list the names of Isabella Crawford, Catherine Campbell, or any of their three potential companions (even with searches for common replacement spellings for their first and last names). In other words, despite the intensive efforts that have been made to document all Mormon pioneer treks to Utah, there is no formal record of any of these young women ever having made the journey.

Official records or not, Isabella obviously did make the journey. Based on the little available evidence, the best explanation for her trek west is that it occurred with the use of a wagon, aided by a hired driver. Although it may seem far-fetched, it is possible that Isabella and her companions made a small, unofficial, "stealth" trek west during the spring and summer of 1858, without the approval or knowledge of church officials who oversaw overland migrations. This explanation could be the reason why they are not listed in any of the formal overland migration rosters. Based on the specifics of the later recollection of Isabella's daughter Catherine (who was apparently named for Isabella's close friend from Scotland and Massachusetts, Catherine Campbell), their trek could be accepted as having been made independently in 1858, and aided by the mysterious hired teamster, "Bob." However possible, such an independent trek by a group of four or five young women aided by a lone teamster is unlikely, given what is known about other overland treks during that period. It is quite possible that Isabella and her companions joined one of the five known 1858 emigration groups (or possibly a group in 1857 or 1859), but their names were never recorded, or that they made the journey during one of those years with a collection of independent groups that never included an official roster. Regarding the notion that Isabella walked "every step of the way across the plains," that is a plausible assumption, given that the wagon was used for supplies. However, even assuming that some or much of the journey was in a wagon, it was likely not any more comfortable than walking, and it would be obvious that they would have spent considerable time on foot anyway. Regardless of the specific time or circumstances of Isabella's journey, it is a remarkable and compelling story.

A PROVIDENTIAL MOVE

An interesting conclusion to the story of Isabella's overland migration to Utah comes from a remembrance in the *Red Book*, which notes that when her party arrived in the public square in Salt Lake City in 1858, there were welcoming friends present to receive everyone in the group except for Isabella, who obviously would have felt very much alone at this point. Without family or friends awaiting her in Utah, twenty-two-year-old Isabella was in a difficult situation, relying wholly on her faith and her wits. Despite the odds against her, she was not left alone. Her supportive relationship with her friend Catherine Campbell (who has also been referred to as Katherine or Katy in written records) is emphasized by surviving family stories, which indicate that after arriving in Salt Lake City, Catherine and her waiting fiancé, William Foreman, seeing that Isabella had no one there to greet her, asked her to go with them, and assisted her in finding living quarters in the Cottonwood area.[20]

Within a short time after her arrival in Utah, Isabella found some type of employment in the Cottonwood area and began to establish herself among the Saints. No written records or family traditions have been located that address her initial years in Utah beyond that terse description. Isabella's close friend Catherine married William Foreman in October of

1859, and the new couple moved to the Upper Provo valley (the Heber-Midway area) five months later, during the spring of 1860. Their move proved providential for Isabella's future marriage, for it was made in the company of John Murdoch and his family. "After laboring in Salt Lake City for some time Isabella came to Provo valley to visit her friends, the Foremans, as the neighbors and friends lived close together and were all young people and very sociable, all soon became acquainted with this young girl. In the course of time she had many suitors for her hand in marriage."[21]

Throughout the remainder of her life, Isabella stayed in close contact with Catherine, with whom she would eventually serve nearly two decades later the presidency of a Stake Relief Society, an LDS women's organization in which the two women worked together for over fifteen years, from 1879 to 1895. Known in the family by the nickname "Bella," she was said to be a pleasant, patient, and congenial person. The two or three photos of Isabella that have survived and made their way into family collections were made in her late middle age and in her advanced years. Even in her old age, these photos show her as having fair, soft, and delicate features, and a pleasant smile. Her small dark eyes and light brows were somewhat high on her face, and she typically wore her hair pulled back in a bun.

LIVING THE PRINCIPLE

After Isabella's marriage to John in late 1862, the Murdoch household consisted of eight persons: three adults and Ann's five young girls. Each of the two wives had her own area of the home, and sometime shortly after Isabella joined the family, John began construction on a larger new home of six or seven rooms to accommodate his growing family.[22]

To understand the social context for the Murdoch household, it is important to consider how their polygamous marriage relationship compared to what was normative in 1860s Utah. Although the image of polygamy tended to define Utah to outsiders from the mid-1850s until the end of the nineteenth century, plural marriage arrangements were not necessarily the predominant form of family life in the region or even among faithful Latter-day Saints. The exact percentages of households wherein polygamy was practiced have been very difficult to establish, but there is general agreement that those who entered into this arrangement were a numerical minority within Utah. At the low end of estimates based on population studies, about 5 percent of married Mormon men and about 12 percent of married Mormon women were involved in polygamous marriage relationships.[23]

One of the early population estimates of polygamy in nineteenth-century Utah, conducted by Stanley Ivins in the 1950s, concluded that about 15 percent of Mormon families in Utah overall were polygamous.[24] More recent estimates, such as those made by prominent historian D. Michael Quinn, place the figure higher, indicating that as many as 20 to 40 percent of married Mormon males and 30 to 55 percent of married Mormon females entered into polygamous relationships during the latter half of the nineteenth century in Utah.[25] Whatever the actual figures, we can conclude that by entering into a church-sanctioned plural marriage relationship, the Murdochs were not the typical family, even in heavily LDS Wasatch County, despite the fact that there was substantial encouragement and pressure for Latter-day Saints of that era to enter into plurality.[26]

Polygamy was practiced at a much higher rate by those Mormon men who were in leadership positions, as was John Murdoch, than among rank-and-file members, because the practice was viewed as an essential step of religious faith and devotion, and men who rejected the practice were not as likely to be given significant ecclesiastical responsibilities. From 1845 to 1888, only a small minority (31.8 percent) of men who were called to be general authorities of the church were monogamous at the time of their appointment.[27] For several decades during the nineteenth century there was a clear understanding that men in high ecclesiastical positions were expected to practice "the principle." Apostle and future church president Wilford Woodruff stated in 1875, "We have many bishops and elders who have but one wife. They are abundantly qualified to enter the higher law and take more, but their wives will not let them. Any man who permits a woman to lead him and bind him down is but little account in the church and Kingdom of God."[28] Church president John Taylor published a revelation in 1882 that mandated all priesthood officers of the church to "conform to my law" of polygamy.[29] Two years later, in 1884, the First Presidency of the church stated that men in high-ranking positions in the church who had not entered into polygamy should resign from their ecclesiastical offices.[30]

In many polygamous families, each wife would maintain her own separate dwelling, and the husband would move from household to household on a presumably agreeable basis. The Murdoch household was an exception to this arrangement, as the entire family generally lived together under one roof. Other contrasts between John Murdoch's marriages and other plural marriages of that era are also worth noting. Like John Murdoch, most men who entered into polygamous marriages had only two wives, whereas about 21 percent of polygamous men married three, about 7 percent married four, and fewer than 6 percent married five or more women.[31]

Most men who had large numbers of wives (for example, five or more) were members of the church hierarchy, at either the general or local and regional levels. Although having one or two plural wives was generally considered to meet the letter of the law with respect to polygamy, there was an understanding at that time that one's glory or station in the hereafter would be higher by adding larger numbers of wives to his family, which would explain why Joseph Smith, Brigham Young, Heber C. Kimball, George Q. Cannon, and many other members of the First Presidency had such a large number of plural wives—*scores* in some cases. Most polygamous men were only slightly older than their first wife, but significantly older than their second wife. Men who took second wives were generally in their thirties, whereas the new wife was generally in her late teens.[32] By contrast, John Murdoch was nearly forty-two and Isabella Crawford was twenty-six years of age at the time of their marriage, another exception to the norms of their time and place.

In modern times, the struggles of what are now termed "blended" families are well known, with step-parents having to negotiate an appropriate parental role with their step-children, even as they adjust to their own complex new marriage relationship. The type of blending that would have been required of polygamous families in nineteenth century Utah was equally complex, and it was compounded by the fact that virtually every element of American society except for "true believer" Latter-day Saints looked down on this arrangement, viewing it as a moral affront, and the federal government was continually trying to stamp out the institution. Although many polygamous families coexisted in harmony, the difficulties encountered among polygamous households were extraordinarily challenging in many cases. In some situations, outright domestic warfare erupted, with some wives and children feeling slighted or treated unfairly in comparison with more favored mothers and children within the family. In other cases, the wives in polygamous households publicly put on a brave face and supported the institution while privately expressing feelings ranging from loneliness to frustration to despair.[33] At one point, Brigham Young became so exasperated with the many complaints he received from women in polygamous marriages in which he was called upon to assist in resolving the domestic conflict that he promised in 1856—at the height of the Mormon Reformation—that he would provide any disaffected wife with a divorce and passage out of the territory within two weeks at no cost. The unexpected number of women who rushed to take advantage of his offer caused him to reconsider and modify this promise.[34]

A Most Harmonious Group

Although the Murdoch family must have experienced particular challenges associated with having two related households living together in a polygamous arrangement, the congeniality and affection shared by John, Ann, and Isabella, as well as their children, is legendary in family lore, and it was widely known also within their community. Even though we must recognize that writings and recollections of those individuals and their descendants may have a tendency to accentuate the positive and downplay the unsavory (a Murdoch family trait in general), there is a great consistency in written family records and oral traditions in describing John Murdoch and his two wives, as well as their family in general, as a most harmonious group. One of Ann's daughters said of them, "The two wives were true wives and true and loving mothers, sharing the burdens of rearing their families together. As I remember, at one time one child had the privilege of nursing both mothers, and did not know which was his own mother."[35] One of Isabella's daughters later recalled in verse: We children never had a quarrel, we were never known to fight. Our mothers wise would stories tell, and soon set things aright... The babies came close together. Kate and Tom like twins seemed to be. They both did nurse at mother's breast, and prayed at Muzz's [Ann's] knee.[36]

One mild exception to the near-unanimous positive descriptions of the Murdochs' polygamous arrangement has been found. In an account of the life story of Isabella's daughter Catherine Campbell Murdoch Hicken, which was written by her granddaughter Rodello Hicken Hunter Calkins in 1979, the writer stated:

> When asked what she thought of polygamy, she would say that their own family was always close and loving, and the names Mother and Muz were always spoken in the same breath; but then she would shake her head and say, "But I'm glad that's in the past; polygamy is not for me!" Once in a while, usually after a visit with her half-sisters, she would shake her head and murmur, "Being a child of the second wife is always down on the stick, no matter how it's whittled!" or "To my way of thinking, it was the first wife who was the 'tony' one." And after the Manifesto, her feeling about the differences in plural wives strengthened, but they were never strong enough nor bitter enough to lessen her brother-sister relationships."[37]

After a thorough examination of everything that has been written, it is no stretch to say that Isabella and Ann were "sister-wives" in the best sense of the term, and they were known for their friendship, courtesy, affection, and respect for each other. One of the Murdoch clan later recalled of them:

> I remember when I was visiting my grandmother Duke when I was very young in Heber City, I saw two darling little ladies arm-in-arm coming up the walk smiling. They were both dressed in black with long full skirts, black silk blouses with high necks over the shoulders, and small black bonnets with brims on them, tied under their chins in a bow. They patted my head and said, "You must be Nettie's little blonde girl." They were so noble and quaint I have never forgotten them.[38]

Isabella's relationship with both John and Ann was so close that in their old age, the three often sat together holding hands, and following the death of the other two, family traditions hold that Isabella said to a daughter, "I am not sure which one I want to see first when I die—John or Muzz (Ann)." After the deaths of John and Ann, when Isabella was left alone, she told family members "if I could have had my choice of any man in the world, I would have still chosen John."

NOTES

1. From the 1850s through the 1880s, Brigham Young, his successor John Taylor, and other leading Mormon authorities taught in unequivocal terms on many occasions that polygamy or plural marriage, sanctioned by church leaders and blessed in temple unions, was absolutely essential for the highest level of exaltation in heaven. For example, Brigham taught: "The only men who become Gods, even the Sons of God, are those who enter into polygamy. Others attain unto a glory and may even be permitted to come into the presence of the Father and the Son; but they cannot reign as kings in glory, because they had blessings offered unto them, and they refused to accept them" (*Journal of Discourses* 11:268–69, August 9, 1866).

2. Among the various historical sources documenting Joseph Smith's introduction of polygamy within the church, and his own personal practice of this principle, three of the best and most detailed comprehensive resources include Todd Compton, *In Sacred Loneliness: The Plural Wives of Joseph Smith* (Salt Lake City, UT: Signature Books, 1998); Linda King Newell and Valeen Tippetts Avery, *Mormon Enigma: Emma Hale Smith*, 2nd ed. (Urbana: University of Illinois Press, 1994); and Richard S. Van Wagoner, *Mormon Polygamy: A History*, 2nd ed. (Salt Lake City, UT: Signature Books, 1989).

3. History of the Church of Jesus Christ of Latter-day Saints, Vol. 5, 134–36. See also Richard S. Van Wagoner, *Sidney Rigdon: A Portrait of Religious Excess* (Salt Lake City, UT: Signature Books, 1994), 295–96.

4. Van Wagoner, *Mormon Polygamy*, 85.

5. Jennie Ann Larson, Information on Isabella Crawford Murdoch (document in author's possesion).

6. Van Wagoner, *Mormon Polygamy*, 90.

7. Gazetteer for Scotland, http://www.geo.ed.ac.uk/scotgaz/Help.html (5 October 2004); The National Library of Scotland, http://www.nls.uk/index.html (accessed June 19, 2005).

8. David Livingstone Visitor's Center, http://www.biggar-net.co.uk/livingstone/ (accessed June 17, 2005).

9. Larson, Information on Isabella Crawford Murdoch.

10. Frederick S. Buchanan, "The Ebb and Flow of Mormonism in Scotland, 1840–1900," *Brigham Young University Studies* 27 (1987): 27–52.

11. Frederick S. Buchanan, ed., *A Good Time Coming: Mormon Letters to Scotland* (Salt Lake City: University of Utah Press, 1988), 11–12.

12. Larson, Information on Isabella Crawford Murdoch.

13. Annie Janett McMullin Rasband, Isabella Crawford Murdoch (document in author's possession).

14. Larson, Information on Isabella Crawford Murdoch.

15. "The Mill Girls," Lowell National Historic Park, National Park Service, U.S. Department of the Interior, http://www.nps.gov/lowe/millgirls.htm (accessed June 19, 2005).

16. *Murdoch Messenger*, 3rd edition, October, 1977.

17. "Church History Library," Church of Jesus Christ of Latter-day Saints, http://www.lds.org/churchhistory/library/ (accessed October 9, 2004). This site contains the most complete listing of individuals and companies in which Mormon pioneer emigrants traveled west to Utah from 1847 through 1868. The site states that it is an incomplete listing, because rosters have not been found for all companies, which is true in the case of Isabella Crawford and her traveling companions, whose names to not appear on any of these lists.

18. Larson, Information on Isabella Crawford Murdoch.

19. Rasband, Isabella Crawford Murdoch.

20. John Murray Nicol, ed., *The James and Mary Murray Murdoch Family History* (Provo, UT: James and Mary Murray Murdoch Family Organization, 1982), 229.

21. Ibid., 230.

22. Ibid.

23. Leonard J. Arrington and Davis Bitton, *The Mormon Experience: A History of the Latter-day Saints* (New York: Alfred A. Knopf, 1979), 133–34; Leroy R. Hafen and

Ann W. Hafen, *Handcarts to Zion: The Story of a Unique Western Migration, 1856–1860* (Lincoln: University of Nebraska Press, 1960), 92; Wallace Stegner, *The Gathering of Zion: The Story of the Mormon Trail* (New York: McGraw-Hill, 1964), 199.

24. Stanley S. Ivins, "Notes on Mormon Polygamy," *Western Humanities Review* 10 (Summer 1956), 229–39.

25. D. Michael Quinn, *The Mormon Hierarchy: Extensions of Power* (Salt Lake City, UT: Signature Books, 1997), 180, 329.

26. Encouragement or pressure on men to enter into polygamy ranged from the subtle to the pointed. Heber C. Kimball's humorous statement "a man who has but one wife, and is inclined to that doctrine, soons begins to wither and dry up, while a man who goes into plurality looks fresh, young, and sprightly" (*Journal of Discourses* 3, April 6, 1856, 291) is an example of encouragement in the subtle form. Brigham Young's more blunt statement in the *Deseret News* of November 14, 1855, "if you deny the plurality of wives and continue to do so, I promise you that you will be damned," is but one among many examples of the more overt type of pressure that Mormons of the mid to late nineteenth century received to enter into the principle.

27. Quinn, *Mormon Hierarchy: Extensions of Power,* 180.

28. Mathias F. Cowley, *Wilford Woodruff* (Salt Lake City, UT: G. Q. Cannon and Sons, 1909), 490.

29. John Taylor's revelation was never included in the English language version of the LDS scripture *Doctrine and Covenants*, because it did not have a new revision until after the church officially disavowed polygamy. However, the revelation did appear in five other editions of *Doctrine and Covenants* that were published between 1882 and 1889 in three different languages, including Swedish, German, and Danish. See Quinn, *The Mormon Hierarchy: Extensions of Power,* 181–82.

30. Ibid., 182.

31. Van Wagoner, *Mormon Polygamy*, 91.

32. Ibid., 91.

33. Ibid., 98–102.

34. Will Bagley, *Blood of the Prophets* (Norman: University of Oklahoma Press, 2002), 40.

35. Nicol, *Family History*, 230.

36. Ibid., 222.

37. Ibid., 479.

38. Ibid., 254.

8

FAMILY, SHEEP, AND WAR

In many parts of Utah, residents were able to move from subsistence farming as the population grew; however, the harsh mountain climate in Wasatch County made raising crops always a gamble. This focus on survival did not encourage the development of industry; everyone had to be a farmer first.

— JESSIE L. EMBRY, *A History of Wasatch County*

We live in an area that we have largely inherited. Some of the familiar things that surround us are of our own making, but largely they are things our fathers did for us. We are heirs of wonderful treasures from the past. But how few of us open our eyes to see those treasures. What a different place this would be if our senses were trained to hear the whisperings of the past and hear how those now gone yearned for this day in which we bear sway.

— J. SYLVAN RASBAND, GLEN M. HATCH, AND WELBY W. YOUNG, Foreword to
How Beautiful Upon the Mountains: A Centennial History of Wasatch County

FAMILY MAN

After John Murdoch's marriage to Isabella Crawford in 1862, the newly blended Murdoch family consisted of John, Ann, Isabella, and Ann's five surviving children. From that time until 1865, the family lived in the one-story log home in Heber that John had built. This structure was small by modern standards, but each of the two wives had her own section of the ranch-style rectangular structure. Drawings and notes preserved in Murdoch family records provide a map of this home.[1] Isabella's area was on the left side looking from the front. She gave birth to her first two children there: Margaret Ann, born May 19, 1863, nine months and ten days after her marriage to John; and Catherine Campbell, born November 15, 1864. Ann's area was on the right side of the home, and she gave birth to three more children there: John Murray was born January 4, 1863, and he died one month later. Isabella Lovina was born April 21, 1864, and John William, also born April 21, 1864, died four months later.

With the deaths of two more infant children, John and Ann had now buried four children during infancy or early childhood, and together they had six surviving children. The infant and child mortality rate in pioneer-era Utah, like that in the rest of nineteenth-century America, was shockingly high. Dietary practices of the day contributed to the scourge (feeding meat and other difficult-to-digest foods to young children), as did unclean drinking water and the abundance of bacterial- and viral-based diseases for which the causes and cures were then unknown: diphtheria, malaria, cholera, smallpox, typhoid, and the ever-present intestinal afflictions (usually referred to as dysentery or bilious fever). Physicians were scarce in frontier areas, more expensive than most poor families could afford, and, in many cases, not particularly helpful. Frontier families of that era relied heavily on plant and herbal remedies to cure various ailments, and the women tended to be more knowledgeable than the men on this subject.[2] Because the Book of Mormon and other Latter-day Saint scriptures also endorsed the use of herbs for healing, Ann and Isabella Murdoch likely had some knowledge regarding herbal remedies and their use, and they would have used these treatments as an adjunct to prayer and priesthood blessings to promote healing.

In 1865 the Murdoch family moved to a new home, a somewhat larger rectangular log structure that John built at the west end of Heber City. This home was at the same location where they later had a large frame home built in 1880, at 251 North 400 West. The family lived in this log structure for several years, and nine more children were born there—four to Isabella (James Crawford, Brigham, Robert, and John Murray) and five to Ann (Thomas Todd, Lucy Veronica, Joseph A., David Steele, and Millicent Sophia). At some point during the mid-1860s, probably during the winter of 1866–67, John was called to leave his family and serve a short-term church mission in Summit and Morgan counties.[3] It has not been recorded what his specific assignment was on this brief missionary assignment, but given that he was the leader of the high priest's group in the Heber area and had significant experience at this point serving in leadership positions, he likely assisted in providing leadership and helping to build the branches of the church in those areas. He may also have assisted in the development of the sheep industry in those communities.

John and Ann lost two more children during the 1870s, while they were still living in the log home in west Heber. Isabella Lovina died in 1870 at age six, and Lucy Veronica died in 1873 at age five, bringing the total of their children deceased during childhood to six. No details remain regarding the specific causes of these deaths, which are probably best attributed to the myriad of diseases and maladies that were common at that time. In analyzing the conditions of that era and the extremely high infant and child mortality rates that resulted, one writer has stated, "In light of modern medical science, it is not surprising that infant mortality was shockingly high, but that any child lived to maturity."[4] Whether or not this statement is an exaggeration, the Murdochs' grim experience with the death of their infants and young children brings home the painful reality of the fleeting nature of life in nineteenth-century America. The survival rate of John and Ann's children—only nine of fifteen lived to adulthood—was only 60 percent. And given that three more of his children died as adults while he was still living (two of his children with Isabella and one of his children with Ann), John ended up burying nine of his twenty-two children, a whopping 41 percent.

The last of the Murdoch children, Isabella Crawford, was born to Isabella on January 8, 1876. She lived to reach adulthood, as did all of John and Isabella's seven children. In 1874, when John and Ann's last child was born, John was fifty-three and Ann was nearly forty-five. Two years later, when Isabella's last child was born, she was nearly forty years old and John was fifty-five. With the conclusion of the childbearing years in 1876, John had fathered a total of twenty-two children with his two wives. Considering Ann's children who had died previously, the Murdoch family consisted of nineteen individuals at this point in time: John, Ann, Isabella, and the sixteen surviving children.

Because of the twenty-four-year time difference between John's oldest living child (Mary Murray) and his youngest (Isabella Crawford), the older children had reached adulthood by the time Ann and Isabella's childbearing days were completed. By 1876, the year Isabella was born, three of John's children were already married: Mary was wed to James Duke in 1868, Ann married William Giles in 1871, and Janett married Henry McMullin in 1875. These marriages were all to the children of fellow early Wasatch County settlers who had helped establish the Heber area along with the Murdochs. Jacobina, the oldest child still living at home, was now sixteen years of age, and Margaret was now thirteen years old. These two girls likely played an important role in helping to run the Murdoch household, and likely assisted in caring for their ten younger siblings and half-siblings.

A recollection of Ann's courtship with William Giles, written by one of the other Murdoch children, sheds some light on the importance of proximity and community in establishing kinship patterns and new families during that era and also illustrates some of the social pastimes in which the young people engaged:

In our childhood home days there came a family from Notingham [Nottingham] England, in 1862, and settled across the street from our residence. Their names were Thomas and Mariah Kirkham Giles and their children were Elizabeth, George M., and William M. Giles. William became one of our intimate childhood friends. As we grew older we were all in our social crowd together, all joined in social pastimes, going to school and plays, meetings and dances and roaming over the green fields and gathering the wild berries and joining in all social life of the young folks together. Then as Ann grew older William selected her for his best girl. Their parents lived just one block apart so they, Wm. and Ann, became very well acquainted with each other and as young people took a large part in building up this western country. She was the daughter of a farmer, he the son of a farmer so they were well suited for each other. William was an Indian war man and when as a young man he was called to go to guard the Indian areas his girl lover would ask the Heavenly Father to protect William Giles and to spare his life so he could return to her, very much to the amusement of the family.[5]

In 1880, the family moved out of the 1865 log home and into a new, large, and modern frame home at 161 West 400 North in Heber. This structure still stands, and it would likely have been one of the nicer homes in town in 1880, pointing to evidence of John's increasing prosperity in his business dealings.

As the Murdoch family grew and matured in the 1870s and later, the children were involved in many aspects of the daily life and commerce of the family. Out of necessity they would have been needed to assist both in running the household and in various domestic tasks, including the home industries that were encouraged at that time to help establish economic self-sufficiency in Utah. Sarah later recalled, "We had to carry our water from a little spring down in the field... in winter father would bring a big log and put it in the fireplace to keep us warm and give us light to read by. It was then that he taught me to knit stockings by firelight."[6] The older children, particularly the boys, were trained to assist in some aspects of managing the sheep ranch and in the self-sufficiency farming that virtually all families in the valley practiced. Because John built a basic ranch home at his property a few miles north of Heber where he worked the sheep, some of the older children likely lived there and helped during the periods when the sheep were not winter grazing to the south. Summers would have involved assisting with the irrigation of the garden crops, caring for the animals, and playing outside in the creeks and fields during the long warm days. As the boys got older, several of them enjoyed playing baseball during the summer months, a very popular activity in Heber by the late 1800s and early 1900s. The lengthy winters provided large amounts of snow and at times excessively frigid cold. A good portion of the winter months were spent indoors trying to stay warm, but there were always chores needing to be done outdoors, and the snowfall would have provided some recreational diversion for the children at times, including the occasional sleigh ride.

Given that John had many children and that he was innately bright and valued learning, he had a particular interest in the development of the schools in the community, and he strongly emphasized learning—both religious and secular—to his children. In fact, in the obituary that appeared in the *Wasatch Wave* on May 13, 1910, one week after his death, John was credited with being instrumental in organizing the first school in Wasatch County. The Murdoch children attended schools in various locations and configurations as the community grew and as the educational system in Wasatch County became more established. Some of the children became excellent students.

Although the territorial legislature passed an act in 1867 that allowed communities to provide free schools through taxation with the majority vote of taxpayers, the fact that the county was so new and still in the settlement phase slowed development for a period of time, and prior to the 1880s, the schools in the Heber area were generally small, serving only a limited number of children. The first school in Heber, which would have been attended by the older Murdoch children, was located in a one-room log structure at the corner of 300 North and 200 West that also served as a church building. This structure was plagued by a leaky roof, and it was so cold in the winter that groups of children took turns studying by the fire and then reciting to the teacher away from the fire.[7] Other school structures followed, including one at 200 North and 300 East, and then another at 200 West and 300 South (the "Sleepy Hollow" school), only a short distance from the Murdoch home. Early schools that the children attended in the 1860s and 1870s were very basic, often the epitome of the "one room schoolhouse," meeting in homes, small log school houses, or other available buildings such as church structures or tithing offices, and with one teacher for a combined age group of pupils.[8]

By the time the younger children attended school in the 1880s, the school system was still rather primitive. It was not until the early 1890s that a larger school building with a more progressive curriculum was put into place at the new Central School on Main Street, headed by educator Henry Aird. By this point in time, the youngest of the Murdoch children, who were born in 1874 and 1876, would have been out of school, as the highest local educational attainment possible during this era was the completion of eighth grade.[9]

With the growth and enhancement of public education in Heber, there were some conflicts, primarily with respect to the connectedness or separation of the LDS Church and the running of the school system. During this era, attendance in some of the public schools diminished as members of non-LDS faiths began to establish private church-operated schools, which were attended not only by their children, but by numerous Mormon children as well. Given that John was absolutely devout in his religious observance, and that he was also strongly interested in education, it is not surprising that his name surfaces in one of the descriptions of the mild conflict that ensued, despite his notable genial disposition. Records from an LDS priesthood meeting that was held in the fall of 1884, in which the topic of Mormon church leaders sending their children to schools run by members of other faiths was discussed, provide a window into this dilemma. John Murdoch was quoted as saying, "A good faithful Mormon teacher would eventually turn out good faithful Latter-day Saints, while the other, the infidel, would turn out infidels." Although John's words from 1884 may sound harsh by modern standards, it is worth putting them in the context of the fact that John and many others made great sacrifices to immigrate to "Zion" with the goal of establishing a theocratic kingdom. John's words also seem less harsh when compared to those of Henry L. McMullin, who was quoted at this same meeting as stating that he "would rather have one of his children die than to go to a non-Mormon school."[10]

Recollections and journals regarding family relationships among the Murdochs during the 1860s and 1870s are sparse, but they provide some additional details to better understand the dynamics and culture of the family. Consistent with the record regarding the unusual harmony between John's wives, Ann and Isabella, all of the available records indicate that John's children retained memories of happy childhood experiences in their family, despite their hardships and the deaths of so many siblings. Without exception, the later autobiographical writings of the Murdoch children, as well as the recollections of the John Murdoch household that the children passed on to their own children, all indicate tender memories, pleasant activities, and a loving and harmonious family constellation, devoid of favoritism, jealousy, coercion, or any significant or long-lasting strife. One of the distinctive aspects of Murdoch family life was the affectionate nicknames that many in the family were given, a tradition that was brought from old Scotland, where such names were used to distinguish people with similar names. Ann was known as "Muzz," and Isabella was known as "Bella." Several of the children were known by their nicknames: Janett as "Net" or "Nettie," Jacobina as "Jake," Millicent as "Gentie," Margaret as "Mag," Catherine as "Kate," Robert as "Boot," John Murray Jr. as "Jock," and Isabella as "Tresa" or "Tressie."

Music was a favorite Murdoch family pastime, and John, Ann, and Isabella all apparently brought with them from Scotland a love for the Celtic and other Scottish music traditions. One of the children of Ann Murdoch Giles, the second oldest Murdoch child who lived to adulthood, recalled that her mother left a strong impression on her own children of her love for music that was cultivated in her childhood home, as well as the pleasant memories she retained from her childhood.

> As children at home, the girls enjoyed singing for their father and mother. Many pleasant times were spent during the long winter evenings in family singing. I remember mother playing the comb while we sat on the floor and sang in the evenings. My mother was very talented musically—she could play most any instrument and had a lovely singing voice. In fact, she used to sing in all the funerals in Wasatch County.[11]

The emphasis on music contributing to a harmonious environment in the Murdoch family home is also documented in several other family history sources. "Their lives were not completely channeled in their occupations, but were richly flavored with music and church activities and recreation."[12] One of the Murdoch grandchildren recalled of her mother Janett's childhood stories, "This family loved to sing, a trait which they passed on to their own families. They loved to gather round in the evenings and sing songs and listen to the stories told by their parents of their native land, of their lives and loved ones, and about crossing the ocean and the plains."[13] Thomas played the fiddle and sang, while Brigham played both the piano and guitar. David also played the violin. As young adults, Thomas and Brigham played together in a band at dances. One of Thomas's children later said of him, "no matter how tired he was, he always brought out his violin and stood in the door of his home in the summer or in the house in the winter and played beautiful music for us. He truly loved that violin."[14] It was apparently a mutual love for music that brought together John and Ann's last child, Millicent ("Gentie") with her future husband, Edward Teancum Murdoch: "Through their musical abilities and willingness to perform, Edward and Gentie were drawn together, and on December 9, 1891, they were married in Heber City.[15]

Although the Murdoch family was ordinary in many respects for the place and time in which they lived, it is no exaggeration to state that their devotion to their religion, coupled with their unusually harmonious family life within a polygamous household, made them quite extraordinary. Several family records have stated that the Murdoch children were raised by both Ann and Isabella, who each treated all of them with equal love and fairness. It might be easy for individuals outside of the family to dismiss such statements as lionized fables, but the frequency with which they appear—in the records of several of the children—is convincing. Perhaps one of the most striking statements to that effect comes from the history of Catherine Campbell Murdoch (Kate), John and Isabella's second child. As an adult, Kate and her children would treasure the visits they had from their "uncle Tom," John and Ann's eleventh child, who was two years younger than Kate. "She once said that she didn't know until she was a girl grown that Tom was a half-brother."[16]

THE SHEEP RANCH

John Murdoch's opportunity to leave Scotland and join the Saints in Zion came as a result of his expertise as a sheepherder. This expertise was hard-earned, honed during the long and lonely days of his youth, after he left his home to work as a shepherd to help support his family following his father's untimely death. Selected personally by Mormon Apostle and President of the British Mission Franklin D. Richards as one of two "Scottish shepherds" that had been requested by Brigham Young, John was poised to help Brigham develop the sheep industry in early Utah, as well as Brigham's own private herd. After arriving in Salt Lake City in September 1852, John met President Young and was surprised to learn that Brigham no longer had any need for his services. "Brigham Young gave us a very hearty welcome, and gave us many words of encouragement. Captain Smoot introduced us to Brigham as his two shepherds with our dogs, and gave me a very good recommend. Brother Brigham informed us that he had rented what few sheep he had left to his Brother Lorenzo for five years and would not need us at the present time for that purpose."[17] This set of circumstances caused John to scramble to find another way to earn a living, but his sheepherding skills ultimately proved to be the means for much of his life's work.

The sheep industry in Utah had a rather inauspicious start, but ultimately it grew into one of the larger and more powerful economic forces of the region in the second half of the nineteenth century and the first quarter of the twentieth century. Domesticated breeds of sheep used for commercial purposes are not native to North America; they evolved from Asian stock, which were later introduced to Europe, and then brought to North America with European immigrants. The first sheep in Utah came westward in rather small numbers with the Mormon pioneers.[18] Most of these few animals would have been brought from the midwest, as there were few or no sheep to be obtained along the overland trail at the time the Saints made their emigration.

Mountain man Jim Bridger began to build a flock of sheep of New Mexican origin at his fort in present-day southwestern Wyoming in 1846 and 1847, and it is possible that some of these animals were traded to the first waves of Mormon pioneers bound for the valley of the Great Salt Lake in 1847 and 1848.[19] The 1850 census listed only 3,262 sheep in the entire Utah territory, and the industry was quite small at that time in comparison with the cattle industry. Gradually, the numbers of sheep within the territory increased, along with the economic power of the industry. Some of the initial growth in numbers of sheep occurred through natural increases in flocks, and some through acquisitions of livestock as larger herds were driven through Utah to destinations westward. In 1850 Santa Fe attorney William Z. Angey brought a large herd through Utah along the Old Spanish Trail, coming through Price Creek, Spanish Fork Canyon, Utah Lake, and the Mormon settlement at Provo on his way to San Francisco. Another early entrepreneur to drive large numbers of sheep through Utah headed for California was Richens Lacy Wooten, who is described as a "mountain man, fur trapper, and frontier raconteur."[20] Wooten brought a herd of over nine thousand sheep through Utah along the old Spanish trail in 1852 and was that summer entertained by Brigham Young, who certainly would have inquired of Wooten regarding the prospects of the sheep industry in Utah. It is a given that some of these two large herds remained in Utah, through either straying or being traded.

A common problem for sheep drovers who were bringing their herds long distances overland was "footsore stock," and one of the solutions was the development of a small industry in communities along the droving trails, where lame stock could be bought cheaply and then sold or traded for a profit after they healed. An early 1850s diary of one drover's experience recorded that while near American Fork, Utah, his group was approached by "the Mormons, numbers of whom are in camp, offering to barter for worn-out sheep, groceries, or anything."[21] The gradual growth of the sheep industry in Utah during this period is evident by the increase in the number of sheep in the 1860 census, which was listed at over thirty-seven thousand, an increase of more than thirty-four thousand over the 1850 census.[22]

By the time John Murdoch and his family moved to the Upper Provo valley in 1860, the timing and conditions were right for him to go back to his knowledge of sheepherding to earn his living, and to help establish the industry in the Heber area. He had the skills and foresight required for the venture, and there was an increasing need for centralized or collective expertise to assist the growing numbers of families in the valley to manage the myriad of challenges they faced in caring for their sheep and making their business profitable. As a history of Wasatch County has recorded of John Murdoch, referring to his contributions within the county, "... pioneered co-operative herding. Those who had sheep banded them together in the co-op herd and Mr. Murdoch took charge of them on range-lands in the summer and on southern ranches in the winter. The venture provided very successful, and families who before had been unable to care for sheep now found it possible to own a herd."[23]

The cooperative nature of this sheep venture was consistent with other similar ventures among the Latter-day Saints in Utah in the 1850s through the 1870s, and it differed substantially from how the sheep industry emerged in surrounding western states such as Colorado and New Mexico, which were much more oriented toward individual ownership and responsibility. "[Utah's] livestock industry had been shaped by the Mormon penchant for cooperation and group life. People lived in towns, farmed small farms, and ran a few cows and sheep. These animals were fed on the farm or grazed on town lands or were part of co-op herds."[24] The sheep cooperative that John Murdoch organized and led followed the basic principles of cooperative ventures from that time and place. The herder gave "as rental to each member a specified number of pounds (usually eight) of wool and twelve head of lambs per hundred head of mixed sheep—ewes, wethers, and lambs—in proportion to each member's share in the cooperative... the old stock in the flocks had to be kept in good condition in case any particular owner desired to sell out."[25]

During the summer months the aggregated herds grazed in the fields north of Heber or in the nearby meadows and forests of the Wasatch Mountains, which provided some of the best grazing lands in the west. In the winter months the herd would be taken to high desert areas to the south—possibly near Utah Lake or in the Sanpete region, where there was less snow and the sheep were well adapted to graze on the tough woody plants that thrived in those areas. Sheep provided these pioneers with many essentials. They were a principal source of meat and a means of exchange or barter for goods and services. To a lesser extent, sheep provided a means for tallow (for candles) and milk for drinking, cooking, and making cheese.

Most importantly, sheep served as the principal material for making fiber for clothing, blankets, and rugs at a time when cotton had to be shipped from long distances and was difficult to obtain in the isolated intermountain west prior to the region being connected to the rest of the nation by rail. Brigham Young's vision of a self-sufficient Zion helped to fuel his support of establishing woolen mills throughout Utah, which helped to increase the demand for wool as well as the markets for wool products. The first large factory in Utah was the Provo Woolen Mills, completed in 1872, the product of a business venture headed by Brigham Young, Abraham O. Smoot, and other leading businessmen of the region as the Timpanogos Manufacturing Association. The four-building factory complex was built on a site along the Provo River, so that both water and power for the mill would be available for the plant. Only a few miles from Heber, the Provo Woolen Mills undoubtedly helped to expand John Murdoch's business and served as a processing center for some or much of the wool from his herds.

In addition to the emphasis on community-based cooperative sheep organizations during the 1850s and 1860s, another unique aspect of the Utah sheep industry during this period of time was the "church flock." The tithing system in place at that time required that one out of every ten lambs be assigned to the church. The bishop in charge of each ward had the responsibility to ensure that the church flock was placed with a shepherd within the community for care. In the case of Heber City during this period, John Murdoch would have been the supervising shepherd, whereas the bishop would have been Joseph Stacy Murdock until 1867, and then Abram Hatch for many years thereafter. The increases in the church flock were used to provide for the care of the poor and to assist new immigrants in getting a start in the area to which they were assigned, an arrangement that required payment at a later time. Because church flock sheep were tended side by side with sheep from private flocks, a system of branding was developed. The original brand used for church flock sheep looked somewhat like a flying cross, with barbed hooks on the four points that ended the lines of the cross, but this brand was later modified into a simple cross.[26] Because John Murdoch was the cooperative shepherd, he would have been involved in working with the two bishops in carrying out the church flock arrangement. Because he lived in close proximity to

Bishop Murdock and then Bishop Hatch, and he himself was a member of the local church hierarchy as the presiding high priest for the area, it is likely that John's ecclesiastical, community, and business lines were quite blended in carrying out his responsibilities for the church flock.

Even though John Murdoch was known for his excellent care of the sheep flocks and for providing individual owners with a consistently good return, the highly successful Wasatch Sheep Cooperative eventually came to an end. As time passed, some of the sheep owners developed larger individual herds and became interested in managing their own flocks full-time on their own rather than in a co-op arrangement. Some of the first sheep owners to develop larger individual flocks in the Heber area included the Jacob brothers, the Lindsay brothers, Jessop Thomas, and the Murdock (no relation to John), Clyde, Clotworthy, Colman, Austin, Smith, and Fitzgerald families.[27] The sheep industry in Wasatch County continued to grow. At one point years later, after Utah was linked to the rest of the nation by railroad, "it was said that there were more milk fed lambs shipped out of Heber City than from any other point in the United States,"[28] which caused a Professor Caine from the Utah State Agricultural College in Logan to state in 1913, three years after John Murdoch's death: "When people speak of sheep, that means Heber."[29]

After the co-op was disbanded, John maintained his own flocks and worked hard to expand them as a means for caring for his growing family. He obtained a large parcel of land about six miles north of Heber and built a sheep ranch there. Later, he built another home in which some family members lived, especially those who were helping with the sheep ranch. John's work in sheep ranching was now an individual and family business, but it followed the same general pattern as during the co-op years. The sheep were grazed in the nearby Wasatch Mountains or at the Murdoch Sheep Ranch during the summer months and were taken south to ranch and graze during the winter months. Shearing time was in the spring and early summer, and the wool was either used locally or transported to other areas within the close-by region, especially Salt Lake City. The sheep tended to reach their best weight during the mid- to late-summer months, after grazing in the rich Wasatch forest regions, which led to the peak time for sending them to market. John was known for his shepherding skills and his general knowledge and skill in caring for livestock. He was credited with introducing to the region "sheep dip," a practice of immersing sheep in vats of disinfectant-infused water to help reduce and eliminate the common problems of scabbing, ticks, and other parasites. In the December 21, 1906, issue of the *Wasatch Wave* an article on "the quiet, reserved, unassuming patriarch" John Murdoch reported, "it was he who built the first dipping vat and introduced that system of treating scab which has now driven that disease from our state." It was also noted that he was well known for taking sheep that were in "poor and scabby condition" into the co-op and in a short time having them vital and healthy.

As the years passed after the Murdochs moved to Wasatch County in 1860 and John founded the first sheep cooperative, the industry grew. The county and other areas of the region proved to have an excellent climate and conditions for sheep production. The Wasatch and Uintah mountains were superb sources for forage during the summer months, and the otherwise overlooked arid desert regions to the south and west were excellent places to ranch sheep during the winter months, because sheep could get their necessary water from snow if required, and they took quite well to the desert brush for feed.[30] As the industry grew, economies of entire counties—including Wasatch County—were centered on sheep production.[31]

The sheep ranching business provided a good living for men like John Murdoch and their families, and some enterprising and driven Utah men—such as John H. Seely of the Sanpete region—accumulated great wealth in the industry. There was a continual emphasis on improving the available breeds to increase production and profits. While the initial sheep in the area were from midwestern and eastern stock, as new introductions occurred, the most common breeds in central Utah during the mid-nineteenth century became Merinos and Rambouillets. Despite some economic downturns in the sheep industry later in the nineteenth and early twentieth centuries because of public image problems (sheep were often looked down on by cattlemen and were incorrectly blamed for introducing a variety of diseases to other animals) and overgrazing of forest lands, the industry had an enormous impact on the economy of Utah, and it dwarfed the cattle industry in terms of sheer numbers and economic muscle for a good part of a seventy-five-year period.

Although no specific records and only a few recollections regarding how John Murdoch earned his livelihood have survived, it is generally understood that his primary occupation after moving to the Heber area in 1860 was his sheep ranching business. Like his fellow pioneers, he would have supplemented this work with a wide variety of self-sufficiency activities, including raising crops, keeping a few cows for milk and cattle for beef, and buying and selling goods and services for barter or cash. After several years of tending his flocks, John lost his sheep through an unfortunate incident. The exact year of this event has never been pinpointed, but the circumstances are documented in Murdoch family histories:

One winter John went south with his sheep, intending to winter them as usual. It was an extra hard winter, and his health failed him. Therefore he leased his sheep to a man who lived nearby and returned home where he could receive the proper care. The man either lost or sold the sheep, but John never saw them again nor did he receive anything for them. This was very unfortunate, as he had spent years in building up the herd. Inasmuch as the man had no other property, John merely dropped the matter.[32]

Whether this incident was the end of John Murdoch's sheep ranching business, or whether he again built the flock up, is unknown. The latter scenario seems likely, as John would have had to continue to make a living and had the experience and resources to do it in the thriving sheep industry, but we can only conjecture. That John never personally left a record of this incident and that it is scarcely mentioned in the scores of Murdoch family histories and recollections that have been handed down suggests a remarkable lack of animosity from John and his descendants regarding his loss. Perhaps we could attribute the lack of vindictiveness to John's generally charitable and optimistic nature. Alternatively, given the enormous personal sacrifices and losses he had already endured during his lifetime, the loss of his flock may have seemed trivial by comparison.

CAPTAIN IN UTAH'S BLACK HAWK WAR

During the early to mid 1860s, Utah was far removed from the American Civil War that occupied much of the nation and caused enormous devastation in the southern and mid-Atlantic states. Because the Mormons were still in a pattern of conflict with the federal government, leaders of the church did not encourage any support of the Union effort in the Civil War, and the massive diversion of energy and resources that the war required actually diverted some of the federal attention away from Utah for a time. Brigham Young held pro-Constitution views, but he also saw the conflict between the states in apocalyptic terms, believing that the carnage it was costing the nation was a result of the wrath of God, and that the bloody civil war would usher in a new era:

> Brigham tended to view the war as divine retribution upon a nation that had allowed the Saints to be persecuted and driven out without extending a hand to protect them. He saw the bloodiness of the conflict as the possible beginning of a national dissolution that would precede the establishment of God's Kingdom on earth."[33]

These views of their prophet led the Saints to not side with either the Union or the Confederacy. Instead they focused on building the kingdom through trying to establish economic self-sufficiency, settling new areas of the territory, and continuing to spread the gospel and invite new converts from Europe to join them in Zion.

Ulysses S. Grant and Robert E. Lee met in the Appomattox courthouse in Virginia on April 9, 1865, to negotiate the terms of the end of the Civil War. That same day in Manti, Utah, a small number of Northern Ute Indian delegates and local Mormon leaders met to try to establish a peaceful resolution to a local conflict that had been brewing for some time and was beginning to escalate out of control, precipitated by starving Indians killing and consuming some of the local settlers' cattle. When one of the Mormon delegates—who was apparently both highly irritated as well as highly intoxicated—lost his temper and pulled a young Ute chieftain from his horse, the insulted Indian delegation abruptly left, promising retaliation.[34] The failure of this peace process and the immediate increase in hostilities marked the beginning of Utah's "Black Hawk War," the longest, bloodiest, and most damaging conflict between Utah's white settlers and Indians.

As the conflict escalated into what was considered an all-out war, the federal government refused repeated requests from the Utah territorial delegation for military assistance. Thus, the responsibility of serving the military interests of Mormon settlers fell to the church militia, the Nauvoo Legion. The reasons for the repeated federal refusal to get involved in this conflict for several years were complex. Because federal resources were scarce and reconstruction of the southern states was a high priority at the conclusion of the Civil War, federal officials were likely not eager to commit military resources to what they viewed as an isolated regional conflict far from the nation's population centers. More importantly, the continuing tension between the leaders of the church and the federal government fueled continuing national resentment toward Utah, and the denial of federal support may have been a form of punishment. Given that many federal officials were outraged over the Mormons having developed separate treaties with the Indians, insisting on political sovereignty, and trying to foster the understanding that the "Big Chief" was in Salt Lake City rather than in Washington, some federal Indian agents in the region possibly saw the difficulties the Mormon settlers were now in as their just deserts.[35]

The Ute Indians who participated in the guerilla warfare that marked this war were led by a charismatic and bright young Ute chief who had been at the failed peace council in Manti in April 1865. He was called

Black Hawk by the Mormons, having been given the name by Brigham Young a few years previously and also recognized as a chief by the church president. Among his own people, Black Hawk was known as Antonguer or Antonga. He had been a witness to the decline of his people's fortunes stemming from the encroachment of the white population in the region, and he was outraged at the result. Having been a witness as a young man to some particularly grisly interactions between the Mormon settlers and his people (he had witnessed the decapitation of the frozen bodies of several of his companions who had been killed by the militia for stealing cattle in 1849), Black Hawk was indignant and threatened to battle to the end to stave off what he saw as the genocide of his people.

Although the incident at Manti regarding the stolen cattle may have precipitated the formal initiation of the Black Hawk War, the roots of this conflict were much more complex and long standing. Most historians have viewed the conflict as the inevitable result of the stresses that white expansion in the Utah territory brought upon the Indians in the form of altering the environment that had sustained them for generations: encroaching on their traditional subsistence patterns, and diminishing their population through the introduction of diseases that were formerly unknown to the native population—smallpox, measles, and syphilis. As a result, the Utes were experiencing widespread starvation and the beginnings of cultural extinction. As the white population increased during the 1860s, plundering and begging by Indians in the region became a widespread problem, as was occurring in other regions of the west as white expansion raced forward. Efforts by white leaders to move Indians to reservation areas—such as the establishment of the Ute reservation under Abraham Lincoln's administration in 1861—tended to aggravate these problems. In fact, the raids led by Black Hawk and his followers were a rejection of the reservation system as well as a response to privations their people had suffered.[36] In many respects, this particular Indian war like so many before and after it was the inevitable result of the clash of cultures and lifestyles where no middle ground or appropriate negotiation was possible. In the view of most of the Indians, the only way to truly solve the problem was for the white settlers to leave the area, something that was simply not going to happen. In the eyes of most of the white settlers, the solution was for the Indians to either take up the ways of the white man in farming and building or be cordoned off in reservation lands. These options were equally repugnant to most Indians.

At the onset of the war, it had been about eight years since John Murdoch's previous service in the militia, when he supervised a group of men in guarding and fortifying Echo Canyon against the movement of Johnston's army into the Salt Lake valley during the winter of 1857–58. John was now in his mid-forties, had two wives and several children to support, and was responsible for managing the sheep cooperative in Wasatch County, where he also had civic responsibilities as county treasurer. Despite these challenges, he accepted the assignment of militia service in this new conflict. Family records and recollections on this aspect of his life are surprisingly brief. "When the Blackhawk Indian War first broke out, John was made a captain in the infantry in the Utah Militia. There were fifty men under his jurisdiction. This lasted almost two years, and he did his share in bringing peace once more to the land."[37]

The two major histories of Wasatch County shed additional light on the scope of the Black Hawk War in that locale, as well as John Murdoch's role in it. Despite the fact that most of the direct conflict in the Black Hawk War occurred some distance south of Wasatch County (in the Sanpete valley, Ephraim, Manti, and southern Utah), Wasatch County was close enough to these regions and isolated enough from the larger population in Salt Lake City to make it a potentially vulnerable target. This concern was heightened by the fact that the nearby Strawberry valley, a traditional Indian hunting ground, had been altered by Mormon settlements, ruining it for the traditional sustenance hunting activities of the Utes. Livestock raids by the Indian warriors occurred in Wasatch County in 1866 and 1867. After one particularly large raid that resulted in the loss of hundreds of sheep and cattle, the entire population of Wallsburg was temporarily moved into homes in Heber, and farmers traveled back and forth to their fields for work for a period of time.[38] The settlement of Midway was also created at this time, as the result of a compromise between the residents of two regions in the outlying Snake Creek area needing to band together into a fort for mutual protection during the raids. Neither of the two groups wanted to move to the site of the other group, so they compromised by creating a fort at Midway—so named because it was halfway between the two communities—and the residents guarded the locked fort at night to prevent raids.[39] The hostilities in the Wasatch County region ceased in late 1867, when a band of Unita-ats led by Tabby-To-Kwana informed the Mormon settlers that they wanted peace. A delegation of Indians was invited to Heber, where John Murdoch presided over a feast in celebration of the peace.[40]

Based on family traditions it is understood that the militia under John Murdoch's leadership primarily served the role of being a "home guard," as they attempted to keep the area secure. Based on anecdotes and formal reports from militia members in other regions during the conflict, we can safely assume that John Murdoch and his men made regular excursions in the general Wasatch County area to observe for signs of encroaching bands of warriors; that they regularly policed the streets of the local settlements; and that they drilled, gathered intelligence, and responded to requests from the general militia commanders. To the best of our knowledge, no direct military confrontation occurred between John Murdoch's group of militiamen and Black Hawk's warriors.

Black Hawk was joined by militants from his own Ute tribe, and from the Southern Paiute and Navajo tribes as well, and accumulated a force of over one hundred men. There were no massed battles in this war. Rather, the battles in this war were primarily guerilla in nature, such as raids on farms and small communities, and similar retaliations on small bands of Indians. The temporary abandonment of at least twenty-five towns in central and southern Utah resulted from the raids, as did the deaths of at least seventy-five whites, both militia and civilians.[41] Many of Black Hawk's fellow militants were killed, at least as many as the number of whites who died. Historian John Alton Peterson has documented evidence of depredations on both sides in this conflict.[42] The peak years of violence were a period of a little more than two years, from 1865 through 1867, a time frame that coincides with the specific concern in Wasatch County. The conflict lessened somewhat after 1868 and actually ended in some areas at this time, but it continued to drag on under a more limited basis for as long as four more years under the leadership of persons other than Black Hawk. In 1870 Black Hawk died of tuberculosis, but the conflict was carried on by some of his zealous compatriots.

The long-standing conflict was brought to a crisis in 1872, when several tribes banded together using the "Ghost Dance" ceremony to prepare for war, after a period of time when the problem of panhandling, stealing, etc., by Indians was becoming uncontrollable and Mormon settlers in the small towns of the central and southern Utah area were demanding swift action of their leaders. Although Brigham Young had been hesitant to use the militia to engage the Indians in battle prior to and even during the conflict, and although he had championed the notion that "it is better to feed the Indians than to fight them," political pressures and the stark reality of great difficulties brought on by cultural displacement and encroachment led him to reluctantly support military action. The Ghost Dance crisis led to federal troops finally being sent to squelch the rebellion. Fearful of the total annihilation of their people as the federal troops entered the region, the militant Indians quickly disbanded.[43] Utah's Black Hawk War was formally brought to an end at this point, but the inevitable tensions and difficulties between the Utah settlers and the indigenous residents continued in different configurations for many years.

In the years that have passed since the 1860s and 1870s, Utah's Black Hawk War has been largely forgotten, relegated to footnote status in most regional histories, and overshadowed by other events of those decades. There has been a recent resurgence of interest in this conflict and its causes, which has resulted in additional light being shed on it, as well as a better appreciation for the difficult times and the context in which it occurred. Black Hawk's remains were unearthed by miners in the early 1900s and were on display for a time in the Museum of Peoples and Culture at Brigham Young University in Provo. In 1996, descendants of Black Hawk demanded that his remains be returned, and they were reburied at the site of his birth in Springville, Utah County, a site that has now been memorialized on a larger scale.[44] John Murdoch's name is listed with other Heber valley veterans of the Black Hawk conflict on a separate plaque atop Memorial Hill near Midway. The foremost historian of this tragic epic has charitably summarized the causes and effects of the Black Hawk War by stating, "The simple fact was that two honorable peoples were hopelessly trapped not only by their own cultures, goals, and interests, but also by the larger political and national forces of their time."[45]

Notes

1. John Murray Nicol, ed., *The James and Mary Murray Murdoch Family History* (Provo, UT: James and Mary Murray Murdoch Family Organization, 1982), 239–43.

2. Daniel E. Sutherland, *The Expansion of Everyday Life, 1860–1876* (Fayetteville: University of Arkansas Press, 2000).

3. John Murray Murdoch, Early History of John Murray Murdoch, written by himself at Heber, Utah, 5 Sept. 1898 (document in author's possession).

4. "Frontier Historian," Regions of Mind, http://regionsofmind.blog-city.com/frontier_historian.htm (accessed July 5, 2005).

5. Joseph A. Murdoch, *A History of the John Murdoch and Mary Murray Murdoch Family* (Salt Lake City, UT: LDS Family History Library, microfilm no. 0,000,156, section 1, area 1, second floor).

6. Nicol, *Family History*, 348.

7. William James Mortimer, ed., *How Beautiful Upon the Mountains: A Centennial History of Wasatch County* (Heber City, UT: Wasatch County Chapter, Daughters of Utah Pioneers, 1963), 190.

8. Jessie L. Embry, *A History of Wasatch County* (Salt Lake City, UT: Utah State Historical Society and Wasatch County Commission, 1996), 32–33.

9. Mortimer, *How Beautiful*, 190–91.

10. Embry, *History of Wasatch County*, 102.

11. Nicol, *Family History*, 274.

12. Ibid., 428.

13. Ibid., 323.

14. Ibid., 397–98.

15. Ibid., 445.

16. Ibid., 474.

17. John Murray Murdoch, Early History.

18. Edward Norris Wentworth, *America's Sheep Trails* (Ames: Iowa State University Press, 1948), 226.

19. Ibid., 308.

20. John O. Baxter, *Las Carneradas: Sheep Trade in New Mexico, 1700–1860* (Albuquerque: University of New Mexico Press, 1987), 119.

21. Wentworth, *America's Sheep Trails*, 171.

22. Ibid., 229.

23. Mortimer, *How Beautiful*, 146.

24. Allan Kent Powell, ed., *Utah History Encyclopedia* (Salt Lake City, UT: University of Utah Press, 1994), 333.

25. Wentworth, *America's Sheep Trails*, 228.

26. Ibid., 229.

27. Mortimer, *How Beautiful*, 146.

28. Ibid.

29. Embry, *History of Wasatch County*, 82.

30. Charles S. Peterson, *Utah: A History* (New York: W. W. Norton & Company, 1984), 126.

31. Ibid.

32. Nicol, *Family History*, 217.

33. Leonard J. Arrington, *Brigham Young: American Moses* (Urbana: University of Illinois Press, 1986), 294.

34. Powell, *Utah History Encyclopedia*, 43–44.

35. Leonard J. Arrington and Davis Bitton, *The Mormon Experience: A History of the Latter-day Saints* (New York: Alfred A. Knopf, 1979), 156.

36. Dean May, *Utah: A People's History* (Salt Lake City, UT: Bonneville Books, 1987), 104–5.

37. Nicol, *Family History*, 217.

38. Embry, *History of Wasatch County*, 37.

39. Ibid.

40. Ibid.

41. May, *Utah: A People's History*, 105.

42. John Alton Peterson, *Utah's Black Hawk War* (Salt Lake City: University of Utah Press, 1998).

43. Ibid., 7.

44. "The death of Chief Antonguer, Black Hawk," Christians Battle Native Americans, Utah History 1865–1872, http://www.users.qwest.net/~philbg/page_2_of_6.htm (accessed June 29, 2005).

45. John Alton Peterson, *Utah's Black Hawk War,* 7.

9

• • •

HARD TIMES ONCE MORE

In the Great Basin they had hoped to distance themselves from American society. That very distance created serious problems of its own, however, and in the end they found America, having let them leave, would nonetheless not let them alone.

There is a profound irony in the fact that Utah's first white settlers, who had felt the solution to their Indian problem was to get the natives to adopt white ways, now suffered from outsiders who tried in the same way to solve the Mormon problem. But people adhere with remarkable tenacity to their old ways.

—DEAN L. MAY, *Utah: A People's History*

It would be a mistake to think that the twenty year period commencing in the early 1870s was a singularly troubled time for John Murdoch and his family. On the contrary, they experienced many joys: the births of their youngest children, the marriages of most of the Murdoch children, increasing success and prosperity, and the simple pleasures of life in the rural Heber valley. In 1878, after more than twenty-five years of separation, John experienced a happy reunion with his younger brother, William, and his family, who emigrated from Scotland to start a new life with the Saints in Utah. Heber and Wasatch County were becoming increasingly established and stable, and John Murdoch was a well-liked and respected member of the growing community. Life was essentially good, and the perpetually cheerful and optimistic John saw it that way, putting the problems and challenges in perspective.

Under the veneer of the essentially hopeful and positive conditions of life for the Murdoch family during this era was a dark cloud of social and political conflict in which the church was continually and increasingly engaged with the United States government. Such tensions and conflicts were not necessarily new. The Murdochs' flight south from Salt Lake City to Goshen during the peak of tensions in the 1857 Utah War, as well as the federal indifference toward the difficulties of the Mormons and Indians during the 1860s and early 1870s Black Hawk War in which John Murdoch served are but two examples of how these Zion–United States conflicts personally affected the family. Beginning in the 1870s, there was a definite increase in the conflict with the U.S. government, and it continued to escalate until it reached its peak in the late 1880s and early 1890s, coming close to unraveling much or all of what the refugee Saints had struggled to achieve in Utah. Despite whatever joys of life were experienced during this time of increased conflict, these were hard times indeed. In the end, they would affect the Murdochs in the most personal and painful of ways.

GOLDEN SPIKE: THE END OF ISOLATION

During the spring of 1869, while John Murdoch was involved in the spring lambing, and while his family was busy with other domestic matters, events of national importance were occurring in northern Utah, about a hundred miles north of Heber City. On May 10 officials of the Central Pacific Railroad and the Union Pacific Railroad met to drive four symbolic spikes—two of them gold—connecting the first transcontinental railroad in North America. The nation was now connected from the Pacific to the Atlantic by a web of railways, allowing for relatively high speed travel, easier shipping of goods, and enhanced commerce and communication across regions of the nation.

With this event, the triumphalism and manifest destiny that had inspired generations of white Americans to move west reached its culmination. The pioneer era was now officially over, and life in Utah would be forever changed. Future immigrants would arrive by rail, avoiding the long and dangerous trek west that had shaped the character of the region and forged the resolve and identity of early pioneers like John Murdoch, Ann Steele Murdoch, and Isabella Crawford. More importantly, Utah was no longer an isolated fortress in the wilderness: Babylon was now connected to Zion.

The completion of the railroad and the interconnection of Utah to the rest of the nation occurred during an era when there were continuing tensions between the Saints and the federal government. Although the immediate crises posed by the Utah War and Mountain Meadows Massacre had somewhat subsided, there was still an underlying element of deep conflict between Zion and "the world." Now that the Civil War had ended and reconstruction of the southern states was under way, the federal government, and more particularly the Republican Party, again made solving the "Mormon problem" in Utah a high priority. Brigham Young's dream of an independent kingdom was now in a state of flux. Twelve years earlier, during one of the peaks in the ongoing tension in 1857, Brigham had warned that "the time must come when this kingdom must be free and independent from all other kingdoms," and stated, "I shall take a hostile movement by our enemies as evidence that it is time for the thread to be cut."[1] It had now become obvious that the destiny of the Saints in Utah was going to be intertwined with that of the rest of the United States, and that "cutting the thread" was no longer a practical threat.

Brigham Young had anticipated the end of Utah's physical isolation. He supported the railroad and was disappointed that the connecting point was not in Salt Lake City, even as he continued to be wary of the social, economic, and political impact that it would have on his people. His wariness was justified. The 1869 completion of the railroad, along with the 1861 connection of Utah by telegraph and the end of the Civil War in 1865, would ultimately set the stage for sweeping changes in the way of life in which the once-isolated Saints existed. Within a short time, the "gentile world" began to gain a strong toehold in the region. When the railway was connected in 1869, there were only three saloons in Salt Lake City, but within five more years there were thirty-eight, one of the changes that must have annoyed Brigham greatly.[2] Within a few more years, these tides of change would bring even greater social upheavals throughout the region, and they would ultimately impact the Murdochs and the rest of Utah in a way that would have been hard for them to imagine.

A Disgrace to the American Name: The Crusade

By the early 1870s, the Civil War was over, the reconstruction of the southern states was in progress, the nation was now linked by a transcontinental railway, and the western regions of the nation were essentially settled. With the passing of these developments the federal government, eastern press, and mainstream Protestant religions now focused an unyielding attention and energy on Utah and the "Mormon problem." Although conflict in one form or another between the church and the federal government was essentially continual from the early 1850s through the late 1860s, it reached new heights beginning with the 1870s, and did not relent for more than another quarter century. Part of this crusade was brought on by continuing dislike of the political power wielded *de facto* by the leaders of the church, but the central issue was clearly the peculiar institution of plural marriage. Having abolished one of the two "twin relics of barbarism" with the end of the Civil War and slavery, the Republican Party, and increasingly the rest of the American political, media, and religious establishments, sought to eradicate the other relic, polygamy.

Church historian and general authority B. H. Roberts, in his *Comprehensive History of the Church*, noted that the beginnings of this round of conflict—which would eventually come close to toppling the church—came in the early 1870s, with a "judicial crusade" against Utah, led by federal Judge James B. McKean.[3] The goals of this crusade were to damage the political power of the church and to chip away at the institution of plural marriage. Some of the specific instruments used to pursue these goals included efforts designed to make it increasingly difficult for Mormon immigrants from Europe to become naturalized citizens, removal of local control over the Utah territorial penitentiary, selecting juries that were packed by persons antagonistic to the church, and using existing laws against adultery to go after practitioners of polygamy. Initially, the targets of this latter effort were rank-and-file Mormons, but ultimately even Brigham Young was arraigned, and the prosecutors made it clear that the objective in the case of *The People v. Brigham Young* (also called *Federal Authority v. Polygamic Theocracy*) was to put the entire system on trial. Roberts, other church leaders, and most members of the church considered these initiatives to be part of a vast "anti-Mormon conspiracy" by the federal government, and, more particularly, the leadership of the Republican Party.

Mormon leaders and other Utah citizens were not the only ones to view these efforts as a politically motivated conspiracy. Although many eastern newspapers sensationalized the events and sided with the federal efforts, some leading national newspapers in the central and western states, including the *Omaha Herald* and the *San Francisco Examiner*, scorned them in 1871 editorials as being un-American and conspiratorial. The *Herald* referred to the federal actions directly as a conspiracy, and posited that "The object was to break down the political power of the people who had conquered Utah from a desert waste into a beautiful garden" to "enable these malignants to occupy, possess, and control it."[4] The *Examiner* editorial was even more blunt, stating that the "Mormon trouble" was "instigated by a 'ring' of Republican politicians, who are looking to the speedy admission of Utah as one of the states of the Union. These small fry, popinjay politicians, and would-be statesmen, know full well that they will have no show for promotion until the Mormon power is broken. Hence, they seek to create a civil war by means of packed juries, unprincipled judges, and perjured witnesses... the whole affair is a disgrace to the American name."[5]

Although some of McKean's rulings were eventually overruled, and his highly personal vendetta against Brigham Young and the church proved so unseemly to even his supporters that he was ultimately dismissed from office, he had set in motion a freight-train-like series of events. As the 1870s progressed, so did the federal efforts to stymie the power of the church and to end polygamy. An increasingly feeble Brigham Young was imprisoned for a short time in 1875, the highest profile incarceration among those of many Latter-day Saint members and officials who would serve prison time for being practitioners of plural marriage over the next two decades. In 1875, George Reynolds, a high-ranking church official and personal secretary to Brigham Young, agreed to serve as the "test case" for the legality of polygamy. He ultimately endured three trials as his case moved from the territorial and district courts all the way to the United States Supreme Court in 1878. To the horror of the church leadership and many members, the Supreme Court ruled against Reynolds in January 1879, with the decision primarily being framed in terms of First Amendment issues of religious freedom. That the Reynolds case was argued in terms of his right to practice freedom of religious expression did not sway the court, which held that justifying polygamy based on this premise would make the professed doctrines of religious belief superior to the highest laws of the land and would thus allow any citizen to become a "law unto himself." "Since the constitution did not recognize a higher authority than itself, neither would the court."[6] Reynolds ultimately served a year in federal prisons, having become the public face of a Mormon "prisoner for conscience sake." He was hailed as a martyr and hero by most of the residents of the Utah territory, and children from Utah's Sunday Schools donated nickels to help pay off his $500 fine.[7]

THE KINGDOM OF GOD OR NOTHING

In August 1877, Brigham Young—the Great Colonizer, church leader, and "Lion of the Lord"—became increasingly ill. He died of apparent complications of acute appendicitis on August 29. With his passing, the man admired above all others by John Murdoch—who considered him "the greatest man on earth"—was gone. Brigham's death raised many questions and anxieties regarding the future course of leadership of the church during a time of unprecedented combative efforts by the federal government against the Saints. Leadership of the church fell to the Quorum of the Twelve Apostles, led by senior apostle John Taylor. In 1880, Taylor was sustained as the new president of the church, and leadership was assumed by a new first presidency. Taylor's personal style, characteristics, and background differed substantially from those of Brigham Young. He was known for his refined and cultured ways, impeccable grooming, and love of literature, whereas Brigham often scoffed at such characteristics and on one occasion even derisively referred to Taylor as "Prince John."[8] Taylor was also a gifted theologian, thinker, and writer, who engaged in significant efforts to clarify doctrinal and policy issues within the church.

Despite these differences in style and substance, John Taylor—who had been shot five times by the mob in Carthage, Illinois, during the murders of Joseph and Hyrum Smith—proved to be at least as fierce and immovable as was Brigham Young in defending the interests of the church and, in some cases, more so. Anyone who was looking for an easily swayed and placated new leader for the church after Brigham's death was sadly mistaken. Being absolutely committed to continuing the work of Joseph Smith and the restoration, and having experienced firsthand the brutal persecutions of the church in the early years, John Taylor was not about to give any quarter to the enemy. Within a short time, his motto as church president became "The Kingdom of God or Nothing."

In 1880, the leadership of the church responded to federal efforts against them by convening a special prayer meeting of general authorities to curse the enemies of the church and to supplicate God for his deliverance from them, as well as his wrath against them. A list of nearly four hundred names of these enemies was entered on a special prayer roll, entitled "Names of Persons to be held in Remembrance before the Lord for their Evil Deeds, and who have raised their hands against the Lord's Anointed." Among the names on the list were those of four presidents of the United States: Martin Van Buren, Ulysses S. Grant, Rutherford B. Hayes, and James Buchanan.[9] This effort did not stop the momentum of the federal government's crusade against the Saints and the institution of plural marriage. In 1882, Congress surpassed the Supreme Court's holding in the 1879 *Reynolds* decision by passing the Edmunds law, which made polygamy a federal crime punishable by up to five years in prison. This act also disenfranchised many Mormons by denying convicted polygamists the right to vote, to hold office, and to serve on juries. The Edmunds law created enormous increases in federal pressure on the Saints to renounce the practice of plural marriage and sent many church leaders into hiding, and it helped to create the "underground" movement.

In the midst of these troubles, John Taylor defiantly continued to advocate "The Principle," urging men and women with even greater zeal to enter into plural marriage. He encouraged the expansion of Mormon settlements into Mexico, where polygamy was illegal but not a particularly high priority for prosecution by government officials. He was absolutely fearless in his resolute stance. During the afternoon session of a general conference of the church held January 4, 1880, in the Assembly Hall in Salt Lake, Taylor discussed the Saints' response to federal efforts to interfere with the practice of their religion, famously stating: "...when they enact tyrannical laws, forbidding us the free exercise of our religion, we cannot submit. God is greater than the United States, and when the Government conflicts with heaven, we will be ranged under the banner of heaven and against the Government...Polygamy is a divine institution. It has been handed down direct from God. The United States cannot abolish it. No nation on earth can prevent it, nor all the nations of the earth combined.... I defy the United States; I will obey God."[10] John Taylor was among the many prominent church leaders who went into hiding during the 1880s. He ultimately spent the final two years of his life—1885 to 1887—in the underground, directing the affairs of the church through an elaborate system of communication among his trusted associates, even as his health failed him and his family suffered from his absence.[11]

TEMPORAL SALVATION: THE MANIFESTO

The year 1887—John Murdoch's sixty-seventh year—was pivotal in the struggle between the church and the United States government. Believing that the 1883 Edmunds law did not go far enough, Congress passed an even more drastic measure. The unprecedented 1887 Edmunds-Tucker law disincorporated the church, confiscated its real estate holdings and business enterprises, and abolished women's suffrage in Utah (in 1870, Utah had became the first U.S. state or territory to grant voting rights to women). Edmunds-Tucker effectively destroyed the political, economic, and social system by which the leaders of the church governed their society and replaced it with federal authority. John Taylor's death in July of 1887 led to a period of two years where the Quorum of the Twelve Apostles assumed church leadership, under the direction of senior apostle Wilford Woodruff, who was eventually sustained as president of the church in 1889 at the age of eighty-three. The election of Republican Benjamin Harrison as U.S. president in 1888 led to even more anti-Mormon activity in Congress, which nearly passed a bill that would have stripped all members of the church of their right to vote.

Wilford Woodruff, a veteran of the church from shortly after its founding, was an avid fly fisherman and diarist, a skilled farmer and rancher, and a legendary missionary who had helped bring nearly two thousand converts into the church during his mission to England in the late 1830s. He was a visionary and a millenialist who believed that the end of the world was at hand, and that the church would ultimately be victorious and emerge as a free and independent theocratic kingdom. But the aging Woodruff was also a pragmatist. He saw that there was no way out of the current conflict with the federal government, and that the United States would have to be satisfied in order to assure "the temporal salvation of the church." Reaching out to the beleaguered Saints, President Woodruff announced a special day of fasting and prayer for all members of the church on December 23, 1889, the eighty-fourth anniversary of the birth of Joseph Smith. The instructions for this fast were to join in prayer that "his Holy Spirit... be poured out upon his servants and upon all the saints as a witness that he was still with them. Also that the enemies of Zion might be confounded in their wicked works and designs." The announcement requested that the exercise "should be done in the spirit of meekness and faith. There ought to be no expressions or desires for the wrath and judgment upon those who have persecuted, reviled, and falsely accused us."[12] A few months later, seeing that the tidal wave of government efforts against the church was threatening its very existence, he felt compelled to take immediate conciliatory actions and to make the difficult decision to abandon the Principle.

On September 24, 1890, Woodruff met with the other members of the First Presidency and a few other invited members of the church hierarchy and announced that he had "sought the will of the Lord, and the Holy Spirit had revealed that it was necessary for the church to relinquish the practice of that principle for which the brethren had been willing to lay down their lives."[13] After a long discussion and many difficult interactions, the group supported the decision, and a press release was sent out that afternoon. The next few days were a flurry of activity, with thousands of copies of Woodruff's announcement being sent to newspapers, church leaders, and government officials. This announcement, which became known as the Manifesto, made clear the intention of the church leadership to submit to the laws of the land and to abandon the principle of plural marriage:

> Inasmuch as laws have been enacted by Congress forbidding plural marriages, which laws have been pronounced constitutional by the court of last resort, I hereby declare my intention to submit to those laws, and to use my influence with the members of the Church over which I preside to have them do likewise... And now I publicly declare that my advice to the Latter-day Saints is to refrain from contracting any marriage forbidden by the laws of the land.

News of the announcement spread quickly and received a mixed response. Some members of the church felt immediately relieved, whereas others were skeptical, stunned that the principle they had sacrificed for was being abandoned, and noted that it was worded as a press release "to whom it may concern" rather than as an authoritative revelation. Some government officials and opponents of the church also viewed the Manifesto with doubt, not convinced that it meant what it said. Despite the initial mixed reception, there is no doubt that the Manifesto unleashed the beginnings of a major change for the church, its members, and the Utah territory, which was now on the road to statehood. It is unfortunate that there are no diaries, letters, or other records regarding how John Murdoch and his two wives heard about the Manifesto, or what was their initial response. Although the Murdochs were staunch in their support of church leaders, the difficult and confusing situation created by the Manifesto and the continued government crackdown would soon result in one of the most trying times of their lives.

PRISONER FOR CONSCIENCE'S SAKE

After the 1890 Manifesto was issued, there was still a considerable amount of confusion regarding how the new policy would be implemented. Did it apply only to ending the practice from that point forward, or was it retroactive to previously existing polygamous unions? Would a husband's cohabitation with a plural wife be prosecuted if the marriage had been in effect for many years and there were children and issues of support to consider? Should men like John Murdoch, who had entered into the practice many years earlier (he married Isabella in 1862, nearly thirty years prior to the Manifesto) abandon their plural wives? These were difficult challenges for the federal government and the First Presidency of the church to consider, and in many cases the answers were not initially clear.

In addition, a huge culture shift was being forced in a short time. It was wholly unrealistic to think that attitudes and practices would change overnight. For years, the general authorities of the church had defended the Principle as being an absolutely essential aspect of the gospel, and vowed that they would resist the laws of the United States with all their might in order to abide by their religious beliefs. Now the president of the church had publicly stated that plural marriages were no longer being performed with his knowledge and consent and was advising members to refrain from entering into such relationships. Some skeptics and outsiders viewed the carefully worded Manifesto statement with suspicion, not really believing that the church leadership would abandon the Principle. These suspicions were given credence when believable reports continued to emerge that numerous polygamous marriages had indeed been authorized by various members of the First Presidency after the 1890 Manifesto.[14] This difficult and confusing state of affairs led not only to a second public declaration in 1904, but to emigration of many polygamists to Mexico and Canada, where they could escape the laws of the United States, as well as the beginnings of an underground polygamy movement outside of the mainstream of the church that would ultimately become associated with Mormon fundamentalism.[15]

When the Manifesto was issued, church leaders had anticipated at least some of these problems. At a meeting of church leaders held October 7, 1890, to discuss implementation of the Manifesto, Wilford Woodruff's First Counselor George Q. Cannon made a bold statement in hopes of stemming neglect of plural wives: "A man who will act the coward and shield himself behind the Manifesto by deserting his plural wives should be damned." Woodruff seconded the sentiment by stating, "I did not, could not, and would not promise that you would desert your wives and children. This you cannot do in honor."[16] Several months later, apostle and future church president Joseph F. Smith was even more emphatic regarding the necessity of maintaining support of and cohabitation with plural wives. In a meeting of general authorities with stake presidents and bishops, he counseled: "God will not justify you in kicking out your families and stultifying yourselves in the eyes of all good men. *We do not want you to leave your wives because of the Manifesto.* Tell your people to take care of their families, just as they have always done."[17]

As the difficult transition into a post-Manifesto Mormon society in Utah was being worked out, John Murdoch continued to live with both of his beloved wives, Ann and Isabella. The aging trio had raised a large and devout family, seen most of their children grow into adulthood, buried some of their children who did not survive, and were now seeing their grandchildren's generation rise. They had worked hard to achieve a measure of stability and comfort, and they enjoyed the familiarity and closeness of their relationship. Perhaps encouraged by the assurances and counsel of church authorities, and perhaps not inclined to worry and take any drastic measures, John had no desire to discontinue living with Isabella, his wife of nearly thirty years, as the letter of the federal law required. Federal judges and marshals thought otherwise. On April 21, 1891, some six months following the Manifesto, seventy-year-old John Murdoch was arrested and taken before a federal judge in Provo. One account states that it was Judge Blackburn, and another account indicates that it was Judge Charles T. Lane. Upon his arraignment, John was sentenced to one month in the penitentiary, plus a fine of $100. Not expecting that his arraignment would result in imprisonment, John was unprepared for this turn of events. He asked the judge to allow him to return temporarily to his home in Heber, so that he could get extra underclothing, and promised that he would return immediately to the penitentiary without an officer or any additional expense to the court. Sympathetic to his plight, the judge agreed to John's request. He was as good as his word. After returning to Heber to get his clothing and put his affairs in order, he immediately returned to the Provo prison to begin his sentence. Asked for his commitment papers, John had none, and the prison warden initially refused to admit him. John then went to the home of his nephew, David Lennox Murdoch, and described the situation. "Uncle left and came up to our place and told his tale. They won't have me, he said. And he seemed very much put out by it."[18] After returning to the prison and insisting to the warden that he serve his time as he had promised, he was incarcerated for thirty days as a "prisoner for conscience sake," for unlawful cohabitation in violation of federal law. It is likely though not certain that John was the oldest inmate in the penitentiary during that period. He was imprisoned with both common criminals and other polygamists who were similarly being incarcerated as part of the post-Manifesto crackdown on cohabitation.[19]

Neither John, Ann, nor Isabella left any written records indicating how the imprisonment affected them or their family. To get a sense of the impact of this pivotal event, we must look carefully at the few writings on this subject that were left by the Murdoch children and other relatives, who were obviously involved in these events, and who would have formed their opinions after listening to John tell his story. It is clear from these accounts that the family viewed the prison sentence as a great hardship, but that they also saw John as a man of integrity for serving time. The writings of John's nephew David Lennox Murdoch indicate support of both these interpretations and also add an element of anger and disgust over the treatment that his uncle received: "...the officers of the law... were using every device and stratagem that the devil could inspire them with to harass, annoy, and imprison...can you imagine a more honorable, honest, and guileless soul than his. He returned to the pen, was admitted, and served his term. He might have gone to California or Timbuktu if he had wanted to. This incident is a wonderful illustration of his honesty, reliability, and dependability and keen sense of right and trust."[20] True to the Murdoch family practice of writing poetry, John and Isabella's daughter Catherine later memorialized her recollections of the way the imprisonment episode was handled by devoting six of the eleven stanzas of her poem "In Our Home" to it:

> We were very happy children until one day
> Our father called us all together
> And to us these words did say:
> "I must obey the laws of the land,
> And we must part for aye;
> But to give up my wives and children
> This I will never do.
> I will go to the penitentiary
> And serve a term or two,
> But that I will never do."
>
> My mother frail and sickly said,
> John I will set you free,
> To send you forth to prison
> Would be the death of me."
>
> Muzz said, "Now dear Bella, this will never do.
> We're going hairts and han's together,
> And to me you've e're been true.
> Now we'll continue onward
> Though demons rage in hell."
> Muzz stood and sweetly sang,
> "All is well, all is well."
>
> My father went to prison,
> Put on those stripes of shame;
> But the angels looking down from heaven said,
> "John, you're not to blame."
>
> A term he served in Prison,
> A fine he had to pay—
> A hundred dollar down in cash
> Before he could come away[21]

Catherine's poem indicates that Isabella—who was apparently quite ill at the time—offered to terminate her relationship with John in order to save him from going to prison, but neither John nor Ann would even consider the possibility. It also clearly indicates, with the emphasis on *that* in the first stanza reprinted, that John was immovable in his commitment to plural marriage and to his wives and children. The fact that John Murdoch ultimately acquiesced to the letter of the law by later separating his households into two while never abandoning Isabella also shows that he was willing to make a compromise to follow the law of the land and the leaders of the church, without violating his commitment to his family. In the post-Manifesto era, when numerous persons continued to secretly enter into new plural marriages, and when an underground polygamous movement that would later be disowned by the church had its beginnings, it is notable that all of the Murdoch children became and stayed monogamists, and that they were by and large highly committed to the church and to the laws of the land.

NOTES

1. Brigham Young, August 2, 1857, *Journal of Discourses* 5: 98–99.

2. Dean May, *Utah: A People's History* (Salt Lake City, UT: Bonneville Books, 1987), 121.

3. Roberts, B. H. *A Comprehensive History of the Church of Jesus Christ of Latter-day Saints*, vol. 6 (Salt Lake City, UT: The Church of Jesus Christ of Latter-day Saints, 1957), 382–98.

4. *Omaha Herald*, October 4, 1871.

5. Roberts, *Comprehensive History,* 393.

6. Bruce A. Van Orden, *The Life of George Reynolds: Prisoner for Conscience' Sake* (Salt Lake City, UT: Deseret Book Company, 1992), 86–87.

7. Ibid., 94.

8. Leonard J. Arrington, *Brigham Young: American Moses.* Urbana: University of Illinois Press, 1986), 198.

9. David John Buerger, *The Mysteries of Godliness: A History of Mormon Temple Worship* (San Francisco: Smith Research Associates, 1994), photograph no. 9.

10. *Salt Lake Tribune*, January 6, 1880, 4.

11. Allan Kent Powell, ed., *Utah History Encyclopedia* (Salt Lake City: University of Utah Press, 1994), 545.

12. Roberts, *Comprehensive History*, vol. 6, 218–19.

13. Richard S. Van Wagoner, *Mormon Polygamy: A History*, 2nd ed. (Salt Lake City, UT: Signature Books, 1989), 139.

14. D. Michael Quinn, "LDS Authority and New Plural Marriages, 1890–1904," *Dialogue: A Journal of Mormon Thought* 18 (Spring 1985): 105.

15. Ibid.; D. Michael Quinn, *The Mormon Hierarchy: Origins of Power* (Salt Lake City, UT: Signature Books, 1997), 183; Martha Sonntag Bradley, *Kidnapped From That Land: The Government Raids on the Short Creek Polygamists* (Salt Lake City: University of Utah Press, 1993), 18–39.

16. Van Wagoner, *Mormon Polygamy*, 145.

17. Abraham H. Cannon journal, October 7, 1891, cited in Van Wagoner, *Mormon Polygamy*, 149.

18. John Murray Nicol, ed., *The James and Mary Murray Murdoch Family History* (Provo, UT: James and Mary Murray Murdoch Family Organization, 1982), 720–21.

19. Ibid., 218.

20. Ibid., 721.

21. Ibid., 222–23.

10

◆ ◆ ◆

THE FINAL YEARS

When their numerous posterity stood around them during the exercises, it caused the words of God to come vividly before our eyes, when he promised Abraham that his posterity should be as numerous as the sands of the desert… at their fiftieth milestone of married life, they still have the love and affection, still the same blissful trust, that characterized their first love missive long, long years ago.

— *Wasatch Wave*, March 4, 1898

During his long residence in this city, he [John Murdoch] has had a most honorable and successful career. His dealings have been honest and upright, and he is at this time one of the most deservedly popular men in Wasatch County.

— *Wasatch Wave*, December 21, 1906

And God shall wipe away all tears from their eyes; and there shall be no more death, neither sorrow, nor crying, neither shall there be any more pain: for the former things are passed away.

—Revelation 21:4

The wave of persecutions and challenges that followed the extreme conflicts between the church and the federal government, including John Murdoch's prison sentence at an advanced age, coupled with the many stresses of day-to-day life, certainly took their toll on John and his family. In his seventies and eighties, his life naturally slowed down, and he along with Ann and Isabella began to experience the common decline in health and vitality that routinely accompanies a long life of challenges and opportunities. Having given his all for his family and religion, John had already greatly surpassed the average life expectancy for men of his era, and he must have believed that the end of his days was not far off. But contrary to what might be expected of most persons under these circumstances, John Murdoch continued to contribute greatly to his family, community, and religion, even as his physical abilities declined. The same can be said of both Ann and Isabella, who also lived long lives, and were not yet done contributing to the greater good by the time their advanced years were upon them. Furthermore, although the Murdochs had been part of some incredible changes and events during their lifetimes, they were on the cusp of being witness to some more dramatic and important events before it was all over.

PATRIARCH: SERVICE IN THE CHURCH

From the time that he was baptized a member of the Church of Jesus Christ of Latter-day Saints in 1850, John Murdoch had willingly accepted every church assignment or calling in which he had been asked to serve. Prior to his 1852 immigration to Utah, he had helped organize, support, and lead the small branches of the church in Scotland to which he belonged. After arriving in Salt Lake City he was asked to serve as a bishop's counselor in the Salt Lake Third Ward, and he filled a similar role for a time in his ward in Heber after his relocation to the upper Provo valley. From 1863 until a few years before his death, John held a position of great responsibility and respect as the leader of the quorum of high priests of the church in his area—men who were experienced and proven in their commitment to the church, and who had served in administrative or leadership positions. Like John, Ann and Isabella were resolute in providing leadership and service in the church. Ann served as a counselor in the presidency of the Female Relief Society organization in the Heber West Ward from the time it was organized in 1879 for several years, and served as the first president of the Wasatch Stake Primary organization for children from the time it was organized in 1883 until 1895.[1] Likewise, Isabella served with Ann for many years as a counselor in the first Relief Society presidency in the Heber West Ward, where her old friend Catherine Campbell Foreman served as the president.[2] Saints of that era, like those of today, varied in their commitment and willingness to build the kingdom by giving of their time and means, and the Murdoch family stood for their willingness to do all that was asked of them, including accepting and magnifying high profile and difficult assignments in the church.

In 1890, at age seventy, John was called and ordained by apostle Francis L. Lyman to serve in the priesthood office of patriarch. He served in this capacity until his health failed him. From the time of Joseph Smith on, the purpose of the office of patriarch, which is held by a spiritually mature and experienced high priest, is to bless the members of the church within their stakes (a stake is a confederation of several wards or local congregations within a common geographical area), by providing them with patriarchal blessings as they feel prompted by the spirit. These blessings are typically performed in the home of the patriarch or of the person who is to receive the blessing. The patriarch places his hands on the head of the seated person, and then verbalizes the blessing as he feels moved by the spirit. A recording of the blessing is made at the same time. In John's day the recordings were made in writing, either in longhand or by shorthand. Blessings are transcribed and stored in the church's historical records department, and can be accessed only by direct descendants of the person who received the blessing. Members receive a copy of their blessing, and are encouraged to read and consider it throughout their lives, as it is considered to be an authoritative personal revelation directly from God. The specifics of the process are described in the *Encyclopedia of Mormonism* as follows:

> An essential part of a patriarchal blessing is a declaration of lineage... [of] the dominant family line that leads back to Abraham.... In addition, as the patriarch seeks the spirit he may be moved to give admonitions, promises, and assurances. Individual traits of personality and strengths and weaknesses may be mentioned. Against the backdrop of the prophetic anticipation of world events, individual roles and callings may be named. One's spiritual gifts, talents, skills, and potentials may be specified with their associated obligations of gratitude and dedication. It is continually taught in the Church that the fulfillment of patriarchal blessings, as of all divine promises, is conditioned on the faith and works of the individual recipient.[3]

Because Mormons view patriarchal blessings as a very important collection of highly personal revelatory messages from God regarding their promise, gifts, and spiritual and temporal destiny, patriarchs are generally accorded a great deal of respect and admiration among members of the church, who are usually very appreciative of the experience, as well as the direction that the written blessing provides to them throughout life. When he was called to the office of patriarch, John had already earned the respect and admiration of those in his community, where even some non-relatives referred to him as "Uncle John," but the important role he played in assisting many members of the church (the figure of two hundred or more is listed several times in family records) receive their patriarchal blessings during his several years in this capacity only increased the esteem in which he was held.

Although patriarchal blessings are considered to come from God by the inspiration of the spirit through the words of the patriarch, it is also widely understood that since the medium—the patriarch who pronounces the blessing—is a person with his own unique characteristics, gifts, and weaknesses, then the blessings might also reflect those characteristics, as

well as the concerns of the times in which the patriarch lived.[4] Commenting on this important issue, John A. Widtsoe, who served as an apostle in
the church from 1921 to 1952, stated, "Since patriarchs are but men, they
are subject to human frailties. Their manner of speech and thinking is
reflected in their blessings."[5] Thus, to understand how John's words in his
many patriarchal blessings were understood and received by those he
blessed, it is useful to read a few phrases from one of them. On December
1, 1905, with his wife Isabella acting as scribe and recorder, John, who was
then nearly eighty-five years old, pronounced a patriarchal blessing on one
of his daughters, who was then middle-aged:

> The Lord has had his eye on you from your earliest infancy up into the present
> time and your life has been preserved for a wise purpose in the Lord. You are
> greatly blessed in being born in the land of Zion amongst the people of God....
> Your mind shall become quick that you shall be able to discern between good
> and evil...You have attained the honors of a faithful mother in Israel.... Your
> children will rise up and bless you in your declining day. You shall never lack
> for friends or for the necessities of life... You shall be able to procure an in-
> heritance in the new Heaven and new earth where all things shall have become
> new...You shall be crowned with honor and glory with many of your kindred
> and friends in the presence of God and the Holy Angels."

Although these words were directed toward his daughter, they provide
an example of some of the ways in which his blessings may have strengthened and encouraged the many other people whom he blessed. This particular blessing stressed the blessings that would come from faithfulness in
keeping God's commandments, the privilege of being born in Zion after
the Saints were driven to Utah, domestic and familial harmony, security in
relationships and in the necessities of life, and the promise of an everlasting exaltation in the presence of God, predicated upon her faithfulness. In
the late nineteenth century, it was not uncommon for patriarchal blessings
to also emphasize living in the last days, the second coming of Christ,
being blessed with the gift of healing, or other spiritual gifts.[6] Although
this particular example of one of John Murdoch's blessings does not emphasize these things, they were part of the culture of Mormonism at that
time, and he may have pronounced blessings to this effect on the heads of
other individuals. Regardless of the specific content of the blessings he
gave, there is no doubt that John's words of encouragement and warning
were an inspiration to many, and that he was appreciated and revered for
his efforts in providing these blessings, even as he was aging and his health

was becoming increasingly frail. "He gave many wonderful patriarchal blessings to the members of the stake. The Lord blessed him with the spirit of the calling, and he took a great deal of joy and interest in pronouncing blessings upon the people."[7]

STATEHOOD AT LAST

From the time that Utah was made a territory of the United States, the territorial legislature repeatedly petitioned Congress for statehood and each time was denied. After Wilford Woodruff issued the September 24, 1890, "Manifesto" formally advising the Saints to no longer enter into plural marriages, there was a lessening of federal hostility toward the territory and the church, and the goal of statehood became increasingly attainable. In addition to the 1890 proclamation, several key events paved the way for Utah's entry into the Union in early 1896. In 1891, church leaders encouraged members to join one of the national political parties rather than to eschew either the Republicans or Democrats and maintain their tradition of small regional parties, such as the People's Party. Because the Republican Party had taken the lead in opposing the Mormons and enacting the federal legislation and enforcement that had nearly toppled the church, most of the Saints were more ideologically aligned at that time with the Democrats, whom they viewed as being more sympathetic to the notion of states' rights. To help achieve a reasonable balance in partisan alignment (and thus enhance Utah's standing with both national parties), church leaders particularly encouraged members to join the Republican Party. By 1893, the local Republican Party had grown several fold and was dominated by prominent Mormons.[8]

In 1893 and 1894, presidents Benjamin Harrison (a Republican) and Grover Cleveland (a Democrat) issued general amnesty and pardons to all polygamists who had refrained from cohabitation since November 1, 1890, a date just a few weeks after the issuance of the Manifesto. Although the amnesty laws forbade polygamous cohabitation, some historians have proposed that there was a general understanding among polygamous Utahns of that time that there would not be any federal prosecution for doing so.[9] If there was such an understanding, it obviously had not been implemented in 1891, when John Murdoch was arrested for participating in the practice.

The U.S. Congress also enacted legislation restoring church property that had been taken by the government during the crackdown of the 1880s and passed a bill that allowed Utah to elect delegates to a constitutional convention. By this time, the aging John Murdoch had established separate households for Ann and Isabella, as required by federal law, and Ann moved to a house at 118 South 500 West in Heber City. However, within a short time, the trio was back together under the same roof, in an arrangement that met the letter of the federal law. John purchased a duplex home at 64 West 100 North that had two separate apartments—one for Ann, one for Isabella, connected by a shared bathroom—and the three of them lived there together until after the deaths of Ann and John. To his credit, John did not abandon or neglect Isabella or her family after the initiation of these federal laws. Sadly, this was not the case for some polygamous wives who did not enjoy legal standing, and who soon found themselves essentially on their own.

On Saturday, January 4, 1896, U.S. President Grover Cleveland issued a proclamation admitting Utah as the nation's forty-fifth state. Two days later, Monday, January 6, was inauguration day for the new state. Ceremonies were held in the Tabernacle on Temple Square, which had been lavishly decorated for the event, and which was packed by an "enormous throng" of citizens. The dignitaries present included not only church and government leaders, but military officers from nearby Fort Douglas and prominent leaders of other churches. The Tabernacle Choir sang "America." The ailing Wilford Woodruff was too ill to speak, and his talk was read by his counselor George Q. Cannon. The governor of the new state, Heber M. Wells, spoke of the need to reconcile and heal after the past several decades of conflict between the Saints and the United States government. National newspapers were replete with the news of the new state. In Washington, D.C., the *Evening Star* editorialized:

> As a territory this new comer has been prosperous and its history unique. The Mormon question was at one time thought to interpose insufferable obstacles to statehood, but with the downfall of polygamy Mormonism has ceased to be viewed as a menace to the institutions of the land. The people who form the new state are enterprising, vigorous types of their surroundings, and from the point of view of wealth, population, and general enlightenment deserve the right to contribute a new star to Old Glory."[10]

In Wasatch County there were also celebrations, including commemorations at both Midway and Heber City. The first two pages of the January 10, 1896, edition of the *Wasatch Wave* were devoted primarily to reporting the exciting events surrounding Utah's admission into the Union. A headline on page 2 enthusiastically gushed, "UTAH!! STATE OF UTAH!! We are now in a government of the people, by the people, and for the people.

Shake!" In an article addressed to his fellow citizens of the county, Judge A. C. Hatch wrote, "I am not able with the language at my command to express a tithe of the joy or thankfulness of the people of Utah for the consummation of their hopes long deferred.... After knocking, knocking, knocking at the door for 47 long and weary years, it has at last been opened unto us and we are welcomed into the Union on equal footing with the original states" (page 2). Having emigrated from their native Scotland several decades previously, John, Ann, and Isabella Murdoch were now residents of the newest member of the United States of America.

THE GOLDEN WEDDING

The year 1898 marked the fiftieth anniversary of John and Ann's marriage in Kirkconnell, Scotland, on February 24, 1848. John was now in his seventy-eighth year, and Ann was approaching age seventy. The two of them, as well as Isabella, who was now nearly sixty-two, had exceeded the average life expectancy of their time by a substantial margin and had experienced the pain of outliving some of their children. Five of the fifteen children born to Ann had died as infants or during childhood, and by 1898, her daughter Ann had died as an adult, leaving behind a husband and eleven children. Although none of the children born to Isabella died during infancy or childhood, she had lost one son as an adult at this point in time—Robert became ill and died in 1893 at age twenty. Together, John, Ann, and Isabella had weathered the storms of life and had seen great sorrow as well as great joy.

In a May 30, 1896, letter to his oldest living child—Mary Murray Murdoch Duke, who was born on the Kansas prairie shortly after the deaths of her two older siblings during the trek west—John alluded to these storms both literally and figuratively, and to his appreciation that better times had come: "I thought of the first time that I looked at your pleasant little face. It was in a very small tent put up in a hurry for the occasion, your mother being already in hard labour. You very soon made your first appearance to us in the midst of the most terrific thunder storm I have witnessed either before or since. The couch on which you and your Mother still lay was yet on the floor, and hail and rain had fallen all over camp to the depth of six inches or more and [was] beginning to come in to the tent... altho in your early life you suffered much privation and passed through many hardships, I am happy to know that you had faith to endure all with patience and womanly fortitude. And thank heaven better days have come to us all."[11]

Despite many continuing challenges, the most notable in recent years being John's imprisonment for being a practitioner of plural marriage, and the forced separation of his families because of anti-polygamy laws, better days had indeed come to the Murdoch family. In celebration of John and Ann's fiftieth wedding anniversary, family and friends held a Golden Wedding reception on February 24 at Turner Hall. This event proved to be one of the social highlights of the year in Wasatch County, and it received a prominent write-up in the March 4, 1898, edition of the *Wasatch Wave*, which referred to it as "one of the most notable reunions in the history of our town," and included a lengthy story on page 3, featuring the following headlines:

A GOLDEN WEDDING

John M. and Ann Murdock Celebrate
Fifty Years of True Happiness

OLD GENTLEMAN IS CANED

And His Venerable Wife "Ringed"
by Members of the Family—Upwards of
Four Hundred Relatives and Friends
Render Homage to the Worthy Couple

The article noted that "Over four hundred people assembled in the new Turner Hall to pay homage to the worthy couple. Some had come from different parts of the state to testify to the love and esteem to which they were held. Right hearty were the handshakes, and merry was the laughter as one by one offered congratulations to the guests of honor."

The event was called to order at 1:00 p.m., by F. L. Clegg, who acted as master of ceremonies. Bishop Allen of Park City read a brief poem composed for the occasion, entitled *A Benediction*, which was sung by the audience to the tune of *America*. Following the singing, an original poem entitled *The Golden Wedding*, written for the occasion by Jane Hatch Turner, was "ably read by that gifted lady." This poem, which consisted of eighteen stanzas of four lines each, addressed the lives, joys, and sorrows of John and Ann. Some of the stanzas dealt specifically with the deaths of their children:

> *Fifty years ago today, dear,*
> *How they've quickly, swiftly fled.*
> *And with them have gone some treasures—*
> *Children, that we now call dead.*

Ah, dear wife, the first that left us
Was our little son so fair,
And the day that he was taken
Seemed we not for life to care.

But a new hope seemed to cheer us,
As we traveled on our way;
Many babies came to love us,
Eight of them are here today.

Although the poem was written in honor of John and Ann, Isabella was not forgotten. True to the type of relationship they had, Isabella was featured as an integral partner, and one of the stanzas made a specific subtle reference to the belief that although their plural marriage was now outlawed, it was only for the duration of this life, and that it would continue in the afterlife:

Bella, come and sit beside us,
We will not put you aside;
What the Lord hath joined together
In the heavens will abide.

Following Mrs. Turner's recitation, other formal presentations occurred. A welcome address was delivered by the couple's son in-law, Henry L. McMullin, which was followed by a soprano solo of *The Holy City* by Mrs. Abram Hatch, and then by a speech by a nephew, James D. Murdoch of Park City. James addressed the audience first, then turned to his honored aunt and uncle with an address that the *Wave* reporter referred to as "one of the most affecting and appropriate speeches ever heard in the town." Gifts were then given as tokens of respect and affection from close family and friends. John was presented with a gold-headed cane with his name engraved on the handle, while Ann and Isabella were each given diamond rings. Following the gift-giving, the reporter noted that "the touching scene brought forth many a tear-dimmed eye."

A dinner was then held, and the three long tables "laden with all that satisfies the cravings of the inner man" were soon surrounded by many guests who enjoyed the celebration feast. The older guests were served first, and then more food was brought out and the younger guests were served. Entertainment was provided during the gala event, which soon proved to overwhelm the *Wave* reporter, who noted, "Here is where the writer lost track of the balance of the program. He became so interested in this part of the day's proceedings that a great part of the entertainment going on in the other part of the hall was missed entirely and he forgot to record what little he witnessed and heard." Dancing followed the meal, and a photographer captured portraits of John, Ann, and Isabella that are still treasured by their descendants. John is holding his gold-handled cane in these photos, and Ann and Isabella appear to be holding or wearing the diamond rings they were given. As the afternoon and evening events moved into the later hours, the older guests departed and the younger participants continued to dance and were joined by many others, until the number present reached over a thousand. The festivities continued until shortly after midnight, when they were brought to a conclusion, and the last of the guests went out into the cold air of a late winter's night in Heber.

A New Century

In contrast to some other periods of their lives, relatively little is known regarding the experiences of John, Ann, and Isabella from the time following the golden wedding anniversary in 1898 until their deaths a few years later. Family recollections indicate that they spent their last years quietly, often at home together in the duplex on First Street, just west of Main, and there are several traditions that the three of them often sat together by the fire, holding hands, reading, talking, or napping. All three of them continued to serve in positions of responsibility in the church. John continued to give patriarchal blessings, sometimes several in a single week. Isabella often served as recorder or scribe, as Ann's health was often poor. When Ann and Isabella were both well and weather permitted, the two of them would sometimes walk together to the businesses of nearby Main Street for marketing and socializing, often arm-in-arm.

John's friends and family gathered in their small home in December 1902, in honor of his birthday. The *Wasatch Wave* noted the occasion, and that John said on this occasion that "he feels better and much younger than he did three years ago." The article further added, "The rooms of the residence were too small to comfortably accommodate the family and friends of Mr. Murdoch who assembled to do him honor, yet a most enjoyable evening was spent in appropriate songs and speeches, and feasting upon the good things prepared for the occasion."[12] Two of the Murdoch children—Isabella and Brigham—had marriages shortly after the turn of the century. Brigham's marriage was his second, following the death of his first wife. These would be the last family weddings that John, Ann, and Isabella would experience.

The Heber community continued to grow and experience modernization. The duplex home included plumbing, and electricity was later added. Such developments would have been an unthinkable advancement and great luxury during the Murdochs' early years in Scotland and Utah. Although the aging John was no longer active in the sheep ranching business, the industry continued to grow in Wasatch County, and by the turn of the century it vastly outranked beef production in the area. The advent of the railroad into the valley helped to make Heber "nationally prominent as a fat lamb shipping center."[13] Irrigation developments in the area made increased and varied agricultural efforts possible.

As the nineteenth century turned into the twentieth, the local newspaper reported on international troubles, such as the Boer conflict in Africa and an American military action in Manila, as well as regional issues such as a smallpox outbreak in Salt Lake City. Although the fervor of the federal anti-polygamy efforts had somewhat lessened in the years since the Manifesto, it was not yet over. The last issue of the *Wasatch Wave* in the nineteenth century provided extensive coverage and an editorial regarding a Colorado congressman's effort to introduce a new bill that would have disenfranchised all practitioners of polygamy from holding public office. An editorial in the *Wave* opined, "We do not think that this should apply to those who entered into polygamy years ago, but we do think that parties who have contracted marriages of this kind in the past few years in direct violation of the law of the land and the manifesto...should be denied the right to hold office in the United States."[14]

CROSSING THE LAST DIVIDE

By 1909, Ann had been in poor health for some time. It was recorded that "she had been failing for several years, sometimes she would have a very severe sick spell, then she would rally and feel better for a short time, but she gradually grew more feeble as the machinery of life weakened and run down from the strain and burdens of years and the load of sorrows, cares, and troubles gathered during a long and active lifetime."[15] She died in the wee morning hours of December 16, 1909, at the age of eighty-two, and her funeral services were held the next day. The December 17th *Wasatch Wave* remarked, "We will miss her pleasant, motherly smile, her wrinkled face, and her gentle voice with its quaint Scotch accent," and expressed sympathy for John, "her aged husband, at whose side she has toiled, shoulder to shoulder, for almost sixty long years of married life." Despite Ann's severe hardships earlier in life, and the fact that she gave birth to fifteen children, she defied the odds and lived much longer than the average life expectancy for women born in the nineteenth century.

After the death of Ann, John's health and vitality continued to slip away at a more accelerated pace. Although he still had the happy association of his beloved Bella, the loss of Ann appeared to sap him of his ability to continue. He became increasingly feeble, and he passed away of "general debility" in his home on Friday morning, May 6, 1910, at the age of eighty-nine, less than five months after Ann's passing. He was surrounded by family at the time of his death, and he passed without a struggle or any final dramatic gestures or communications.

Funeral services were held two days later, Sunday afternoon, May 8, at the Heber Stake Center, under the direction of the stake presidency. A formal "line of march" was held from his residence on 64 West 100 North Street to the nearby stake center, headed by members of the high priests' quorum, over which John had presided from 1862 until shortly before his death. This march was an orderly and somber event. After the high priests, the stake presidency and patriarchs followed, and they were trailed by the bishoprics of three Heber wards. Isabella and John's only surviving sibling, William, came next, followed by John's children, grandchildren, other relatives, and then by friends and well-wishers. The packed stake center was filled with potted plants and the chapel podium was draped in white. The patriarchs and members of the presidency of the Heber Stake all spoke, "bearing testimony of the faithfulness and sterling worth of brother Murdock." Music was provided by a mixed chorus and a male quartet, under the direction of a Professor Whitaker.

The May 13, 1910, issue of the *Wasatch Wave* reported prominently the news of John Murdoch's death and funeral, along with stories about the death of King Edward VII of Great Britain, the anti-tuberculosis movement, the expansion of the homeopathic approach to medicine, an "insane farmer on a rampage" in Colorado, and the usual local news. The paper noted that at the time of his death, John had 101 grandchildren and six great-grandchildren, and it added that he was "one who has been a useful citizen and an energetic worker for the betterment of the community in which he lived.... In 1860 he moved his family to Heber where they have resided ever since. He conceived the idea and supervised the building of the first school house in the valley and was always an energetic worker for the upbuilding of the community, having taken an active part in all public enterprises. He has lived an honest, upright life and the memory of his many kind acts and noble deeds will ever be cherished by his numerous posterity and friends." Notices regarding John's death also appeared in the *Salt Lake Tribune* and the *Deseret Morning News*, evidence that his reputation and impact was regional, not just local.

Knowing that the legal system did not recognize his marriage to Isabella and thus did not provide any default rights of survivorship for her as it would have for Ann, John had planned carefully during the final years of his life to make sure that she would be provided for after his death. His will was written when he was seventy-one years old, on January 16, 1892. It seems almost certain that the timing of the will, with most of the text stipulating benefits for Isabella and her children, was precipitated by the federal anti-polygamy laws, the Woodruff Manifesto, and the prison sentence John had served only a few months earlier. The will appointed Isabella and their son James C. Murdoch as the executors of his estate after his death. The first portion of the will was focused on provisions for Isabella and their children, and in it he gave her and their children a "house, consisting of ten rooms with cellar, pantries, wood and outhouses, all under one roof," along with the furnishings and improvements of the dwelling. John also gave to Isabella and her children several acres of land in various locations, some horses, cows, and pigs, a wagon and various implements, and the interest on five hundred dollars "so long as the principal shall remain unbroken." In addition, the will stipulated that "the right of the Female Relief Society to remove their Grainery" from one of the lots "at any time they may wish to do shall not be impaired, interfered with or hindered in any way." John may have amended this will at a later time, or provided additional instructions, but any such additional records have not been located. It is likely that this will was not the sole set of instructions or legal directives he left, because some family records indicate that he appointed his son Joseph as administrator of his estate, and that each of the children received an equal share, which ended up being about $900 apiece. "There was no dissension or controversy in the settlement, as each felt the property had been fairly and equally divided."[16]

John's death left Isabella alone at age seventy-four. She was still in relatively good health and had children and grandchildren nearby, but she now became terribly lonely, and she grieved the loss of both Ann and John. About six months after John's death, Isabella left the duplex home near Main Street and moved into the home of her daughter Catherine (Katie) Campbell Hicken and her son-in-law, David W. Hicken. She spent the last years of her life living in the "house of many rooms" with Kate and her family. Following a few years of continually declining health and some severe illness at the end of her life, Isabella died of "general debility" about six years after the passing of Ann and John, on April 10, 1916, two days shy of her eightieth birthday. Funeral services were held at the Heber Tabernacle building on April 12, her birthday. The several speakers at the service, including John's son-in-law Henry L. McMullin, praised the goodness of her life and recollected the amazing story of her journey from Scotland to Massachusetts to Utah as a young woman. In the coverage of her passing and funeral, the local newspaper reported "Bishop Crook said he had been intimately acquainted with the Murdock family, and wished to testify that the family of John M. Murdock had lived in peace and harmony notwithstanding there were two wives rearing families together." [17]

THE LAST PIONEERS

With Isabella's passing, the last of the Murdoch trio was gone. An era was coming to an end, as the last of the pioneers who trekked across the vast plains of America and endured unimaginable hardships along the way were gradually dying. The Murdochs and many other Saints of their generation represented the last of the practitioners of plural marriage who did so with the blessing of the church. By the early 1900s, those who continued to enter the practice of "the Principle" revealed by Joseph Smith over a half century earlier were not only in defiance of the laws of the land, they were increasingly shunned and punished by the church, leading to the establishment of the "Mormon Fundamentalist" movement that lives on today in several areas of the Great Basin and elsewhere. The pioneering lives of the Murdochs and other early Utah settlers began to be remembered with greater interest and appreciation by their descendants, who sometimes recollected, wrote, and talked about their forebears in a way that nearly lionized them. Stirred by the religious overtones that in great measure drove the settlement of Utah, the early history of the area and the movement to Zion began to evoke a fervent and zealous interest in regional history among local citizens that no other areas of the western or midwestern states could come close to matching.

John Murdoch was born in obscurity, to a poor family in Scotland at a time when the influence and social conditions of his nation were in decline. The death of his father while John was still a young boy, and the poverty and premature responsibility that were then thrust upon him, should have destined him to a life that would end at an early age, with little to show for it, and few things about it that future generations would care to remember. The crushing losses that he endured during his adult life could very well have sapped his spirit and left him a broken and embittered man who might simply give up the struggle. And yet despite all the odds against him, John Murdoch was destined for more than these external forces and conditions would indicate. In one sense, he was a common man who happened to live in an uncommon time and situation. But in a greater sense, he represents the struggle of every man to reach within himself, throw off the limitations that hold him back, and achieve the very best of the promise within him.

NOTES

1. Annie McMullin Rasband, Ann Steele Murdoch: First Wasatch Stake Primary President (document in author's possession).

2. William James Mortimer, ed., *How Beautiful Upon the Mountains: A Centennial History of Wasatch County* (Heber City, UT: Wasatch County Chapter, Daughters of Utah Pioneers, 1963), 119.

3. Daniel H. Ludlow, ed., *Encyclopedia of Mormonism,* vol. 3 (New York: Macmillan Publishing, 1992), 1066–67.

4. Irene M. Bates, "Patriarchal Blessings and the Routinization of Charisma," *Dialogue: A Journal of Mormon Thought* 26(3), Fall 1999: 1–29.

5. John A. Widtsoe, *Evidences and Reconciliations,* comp. G. Homer Durham (Salt Lake City, UT: Deseret Book Company, 1954), 234.

6. Bates, "Patriarchal Blessings," 21–22.

7. John Murray Nicol, ed., *The James and Mary Murray Murdoch Family History* (Provo, UT: James and Mary Murray Murdoch Family Organization, 1982), 218.

8. Dean May, *Utah: A People's History* (Salt Lake City, UT: Bonneville Books, 1987), 128.

9. Ibid.

10. *Wasatch Wave*, January 10, 1896.

11. Nicol, 250.

12. *Wasatch Wave*, January 3, 1902.

13. Jessie L. Embry, *A History of Wasatch County* (Salt Lake City, UT: Utah State Historical Society and Wasatch County Commission, 1996), 82.

14. *Wasatch Wave*, December 22, 1999.

15. *Wasatch Wave*, December 17, 1909.

16. Nicol, *Family History,* 220.

17. *Wasatch Wave*, April 14, 1916.

EPILOGUE:
BEACON ON A HILL

I have been asked repeatedly to write something about our ancestors, where they hailed from—what were their avocations, where they resided etc. I fully realize unless this is at least attempted soon, the generation of people to which I belong will soon all have passed away and the succeeding generation will be left without much information pertaining to those times, circumstances and events. With these thoughts then, and with a desire to comply with the request so made, I will attempt to put in writing what little I know of the past of our ancestors...

— David Lennox Murdoch, nephew of John Murdoch

To keep our faces toward change, and behave like free spirits in the presence of fate, is strength undefeatable.

— Helen Keller

John Murdoch experienced an extraordinary amount of change during his lifetime. Born in rural Scotland during an era when travel by horse-drawn carriage or wagon was a luxury in comparison with the usual option of walking, he ultimately walked across the vast plains of America to the Rocky Mountains, but lived to see the beginnings of the automobile era. Although most of John's life was lived during an era when water needed to be drawn from wells or carried from streams, he lived to enjoy the comforts of indoor plumbing in the home of his later years. Despite the fact that Utah was an isolated territory of the United States in a vast arid wilderness when John arrived in 1852, he lived to see it connected to the rest of the nation by the transcontinental railroad, become a state, and begin the process of modernization in the twentieth century. John also lived to see the beginnings of social and cultural changes that would eventually sweep across the region and the world.

Mountains of Change

In the years immediately following John's death, change began to come to his beloved valley and his adopted country at an accelerated rate, providing a whisper of the times of massive technological, political, and social-cultural change that would be faced by future generations of his descendants. Less than a decade after his death, some of his descendants fought for the United States in World War I, a "War to End All Wars." They then faced an influenza epidemic in 1918 that essentially put an end to large public gatherings in Utah for months. They struggled through the great depression of the 1930s, not knowing if the times of plenty were just on hold or were over for good. In the 1940s many of John's descendants served their country in far-flung regions of the planet during World War II, proving that all wars had not ended, and bearing witness to enormous horrors and atrocities in the darkest years of the twentieth century. After the World War II generation of John's descendants—primarily his great-grandchildren—started their own families in the 1950s and raised them in the 1960s and 1970s, these families coped with massive social and cultural unrest. Although Utah was not a hotbed of radicalism and civil unrest during the 1960s and 1970s, it did not escape the waves of change brought by these times, even in remote Wasatch County. These changes would be a harbinger of even more rapid changes and challenges that would occur at the end of the twentieth and beginning of the twenty-first centuries and that would cause some of the next generation of John's descendants to wax nostalgic for the "simpler" times of their youth.

The names of men and women from Wasatch County who served their nation in wars and in other conflicts are listed on metal plaques atop Memorial Hill in Midway, just a few miles from the old Murdoch sheep ranch. John's own name appears there, as a veteran of the Black Hawk War of the 1860s. As one ascends up the spiral-like narrow gravel road that leads to the top of this hill, a panoramic view of the Heber valley begins to unfold, leading to a complete sweep of the region on top, where the plaques not only commemorate many of John's descendants who retained the Murdoch surname, but many who were given other surnames through marriage: Hicken, Duke, Giles, Clegg, Nicol, Moulton, Rasband, and others.

The view from the top of Memorial Hill also informs the observant eye that changes of other types have continued since the days of John Murdoch. Although many cattle are visibly present in Wasatch County— a few large commercial herds on larger ranches and many smaller collections of cattle on small spreads—sheep have become much less common since the days of the Murdoch sheep ranch. In the first quarter of the twentieth century, with increased population pressures, the establishment of national forest preserves in the Wasatch Mountains, and increasing concerns about overgrazing, the stage was set for the eventual decline of the local sheep industry. Summer grazing rights in the mountains became more competitive and difficult to obtain, and tension between cattlemen and sheep ranchers over increasingly tight resources escalated at times. Eventually, the need for wool fiber began to diminish as other materials became more widely available and affordable, with the advent of a world-wide economy, and the use of lamb in the American diet slowly began to decrease in popularity. Although the sheep industry that John was instrumental in establishing in Wasatch County and that sustained his family rebounded at times, it has never regained its position of prominence from the late nineteenth and early twentieth centuries, and the era of the small operator eventually gave way to a new era of larger and more centralized ranching operations.[1]

During the twentieth century, the Anglo-Celtic cultural traditions brought by the first settlers of the upper Provo valley—most of whom were recent British or Scottish immigrants—gradually took backstage to new ways. John's descendants, as well as most other residents of the Heber area, began to establish new traditions, while many of the old ways became gradually forgotten or unrecognized as to their origin. The distinct forms of an immigrant culture became less prominent as a new hybrid culture was formed, consisting for the most part of a blend of emerging Mormon cultural patterns, American traditions, and the individualistic and conservative world view that was shaped by the geography and demands of the intermountain west region. As the sheep industry declined, events such as rodeos became an important part of the local cultural life in the county, and residents of the valley were more likely to have an affinity for American country and western music than for the old Celtic folk ballads, perhaps not recognizing the strong connection between the two.

As the population of Wasatch County grew, the economy became less dependent on agriculture and more dependent on tourism, recreation, and the jobs supplied in the urban region along the Wasatch Front. Increased pressures related to population growth and development led many residents and public officials of the region to have a strong nostalgia for the previous days of an exclusively rural society, and to have concerns over the inevitable changes to the way of life that they loved. Heber and the rest of Wasatch County remain rural by contemporary American standards, but they have experienced significant population pressures, conflicts over development, and a constant influx of outsiders who are often lured to the region by its scenic beauty and outdoor-oriented lifestyle. Like housing gentrification and other changes in urban areas that displace old residents as new residents establish enclaves, the changes that have occurred in the region that John Murdoch helped to establish often produce resentment as the old ways become harder to maintain. As one former county commissioner put it, "We are tired of giving up our land in Wasatch County so that others can come in here."[2]

Not only did Wasatch County experience significant changes in the decades following John Murdoch's death, but the state of Utah, no longer an isolated fortress, changed in ways that would have been difficult to imagine during John's lifetime. By the late 1940s, the once hated Republican Party, which had only a few decades earlier been the instrumentality behind the near-toppling of the LDS Church and the imprisonment of John and many others over the practice of plural marriage, became the dominant political force in the region. By the early twenty-first century, Utah had become the most Republican state in the Union, a seemingly unbreakable "Red State" stronghold that not only had a vastly Republican-controlled legislature, but routinely elected Republican candidates with margins over 70 percent. The one-party mentality created by this trend caused many Mormons in Utah to believe privately, and some Republican leaders in the state to exclaim publicly, that being affiliated with any party other than the Republican was incompatible with being a good Latter-day Saint, despite oft-repeated official church statements of political neutrality.[3]

When John Murdoch and his fellow Mormon pioneers descended through the mountain passes and into the valley of the Great Salt Lake, they hoped to find a New Jerusalem, a Zion community where the vast majority of residents were Latter-day Saints, and where most longed to be left alone and not tampered with by outside forces or trends. The theocratic kingdom of God that was originally envisioned by Joseph Smith in the midwest was attempted to the utmost in early Utah. Brigham Young initially had great success in his efforts to establish this dream, but he could never fully isolate the Saints in Utah from the rest of the world, and he came to realize that coexistence was going to be a fact of life, even if this coexistence was an uneasy *détente* at times and brought unwanted changes. Brigham's successor, John Taylor, refused appeasement or acquiescence to these tides of change to the end, and he spent his last years in hiding, unwilling to compromise the kingdom until his death. The winds of change ultimately swept through Utah, and they continue to do so to the present day, every bit as powerful as in John Murdoch's day, even if less dramatic.

Inevitably, Mormonism adapted to the times. When John Murdoch was baptized into the Church of Jesus Christ of Latter-day Saints it was a young movement, with a modest but rapidly growing population of several thousand members. By the time of his death in 1910, there were over three hundred thousand Mormons. In 1984, noted sociologist of religion Rodney Stark examined growth patterns of the LDS Church—now several million in size—and predicted that the movement was well on its way to becoming a major world faith tradition, similar in scope, size, and influence to Islam and Catholicism.[4] By the beginning of the twenty-first century, the third and fourth generations of John's descendants who remained faithful Latter-day Saints belonged to a movement nearly twelve million strong, and although the growth of church membership began to slow in the early twenty-first century in comparison with the unprecedented rates of increase during the second half of the twentieth century, new members worldwide continued to be attracted to the message of the restoration.[5]

Within a century after John's death, the fiery rhetoric and uncompromising toughness of Brigham Young, Jedediah M. Grant, George A. Smith, John Taylor, and other Mormon leaders who were influential in his life had given way to more accommodating teachings by church leaders, who were much more likely than their predecessors to emphasize the church's ecumenical place within the Christian tradition, preach cooperation with governments and other faiths, unfailingly promote a positive public image, and strive scrupulously to avoid controversy. The doctrine of plural marriage, officially abandoned after the 1890 and 1904 manifestos, became a most uncomfortable subject within the church. By the late twentieth century, members who raised questions about the historical place or doctrine of plurality during talks or discussions in church meetings risked offending the sensibilities of other members, and of violating a major social norm of silence on the subject. Although the descendants of early Mormon pioneers like John Murdoch who practiced plurality and had large numbers of children were likely to honor their forebears and respect greatly what they did, they themselves would be mostly appalled at the thought of living such a lifestyle.

By the beginning of the twenty-first century, the percentage of Utahns who were Latter-day Saints was on a downward trajectory, with Mormons projected to become a numerical minority in the state by as early as 2025 if present demographic trends continue.[6] In-migration to Utah is today more likely to be stimulated by the unique geography and outdoor recreation-oriented lifestyle that the region provides than by the quest for a religious homeland. The area adjacent to the old Third Ward neighborhood just south of downtown Salt Lake City, where John got his initial toehold as an immigrant and built his first home, continues to shelter new waves of immigrants. The current waves of international immigrants who try to establish a new life in the old homes just south of downtown Salt Lake City are seldom from Europe, as John and most of his fellow Mormon pioneer immigrants were. Rather, they are more likely to be from places such as Mexico, Central America, Africa, and Southeast Asia; they are mostly not Latter-day Saints, and they tend to be economic and political refugees rather than religious pilgrims. Utah continues to be a beacon on a hill for many, but usually for different reasons than those that motivated the Murdoch family to leave Scotland.

Although there are still descendants of John Murdoch in Wasatch County, this locale contains but a fraction of his current progeny. Lured by opportunities and dreams in other places, some of John's children and many of his grandchildren gravitated away from Heber, although many kept close ties to it and considered it a precious ancestral homeland. Their own migration patterns, and the patterns of the generations after them, first took them to the more densely populated areas along the Wasatch front, and to the farming regions of eastern Idaho. The next wave of movement took family members to adjoining states in the west, but many of them continued their frequent visits to Heber, pilgrimages in some respects, to keep alive the memories and relationships that were originally nurtured there. The current generations of John's descendants are found across the United States, mostly in the west, but in every region of the nation and in other parts of the world as well. Like John, Ann, and Isabella, they are pursuing their dreams and in many cases making new starts, sometimes reaching those dreams and sometimes finding challenges that they could not have imagined previously.

PRESERVING THE PAST

John's nephew, David Lennox Murdoch, returned to his native Scotland as a missionary for the LDS Church in 1905–7. During his time in Scotland he became reacquainted with old friends and family, visited sites of importance to the family in the Auchinleck area, and made some keen observations about the Murdoch family heritage. David possessed a sharp intellect and was an able writer, unafraid to express his views boldly. It was fortunate that his written record of the history of the James and Mary Murray Murdoch family was preserved. His writings were apparently the first attempt at a comprehensive history of the family, and they also include his journals from the voyage home from Scotland. In his preface to the

Murdoch history, he expressed concern over the possible loss of knowledge of those who came before him and the old ways, observing, "I fully realize unless this is at least attempted soon, the generations of people to which I belong will soon all have passed away and the succeeding generation will be left without much information pertaining to those times."[7]

Within a few years after he wrote these words, an extraordinary chain of events was set into motion that would ensure that the story of his people would be preserved. Murdoch family gatherings began to be held in the summers on an annual basis in the Heber or Provo Canyon area, with family members arriving by train, horse and buggy, or wagon. The first reunions were informal, but by the 1920s they began to be more established, as traditions emerged, and as records were kept of the proceedings. In a culture region where large family reunions were not unusual, the Murdoch reunions stood out for their size, organization, and the devotion with which many of the family attended and participated. Socializing and recreation were important activities, but the persons who organized these reunions ensured that family histories would be read, cultural traditions passed on, and the old family stories retold. The Murdoch reunions grew over the years into exceedingly large affairs, even as the older generations passed away and most of those in attendance had no immediate personal connection with John Murdoch, Wee Granny, or the other family pioneers.

In 1973, the James and Mary Murray Murdoch Family Organization was established, with a constitution and by-laws. One of the key efforts resulting from this organization was the establishment of officers and activities to ensure that family histories would be collected and disseminated. John Murdoch's great-grandson Dallas Murdoch helped to organize this effort, and the collection of biographies and histories was spearheaded in great measure by his sister, Ruth Schulz. In 1982, the James and Mary Murray Murdoch Family History was published by the family organization, edited by John's grandson John Murray Nicol. This 784-page volume was a Herculean effort, pulling together a vast amount of information and including diaries, letters, personal histories and recollections, and genealogical records. In the Mormon culture where individuals and families are encouraged to write journals and keep family histories, such compilations are not unusual. However, the Murdoch history, known as the "Red Book" by family members because of the color of its cover and binding, stands out as extraordinary in its depth, breadth, detail, and organization, and in the affectionate and articulate way in which many of the contributions were written. Many of the principal contributors to the Red Book are now gone, but the impressive record contained in it ensured that the lives of John Murdoch, Wee Granny, and others would not soon be forgotten.

In Our Mind's Eye We Can Visualize the Journey

At the start of the twenty-first century, just a few years short of a hundred years since John Murdoch's passing, a remarkable series of events was put into motion by the modern Murdoch family, ensuring that the legacy of John and his family, Wee Granny, and their immediate descendants would not yet be forgotten. These events came together not just because of the extraordinary life stories of these Murdoch pioneers, but because an extraordinary constellation of family organizations and traditions had developed and evolved, making such grand memorials possible.

On June 24, 2001, a memorial service was held by the Murdoch family for John's mother, "Wee Granny," in Scottsbluff, Nebraska, the closest town to the nearby Chimney Rock area, where she passed away in October 1856 at age seventy-three. Through word-of-mouth announcements and flyers mailed to family members, a groundswell of interest emerged. Approximately 450 descendants of James and Mary Murdoch—the majority of them being descendants of John Murdoch and his wives—came from across the United States to attend these activities, filling to near capacity the motels and campgrounds of the Scottsbluff community. Some vehicles arrived bearing Wee Granny flags. Several major activities were held as temperatures as high as 107 degrees were reached. An LDS sacrament meeting was held in the Scottsbluff chapel, filling it well beyond normal capacity and into the cultural hall, stage, and hallways. Special musical performances and talks occurred during the evening hours, including comments by an official from the Mormon Trails Association and by members of the Murdoch family.

An original painting by prominent intermountain west artist Clark Kelly Price, inspired by Wee Granny's last moments and passing near Chimney Rock, was unveiled. This painting was commissioned by the Murdoch Family organization specifically for the event. In a talk about the painting, comments from the artist regarding his experience in creating the painting were read:

> As I started to draw her, she came together very easily. I generally have a hard time portraying women but when she came so easily, I felt I was on the right track and had a very good feeling about her.... I prayed about who should be in the scene and I felt good about who I portrayed. I felt impressed that I should show the other handcarts in the distance, and that because of Wee Granny's

difficulties, her group was left behind and were the last of her company. I also attempted to show that the weather was hot and dry and that it was late in the fall. I took great pains to show the struggle of those who were with her, both in their faces and in the clothing they wore. I took some liberty with the placement of Chimney Rock and also the bluffs, but I wanted them to be prominent landmarks in the scene. The trail was on the north side of Chimney Rock and she died some miles east of it, about 4:00 in the afternoon, facing toward Zion or toward the west. That is why James is shading her face from the late afternoon sun. That is also why she could say, "Tell John I died with my face toward Zion". The scene portrayed what I came to know about the circumstances of her death....[8]

Since its completion in 2001, Price's painting has become increasingly well-known. A few weeks after the memorial service, the painting was featured in an article about the event that appeared in the *LDS Church News* supplement published by the *Deseret News*. The painting was also featured on the inside of the back cover of the August 2005 issue of the church's *Ensign* and *Liahona* magazines, distributed to church members worldwide. Currently, there are plans to feature the painting in a documentary film about the Martin Handcart Company by director Lee Groberg, anticipated to be shown on some PBS stations in the fall of 2006.[9]

For many the highlight of the Scottsbluff event was the dedication of a stone marker commemorating Wee Granny. This marker was placed in a small private cemetery east of Chimney Rock, not far from the spot where it is thought that she died. Comments and dedicatory prayers were offered at the dedication, which was held in two separate sessions in order to accommodate the large number of people present. Following the dedicatory prayer, David Barclay, dressed in formal Scottish garb, played John Newton's Protestant hymn, "Amazing Grace," on bagpipes. In his dedicatory prayer, Robert R. Lee stated:

Gratefully, we remember those who left their homelands to come West to the Rocky Mountains to help build a Zion society and live in peace and harmony. In our mind's eye, we can visualize the journey by the ship Horizon to America, the railroad trip to Iowa City and the handcart trek from there west. We can almost see those faithful saints pushing and pulling handcarts along the dusty trails not far from here. In amazement we recognize the faith of Wee Granny, who at nearly 74 years of age made the arduous trip from Scotland by sea, rail and handcart to this area where she simply gave out. It is hard to believe that she could walk 700 miles from Iowa City to near Chimney Rock. For her faith, perseverance and courage we thank thee. The presence of this large crowd witnesses the inspiration that her life and memory brings to the Murdoch Family and friends. Her words to her son John, shortly before she died, "Tell John I died with my face toward Zion" will be forever treasured and remembered by all present today. We pray that we will repeat and keep alive Granny's story of faith to our children and grandchildren so that she may inspire them and those who follow." [10]

The Wee Granny memorial was a watershed event in stimulating interest in the history of the Murdoch family. It generated a strong response not only from members of the large extended Murdoch family, but from many others who had an interest in western U.S. history, Utah history, and the story of the Mormon pioneers who were not members of the family. Only fourteen months after the Wee Granny commemorative event, a memorial program was held in honor of John Murdoch and his two wives, August 23–24, 2002, in Heber City. The primary purpose of this event was to dedicate a large new gravestone at the burial site of John, Ann, and Isabella, to replace the original marker that had fallen into disrepair and was becoming difficult to locate and read.

About three hundred persons attended the events held in conjunction with the gravestone dedication, which included a memorial service and social, a luncheon, tours of the homes in which the Murdoch family lived, and a "museum," which included displays of items belonging to John (his fiftieth wedding anniversary cane), Ann (salt and pepper shakers, a brooch, and a handkerchief), and Isabella (two pairs of glasses). Among those in attendance were five surviving grandchildren of John Murdoch: Tressa Murdoch Garrett (daughter of Brigham Murdoch, son of Isabella), Howard Murdoch (son of Brigham Murdoch, son of Isabella), Della Murdoch Perry (daughter of Thomas Todd Murdoch, son of Ann), Jennie Ann Hicken Larsen (daughter of Catherine Murdoch Hicken, daughter of Isabella), and John Nicol (son of Isabella Crawford Murdoch, daughter of Isabella, editor of the "Red Book").

At the gravestone dedication, bagpiper David Barclay once again played "Amazing Grace," as well as the Mormon hymn "Praise to the Man" (a tribute to Joseph Smith), which was written by William W. Phelps to the tune of a popular Scottish folk song from the eighteenth and nineteenth centuries. A dedicatory prayer was offered by Gary Lloyd of Midway, Utah, who served as chairman of the event. A painting of John Murdoch and his two wives, by artist Clark Kelly Price, was unveiled, and prints were made available for sale. This painting portrayed the middle-aged trio working together in the outdoors.

On April 15, 2005, a dinner and special dedication ceremony was held in conjunction with the unveiling of a painting by artist Mel Hillerup, celebrating the prominence of the sheep ranching industry in Wasatch County's past. This painting is located on the wall of the main foyer entrance inside the Wasatch Branch Campus of Utah Valley State College, located in north Heber, not far from the area of John Murdoch's sheep ranch. The painting is clearly inspired by the location and impact of John's ranch. It shows a man on a horse, accompanied by two sheep dogs, watching over a large flock of sheep. In the background are the Wasatch Mountains, with Mount Timpanogos particularly identifiable. In the right foreground is a sheep trailer, with a stove pipe projecting from its characteristic rounded fabric roof.

An Exceptional Legacy

It is not possible to predict whether the prominent commemoration events of the first few years of the new century will prove to be singular moments in time, or whether they will spawn future events. Clearly, the Murdoch family has grown exponentially since the time of John's death in 1910, to the time of the completion of this volume, some ninety-five years later. Although it would be most difficult if not impossible to make an exact estimate of the number of John's descendants who are living at the present time, it is not inconceivable that they could be as many as six thousand or even more, assuming that his grandchildren and their descendants bore children at a rate slightly higher than the national averages, an assumption that would be consistent with fertility rates among American Mormons of these eras. Whether or not future generations of John Murdoch's descendants will continue to know his story and look to his legacy as an inspiration for their lives, or whether the current interest in their history will prove to be only a passing fad is unknown. However, the impact of John's life on the lives of his descendants is undeniable, and the legacy he left for them is truly exceptional.

What makes an extraordinary life? To some extent it begins when extraordinary persons begin their sojourn on earth, but to a great extent it is the times and circumstances in which these persons live that push them to live a life that is truly exceptional. Extraordinary times, especially times of great challenge and stress, provide a crucible that defines and shapes a life, relegating it to the ordinary or moving it into the pantheon of the noteworthy. Had John Murdoch, Ann Steele, and Isabella Crawford been born into our time they may have lived exemplary lives of character, determination, and service, but it is highly unlikely that the circumstances of their lives would have pushed them into making the kind of impact that the times in which they lived helped to assure. Although the pioneering era in the American west is long gone, John's present-day descendants live in times of great change and confusion and have their own crucibles that will ultimately define their lives. They will not sail across the Atlantic, bury their children along the banks of the Mississippi River, or walk halfway across the American continent, but they will be tested by their own times of duress. Through it all, they can look to the extraordinary life of their forebear John Murray Murdoch as a pattern for coping with whatever challenges are placed in their paths.

NOTES

1. Jessie L. Embry, *A History of Wasatch County* (Salt Lake City, UT: Utah State Historical Society and Wasatch County Commission, 1996), 135–36.

2. Embry, *History of Wasatch County*, 299.

3. Greg Burton, "A Small Tent: Lawmakers Say No Room for Demos in LDS," *Salt Lake Tribune*, October 27, 2000.

4. Rodney Stark, "The Rise of a New World Faith," *Review of Religious Research* 26, no. 1 (1984): 18–27.

5. "Keeping Members a Challenge for LDS Church," *Salt Lake Tribune*, July 25, 2005.

6. "Dixie Diversity," *Salt Lake Tribune*, July 25, 2005.

7. John Murray Nicol, ed., *The James and Mary Murray Murdoch Family History* (Provo, UT: James and Mary Murray Murdoch Family Organization, 1982), 712.

8. "Comments by Clark Kelly Price," James and Mary Murdoch Family website, http://murdochfamily.net/misc/comments_clarkkellyprice.htm (accessed August 2, 2005).

9. *The Murdoch Messenger*, vol. 2, July 2005: 1.

10. "Wee Granny Memorial Service Dedication of Wee Granny Monument," James and Mary Murdoch Family website, http://murdochfamily.net/misc/dedicatory_prayer.htm (accessed August 2, 2005).

APPENDIX

◆ ◆ ◆

THE CHILDREN
OF
JOHN MURRAY MURDOCH

ORDER OF CHILD	NAME	NAME OF MOTHER (ORDER OF CHILD FOR HER)	DATE OF BIRTH / DATE OF DEATH	AGE AT DEATH	NAME OF SPOUSE (DATE MARRIED)	NUMBER OF CHILDREN
1	Elizabeth	Ann (1)	21 Nov 1848 / 4 Apr 1852	40 mo.	NA	NA
2	James	Ann (2)	June 1850 / 20 Mar 1852	22 mo.	NA	NA
3	Mary Murray	Ann (3)	20 May 1852 / 20 Dec 1917	65	James Duke (3 Oct 1868)	8
4	Ann	Ann (4)	12 Sep 1854 / 2 Jan 1890	35	William M. Giles (5 Jun 1871)	11
5	Janett Osborne	Ann (5)	20 Dec 1856 / 11 Jun 1949	92	Henry Lufkin McMullin (6 Dec 1875)	7
6	Sarah Jane	Ann (6)	15 Jan 1859 / 16 Jan 1933	74	Thomas Heber Rasband (28 Nov 1878)	4
7	Jacobina Wells Osborne	Ann (7)	7 Nov 1860 / 18 Oct 1933	72	William Jonathon Clegg (2 Dec 1880)	15
8	John Murray	Ann (8)	4 Jan 1863 / 4 Feb 1863	1 mo.	NA	NA
9	Margaret Ann	Isabella (1)	19 May 1863 / 11 Mar 1904	40	Lewis Joshua Hawkes (7 Nov 1889)	7
10	Isabella Lovina	Ann (9)	21 Apr 1864 / 17 Jun 1870	6	NA	NA
11	John William	Ann (10)	21 Apr 1864 / 28 Aug 1864	4 mo.	NA	NA

Order of Child	Name	Name of Mother (Order of Child for Her)	Date of Birth / Date of Death	Age at Death	Name of Spouse (Date Married)	Number of Children
12	Catherine Campbell	Isabella (2)	15 Nov 1864 / 6 Mar 1945	80	David William Hicken (21 Jul 1886)	9
13	Thomas Todd	Ann (11)	4 Mar 1866 / 21 Oct 1953	87	Sarah Ingerborg Hansen (15 Jul 1915)	7
14	Lucy Veronica	Ann (12)	25 Nov 1867 / 6 Jan 1873	5	NA	NA
15	James Crawford	Isabella (3)	11 Feb 1869 / 14 Aug 1959	90	Sarah Elizabeth Giles (27 Nov 1901)	8
16	Joseph A.	Ann (13)	11 Mar 1870 / 27 Aug 1943	73	Martha Ellen Fortie (20 May 1891)	12
17	Brigham	Isabella (4)	2 Nov 1870 / 13 May 1947	76	1. Mary Blanche Alexander (16 Dec 1891); 2. Martha Louannie Hammon (8 Apr 1903)	11
18	David Steele	Ann (14)	31 May 1872 / 1 Oct 1950	78	Mary Emily Van Wagenen (21 Oct 1891)	15
19	Robert	Isabella (5)	12 Sep 1872 / 3 Sep 1893	20	NA	NA
20	John Murray	Isabella (6)	1 May 1874 / 26 Apr 1928	53	1. Minnie Marie Miller (30 Jan 1904); 2. Cora Leona Vail (5 Jan 1921)	5
21	Millicent Sophia	Ann (15)	21 Aug 1874 / 7 Feb 1916	41	Edward Teancum Murdock (9 Dec 1891)	10
22	Isabella Crawford	Isabella (7)	8 Jan 1876 / 1 Dec 1940	64	Hyrum Chase Nicol (23 Sep 1903)	8

BIBLIOGRAPHY

Arrington, Leonard J. *Brigham Young: American Moses.* Urbana: University of Illinois Press, 1986.

Arrington, Leonard J., and Davis Bitton. *The Mormon Experience: A History of the Latter-day Saints.* New York: Alfred A. Knopf, 1979.

Bagley, Will. *Blood of the Prophets.* Norman: University of Oklahoma Press, 2002.

Bates, Irene M. "Patriarchal Blessings and the Routinization of Charisma." *Dialogue: A Journal of Mormon Thought* 26, no. 3 (Fall 1999), 1–29.

Baxter, John O. *Las Carneradas: Sheep Trade in New Mexico, 1700–1860.* Albuquerque: University of New Mexico Press, 1987.

Bell, Stella Jacques. *Life History and Writings of John Jacques.* Rexburg, ID: Ricks College Press, 1978.

Berlin, Elliott C. Abraham Owen Smoot, Mormon Pioneer Leader. Provo, UT: Brigham Young University, Master's Thesis.

Black, George F. *The Surnames of Scotland: Their Origin and Meaning.* New York: New York Public Library, 1999.

Blundell, Nigel. *Scotland.* New York: Barnes & Noble Books, 1998.

Bradley, Martha Sonntag. *Kidnapped from That Land: The Government Raids on the Short Creek Polygamists.* Salt Lake City: University of Utah Press, 1993.

Buchanan, Frederick S. "The Ebb and Flow of Mormonism in Scotland, 1840–1900," *Brigham Young University Studies* 27 (1987): 27–52.

———, ed. *A Good Time Coming: Mormon Letters to Scotland.* Salt Lake City: University of Utah Press, 1988.

Buerger, David John. *The Mysteries of Godliness: A History of Mormon Temple Worship.* San Francisco: Smith Research Associates, 1994.

Burton, Greg. "A Small Tent: Lawmakers Say No Room for Demos in LDS." *Salt Lake Tribune,* October 27, 2000.

Compton, Todd. *In Sacred Loneliness: The Plural Wives of Joseph Smith.* Salt Lake City, UT: Signature Books, 1998.

Cowley, Mathias F. *Wilford Woodruff.* Salt Lake City, UT: G. Q. Cannon and Sons, 1909.

Devine, T. M. *Scotland's Empire and the Shaping of the Americas, 1600–1815.* Washington, DC: Smithsonian Books, 2003.

Embry, Jessie L. *A History of Wasatch County.* Salt Lake City, UT: Utah State Historical Society and Wasatch County Commission, 1996.

Fenton, Alexander. *Country Life in Scotland: Our Rural Past.* Edinburgh, Scotland: John Donald Publishing, 1987.

Finn, Michael, ed. *Scottish Population History from the 17th Century to the 1930s.* Cambridge, England: Cambridge University Press, 1977.

Frye, Peter, and Fiona Somerset Fry. *The History of Scotland.* London: Routledge, 1982.

Glasgow, Maude. *The Scotch-Irish in Northern Ireland and the American Colonies.* New York: G. P. Putnam's Sons, 1936.

Grant, Neil. *Scottish Clans and Tartans.* New York: Octopus Publishing, 2000.

Hafen, Leroy R., and Ann W. Hafen. *Handcarts to Zion: The Story of a Unique Western Migration, 1856–1860.* Lincoln: University of Nebraska Press, 1960.

Hankins, Nelli Potle, and John Strawthorne. *The Correspondence of James Boswell with James Bruce and Andrew Gibb, Overseers of the Auchinleck Estate.* Edinburgh, Scotland: Edinburgh University Press, 1998.

Hanley, Clifford. *The Scots.* New York: Times Books, 1980.

Herman, Arthur. *How the Scots Invented the Modern World: The True Story of How Western Europe's Poorest Nation Created Our World and Everything in It.* New York: Crown Publishers, 2001.

Hibbs, Bob. "Sunday Post Card: Railroads." *Iowa City Press-Citizen*, December 17, 2000.

Ivins, Stanley S. "Notes on Mormon Polygamy." *Western Humanities Review* 10 (Summer 1956), 229–39.

Jensen, Andrew. *Historical Record, vols. 5–8, Church Encyclopedia, Book 1.* Salt Lake City, UT: Church of Jesus Christ of Latter-day Saints.

Larson, Jennie Ann. Information on Isabella Crawford Murdoch. Document in author's possession.

Ludlow, Daniel H., ed. *Encyclopedia of Mormonism.* Vol. 3. New York: Macmillan Publishing, 1992.

May, Dean. *Utah: A People's History.* Salt Lake City, UT: Bonneville Books, 1987.

McConkie, Bruce R. *Mormon Doctrine.* 2nd ed. Salt Lake City, UT: Bookcraft, 1966.

McDonald, Anne Rasband. History of James and Mary (Wee Granny) Murdoch. Document in author's possession.

McDonald, Hiram, and Anne Rasband McDonald, eds. *Our Generations: A Legacy of Faith.* Bountiful, UT: Hiram and Anne Rasband McDonald, 1996.

McMullin, Annie Janett. Description of an Early Home in Wasatch County. Document in author's possession.

Mortimer, William James, ed. *How Beautiful Upon the Mountains: A Centennial History of Wasatch County.* Heber City, UT: Wasatch County Chapter, Daughters of Utah Pioneers, 1963.

Murdoch, Dallas Earl. *The Brigham and Thomas Todd Murdoch Family Histories.* The Brigham and Thomas Todd Family Organization, 1998.

Murdoch, John Murray. *Early History of John Murray Murdoch, written by himself at Heber, Utah, 5 September 1898.* Document in author's possession. This document also appears in some other family compilations, most notably including Hiram McDonald and Anne Rasband McDonald, eds., *Our Generations: A Legacy of Faith* (Bountiful, UT: Hiram and Anne Rasband McDonald, 1996).

Murdoch, Joseph A. *A History of the John Murdoch and Mary Murray Murdoch Family.* Salt Lake City, UT: LDS Family History Library, microfilm no. 0,000,156, section 1, area 1, second floor.

Newell, Linda King, and Valeen Tippetts Avery. *Mormon Enigma: Emma Hale Smith.* 2nd ed. Urbana: University of Illinois Press, 1994.

Nicol, John Murray, ed. *The James and Mary Murray Murdoch Family History.* Provo, UT: James and Mary Murray Murdoch Family Organization, 1982.

Peterson, Charles S. *Utah: A History.* New York: W. W. Norton & Company, 1984.

Peterson, John Alton. *Utah's Black Hawk War.* Salt Lake City: University of Utah Press, 1998.

Powell, Allan Kent, ed. *Utah History Encyclopedia.* Salt Lake City: University of Utah Press, 1994.

Quinn, D. Michael. "LDS Authority and New Plural Marriages, 1890–1904," *Dialogue: A Journal of Mormon Thought* 18 (Spring 1985): 9–105.

———. *The Mormon Hierarchy: Extensions of Power.* Salt Lake City, UT: Signature Books, 1997.

———. *The Mormon Hierarchy: Origins of Power.* Salt Lake City, UT: Signature Books, 1997.

Rasband, Annie McMullin. Ann Steele Murdoch: First Wasatch Stake Primary President. Document in author's possession.

Rasband, Annie Janett McMullin. Isabella Crawford Murdoch. Document in author's possession.

Report of the Glasgow Conference, 1849. Copy located in Box 100, Folder 16, of the Frederick S. Buchanan Collection, accn. #379, Special Collections, Marriott Library, University of Utah, Salt Lake City.

Roberts, B. H. *A Comprehensive History of the Church of Jesus Christ of Latter-day Saints.* Vol. 5. Salt Lake City, UT: The Church of Jesus Christ of Latter-day Saints, 1957.

———. *A Comprehensive History of the Church of Jesus Christ of Latter-day Saints.* Vol. 6. Salt Lake City, UT: The Church of Jesus Christ of Latter-day Saints, 1957.

Sage, Leland L. *A History of Iowa.* Ames: Iowa State University Press, 1974.

Schlissel, Lillian. *Women's Diaries of the Westward Journey.* New York: Schocken Books, 1982.

Shaw, James Edward. *Ayrshire, 1745–1950: A Social and Industrial History.* Edinburgh, Scotland: Oliver and Boyd, 1953.

Smith, Joseph Jr. *The Pearl of Great Price.* Salt Lake City, UT: The Church of Jesus Christ of Latter-day Saints, 1981.

Smith, Joseph Fielding, comp. *Teachings of the Prophet Joseph Smith.* Salt Lake City, UT: Deseret Book, 1951.

Stark, Rodney, "The Rise of a New World Faith." *Review of Religious Research* 26, no. 1 (1984): 18–27.

Stegner, Wallace. *The Gathering of Zion: The Story of the Mormon Trail.* New York: McGraw-Hill, 1964.

———. "Ordeal by Handcart." *Collier's,* July 6, 1956, 85.

Sutherland, Daniel E. *The Expansion of Everday Life, 1860–876.* Fayetteville: University of Arkansas Press, 2000.

Tuchman, Barbara W. *A Distant Mirror: The Calamitous 14th Century.* New York: Alfred A. Knopf, 1978.

Turner, Lynn Slater. *Emigrating Journals of the Willie and Martin Handcart Companies and the Hunt and Hodgett Wagon Trains.* Lynn Slater Turner, 1996.

Van Orden, Bruce A. *The Life of George Reynolds: Prisoner for Conscience' Sake.* Salt Lake City, UT: Deseret Book Company, 1992.

Van Wagoner, Richard S. *Mormon Polygamy: A History.* 2nd ed. Salt Lake City, UT: Signature Books, 1989.

———. *Sidney Rigdon: A Portrait of Religious Excess.* Salt Lake City, UT: Signature Books, 1994.

Wentworth, Edward Norris. *America's Sheep Trails.* Ames: Iowa State University Press, 1948.

White, Timothy. *Long Ago and Far Away: James Taylor, His Life and Music.* London: Omnibus Press, 2001.

Widtsoe, John A., ed. *Discourses of Brigham Young.* Salt Lake City, UT: Deseret Book Company, 1971.

———. *Evidences and Reconciliations.* Compiled by G. Homer Durham. Salt Lake City, UT: Deseret Book Company, 1954.

Wier, Alison. *Mary, Queen of Scots and the Murder of Lord Darnley.* New York: Ballantine Books, 2003.

Wilson, Thomas. The Journal of Thomas Wilson. Microfilm copy in Brigham Young University Library, Provo, UT.

INDEX